ALL AMERICAN MUSIC

ALL
AMERICAN
MUSIC

Composition in the Late Twentieth Century

JOHN ROCKWELL

Vintage Books
A Division of Random House
New York

First Vintage Books Edition, updated, April 1984

Copyright © 1983 by John Rockwell

All rights reserved under International and Pan-American Copyright Conventions. Published in the United States by Alfred A. Knopf, Inc., New York, and simultaneously in Canada by Random House of Canada Limited, Toronto. Originally published by Alfred A. Knopf, Inc. in 1983.

Owing to limitations of space, all acknowledgments for permission to reprint previously published material may be found on page 287.

Library of Congress Cataloging in Publication Data
Rockwell, John.
All American music.
"Bibliography and discography": p.
Includes index.
1. Music—United States—20th century—History and criticism.
I. Title.
ML200.5.R6   1984   781.773'09'04   83-40299
ISBN 0-394-72246-9 (pbk.)

Manufactured in the United States of America

For my parents,
and to Linda and Howard,
with gratitude

Thanks for advice and information
to Robert Christgau, Robert Cornfield and Robert Gottlieb,
and also to Holly Fairbank, H. Wiley Hitchcock, Honey Hoffman,
Lawrence Loewinger, Robert Palmer, David Reneric,
Patrick J. Smith and Roger Trilling

CONTENTS

Introduction   *3*

1   The Rise of American Art Music   ERNST KRENEK   *14*
     & the Impact of the Immigrant Wave
     of the Late 1930's

2   The Northeastern   MILTON BABBITT   *25*
     Academic Establishment
     & the Romance of Science

3   American Intellectual Composers   ELLIOTT CARTER   *37*
     & the "Ideal Public"

4   The American Experimental Tradition   JOHN CAGE   *47*
     & Its Godfather

5   Romantic Defiance,   RALPH SHAPEY   *60*
     Enlightened Patronage
     & Misanthropy in the Midwest

6   The Return of Tonality,   DAVID DEL TREDICI   *71*
     the Orchestral Audience
     & the Danger of Success

7   The Romantic Revival & the   FREDERIC RZEWSKI   *84*
     Dilemma of the Political Composer

8   Post-Cageian Experimentation   ROBERT ASHLEY   *96*
     & New Kinds of Collaboration

9	The Orient, the Visual Arts & the Evolution of Minimalism	PHILIP GLASS	109
10	Women Composers, Performance Art & the Perils of Fashion	LAURIE ANDERSON	123
11	Electronic & Computer Music & the Humanist Reaction	DAVID BEHRMAN	133
12	Environmental Composers & Ambient Music	MAX NEUHAUS	145
13	Musique Concrète & Composition Beyond Music	WALTER MURCH	154
14	Jazz, Group Improvisation, Race & Racism	THE ART ENSEMBLE OF CHICAGO	164
15	Mystical Romanticism, Popularity & the Varied Forms of Fusion	KEITH JARRETT	176
16	Free Jazz, Body Music & Symphonic Dreams	ORNETTE COLEMAN	185
17	Latin Music, Folk Music & the Artist as Craftsman	EDDIE PALMIERI	198
18	Urban Popular Song, the Broadway Musical, the Cabaret Revival & the Birth Pangs of American Opera	STEPHEN SONDHEIM	209
19	Rock, Populism & Transcendental Primitivism	NEIL YOUNG	221
20	Art-Rock & the Fusion of Races & Styles	TALKING HEADS	234
	Bibliography and Discography		247
	Index		263

ALL AMERICAN MUSIC

INTRODUCTION

This is a book about new American music as it really is. Music's range has always reached from the complicated to the simple, from cathedrals and concert halls to fields and streets. In America today, the diversity seems greater than ever. Yet even as the separate styles maintain their vitality, they are also coming together in subtle and unexpected ways. That can be perplexing and disturbing, but it can also be enormously exciting. Music in the late twentieth century exists on myriad levels of technical complexity, historical tradition, technological discovery and hybrid interaction. And no culture in the world has a richer confluence of these cross-currents than the United States, where the old battles about what is European and what is American, what is popular and what is "serious," are being fought with a new fierceness—and resolved with a new confidence.

One way of looking at American music from the earliest times is as a dialogue between the "cultivated" and the "vernacular." The terms are borrowed from H. Wiley Hitchcock, whose *Music in the United States: A Historical Introduction* is one of the three succinct histories of American music that treat the balance between those extremes judiciously; the others are Wilfrid Mellers's *Music in a New Found Land* and Charles Hamm's *Music in the New World.* But if American music is such a dialogue, it has only quite recently been regarded as such. Before the 1960's, by and large, the vernacular side of the dialogue was mute, silenced by the academic, cultivated view of what music was and should be. Establishment histories traced "serious" American music in terms of its European-derived classical tradition. Some such histories treated with solemn seriousness the generations of worthy but faceless imitators of European models who defined our art music up until the end of the last century. Others paid deference to our pioneering eccentrics, but held that this country did not really find its own musical voice until the early twentieth century, with Charles Ives. By any standard, the first three decades of this century were exciting and promising ones for the evolution of an indigenous American art music. There was the growth of the American symphonists, many of whom were trained in France, and the simultaneous appearance of an experimental tradition inspired above all by Henry Cowell.

But there was more to American music than this. Indeed, our country's musical history can be seen as a happy babble of overlapping dialogues—not just cultivated and vernacular, but European and American, white and black, male and female, East Coast and West Coast, Occidental and Oriental, urban and rural, secular and sacred, consonant and dissonant, German and French, even English language and all the others. And while there have been many histories of the various sacred, folk and popular traditions, they have rarely attempted a connection to the cultivated, "serious" mainstream.

Just as nineteenth-century European composers turned to the folk traditions of their own countries, so did cultivated composers here begin to explore our folk heritage, from British secular songs and psalmody to spirituals to minstrelsy and the waves of musics that arrived with the nineteenth-century immigrants. At the same time, our growing population, improved communications and capitalist ethos were conspiring to make popular music something more than a local phenomenon. First sheet-music sales and eventually recordings gave popular composers and performers a national reputation. By the 1930's, popular music included Broadway and Hollywood musicals and their attendant Tin Pan Alley songs, jazz and that special style of "crooning" designed for the radio.

The composers of these various cultivated and vernacular genres were not unaware of one another. George Gershwin was admired in "serious" circles; many young classical composers were fascinated by the formal procedures of jazz; Kurt Weill crossed over boundaries both in Berlin and in New York; classical styles influenced Hollywood film composers. In the thirties, a vigorous leftist populism proclaimed the seriousness of the popular and folk traditions, and such composers as Aaron Copland, Roy Harris and Virgil Thomson all strove to achieve a folkish directness within a cultivated context.

Such "fusions" have become endemic in our own time. One reason is the easy accessibility of all kinds of music, with the proliferation of discs, cassettes and radios. Unique styles flourish in isolation. It is difficult to remain isolated in contemporary American culture, and as a result we have more hybrid musics than ever before. And just as there is ever greater stylistic cross-pollination within the United States, so is the Western world as a whole increasingly influenced by the music and culture of alien civilizations. Many of our brightest young composers have begun to question the basic assumptions of the European tradition—to doubt an automatic equation of artistic worth with complexity, for instance, or of artistry with a distinguished pedigree or elaborate technical virtuosity.

This book does not try to recount that story in precise chronological detail, or to extend it systematically up to the present moment; the title has multiple meanings, but absolute inclusivity is not one of them. This is not a survey, guide or encyclopedia. I offer, instead, a more personal approach to my subject. If this book seems idiosyncratic, that is perhaps partly, and unfortunately, because of its catholicity, which seems self-evident to me but not yet to everyone else. Catholicity is difficult both to comprehend and to accept. Those especially perplexed by it are those with a special loyalty to one particular tradition. When a person comes to music through a certain style, as a listener or after long years of practice, other styles may seem inimical to that first love. For composers, insularity is almost a prerequisite—a jealous concentration on one's own work can, and perhaps even should, lead to ignorance or uncharitableness about the work of others. But in American culture today, in part because of the very onslaught of diverse musics, too many music-lovers have retreated defensively behind the walls of that which they like best, slighting or damning everything else. Even if one feels the stirrings of sympathy for a different kind of music, the sheer bulk of sound available today and the sheer weight of the traditions that underlie any style make the effort at ecumenicalism daunting. A specialist in classical music may grudgingly concede that interesting developments are taking place within what was once called "jazz." But the bristling cult of jazz fans, critics and experts seems so feistily self-contained, and the amount of information to be mastered so prolific, that one is easily dissuaded. Still, we must make the effort, if we are to serve as honorable citizens of our musical state; anything less is laziness at best and pernicious distortion at worst.

But more than its catholicity, what is really unusual about this book is its organization. What I offer here is twenty essays. The subjects of those essays are twenty living, actively creating American composers (or, in two chapters, groups of composers). But I also attempt in each chapter to consider broader issues epitomized by those composers, their music and their place in American cultural life. Thus, my selection of chapter-subjects was based not just on the inherent quality of each composer's music (indeed, in a few cases I don't find the music of paramount interest) but also on what they suggest about contemporary American composition in general.

A quick glance at the table of contents will reveal the balance I have established, and what I have left out—both types of music and specific composers. These choices are inevitably arbitrary, or will strike others as such. The balance between various kinds of music, for instance, will offend classical-music traditionalists who regard all pop as an affront, and populists who despise art music as the played-out amusement of the ruling classes. There will be those who protest the omission of Leonard Bernstein, George Crumb, Steve Reich, Cecil Taylor, Miles Davis, George Clinton or Bob Dylan. As it happens, all of those names are mentioned in the book. But I have my reasons for picking the people I picked.

I began my critical career writing about classical music. I had what I now realize was a preternaturally intense relationship to popular music as a young teenager, awaiting with breathless expectation the results of the weekly "Hit Parade." But soon classical music seized me, and it was as a writer about serious art music, and about how such music related to society at large, that occupied me in my graduate studies and in my first years as a critic. I subsequently came to believe that experimental music, vernacular music and non-Western music were important and enjoyable, too, and that a "music critic" had no business excluding entire traditions that most of the world thought of as "music" just because they didn't conform to his own cultural prejudices. Hence my writing in recent years has reflected a very deliberate attempt to open myself up to all forms of musical expression. That may make the process sound too much like grim duty, driving myself on out of moral conviction to listen to all sorts of horrible noise. The fact is, pleasure coincided with principle: I write about all kinds of music because I now love all kinds of music, and want to share that love as best I can.

But "classical music"—the tradition of Western art music and the individualized artistic selfawareness that tradition entails—came first, and its primacy has shaped this book. The choice of composers and subjects here, and the balance between different kinds of contemporary music, is the result of my desire to reach out from the perspective of art music to embrace other kinds of music into that tradition. Thus this book may also disappoint those populists who espouse a strict equilibrium between the cultivated and the vernacular. To the staider sort of "classical music lover," experimentalists and electronic musicians may seem very far removed from traditional classical music. But they *are* part of that tradition, and when they are counted as such, they tip the balance of the chapter-subjects decisively toward the classical.

This means that there are more varieties of overt art music than vernacular music represented here, and that the vernacular musicians were chosen in part because in some, sometimes intangible, sense they have a selfconsciousness as artists, as composers with a relationship—even an adversary relationship—to the heritage of Western art music. Much wonderful music has come from unadulterated folk and popular traditions, and I touch on some of it here. One of my recurrent themes, in fact, is that an excessive selfconsciousness can rob a composer's music of its vitality. Perhaps I am struggling with an indefensible criterion in my espousal of compositional artistry, one that must wither in the face of any attack that challenges such distinctions as delusions of race and class. But still, my concern here is for composers, as opposed to defiant entertainers or humble craftsmen or embodiments of the folk spirit, and I am trying to explore in as broad and realistic a way as I can what it means to be an American composer today.

Our composers and, indeed, American intellectuals and artists of every sort have felt estranged from the mercantile and bellicose aspects of the culture as a whole since before the republic was born. In that sense, and given our atomistic notion of individuality, every American artist is an outsider, and perceives himself as such. But I am interested in a special kind of outsider—the composer who has refused to accept whatever it was that was expected of him. Those expectations can come in the form of a cultivated tradition, an academic or popular fashion, a commercial imperative or a folk style. The composers with whom I am particularly concerned have struck out on their own, even if they simultaneously longed for the spiritual kinship of their fellow artists and the culture itself. Determinedly or in despair, they struggled against what seemed inevitable, and were often forced into marginality by the very intensity of their convictions. The prevalence of such men and women among those now recognized as our important composers and artists has disrupted whatever equivalent we have here of the tradition that sustains so much European culture. And yet such independence itself contributed to the European classical music that now dominates our concert life. Haydn, the creator of the sonata form, the string quartet and the symphony as we know it, accomplished all those tasks in isolation at Esterházy. "I was cut off from the world," he wrote. "There was no one to confuse me, and so I was forced to become original." It is just that kind of spiritual independence that seems, better than anything else, to define what is characteristic about the best American music.

It must be reiterated that the essays here are not intended as comprehensive studies of their ostensible subjects' lives and work. I chose these composers because they seemed particularly representative of different kinds of music and more general ideas. But I also wanted to consider those ideas in terms of living personalities and actual music, which could be evoked by me and then confirmed through a consultation with the bibliographic and discographic information at the back of this book. I could have written a more conventionally coherent sociological-historical-musicological essay, or a straightforward history full of superficial thumbnail sketches, or a series of unashamedly discrete essays. In the end, I tried to do a little of all three things, in the expectation that a bit of each would enliven the others.

My intended reader is any generally cultured person with an interest in music—altogether, or any particular kind considered here. There is practically no technical language; I have written very deliberately for the layman and the non-specialist. This book is for anyone who likes to think about music, a category that does not necessarily include all musicians. Nor should it. Music is a non-verbal art, and at best a verbal gift provides a lively adjunct to musical talent, as with Thomson. I wish to address those who enjoy combining aural sensation with thought, and not just thought about aural sensation, but about history, sociology, economics and politics, too. My academic training was as a cultural historian, and I hope it shows.

Although the book as a whole hardly offers a smooth narrative sequence, it is my intention that a reader will gradually perceive it as the telling of a tale—a tale of traditional, cultivated music opening itself up to the diversity of the true American musical experience, just as the finest American artists and intellectuals have always been attuned to the breadth of American life as a whole.

The first group of four composers consists entirely of older men whose roots reach back to the inter-war period in which populism, experimentalism, German and French influences and a nascent nationalism all helped shape our musical climate. The narrative begins with a composer most people do not even think of as American—Ernst Krenek. The Krenek chapter is introductory to the other classical chapters, intended to establish the climate in which American art music evolved after the end of World War II. Krenek is important as a symbol of the Central European emigrants who arrived in America in the late thirties and deflected the course of American musical history, for better and for worse. Milton Babbitt is the patriarch of American musical rationalism, the avatar of European-oriented ultra-complexity. Elliott Carter represents another kind of complexity, a man who grew out of the Francophile tradition into a curious Franco-Germanic mutation, alienated and alone, yet also the honored epitome of the Northeastern establishment. And finally in this first part, there is John Cage, whose position as the progenitor of American experimental music in our time is unchallenged.

The next section is devoted to composers who, in their very different ways, make music that conforms to accepted notions of what "classical music" has been and should be, and who exemplify the inclination in the past few years to reach out once again to willing audiences. Ralph Shapey may be a misanthropic curmudgeon, but his esthetic ideas as well as his music amount to a deliberate reversion to a romanticism for our time. David Del Tredici and Frederic Rzewski are even more overt in their own "return to romanticism"—Del Tredici, though trained as a strictly rational modernist, with the popsy openness of his recent scores; Rzewski with politically inspired adaptations of nineteenth-century idioms.

Three composers stand for the experimental tradition descended from Cage. Like Del Tredici and Rzewski, they suggest a swing from complexity to simplicity, and also a tendency among the present-day experimentalists toward musical theater and even opera. Robert Ashley was the archetypical sixties bohemian wild man, but also a pioneer in new forms of mixed media, and someone who has worked in and been influenced by new-music scenes in three widely varying parts of the country. Philip Glass is perhaps the most popular "serious" composer today, an early minimalist who has now reached out to opera and rock. Laurie Anderson is a composer and "performance artist" who operates on the increasingly fluid borders of art-rock, theater and poetry. She also indicates, by her very isolated position in this book, the difficult task women have had in establishing themselves as composers in our culture.

All three men in the section on electronic music work with electronic instruments, but otherwise differ widely. David Behrman is the most traditional of the three; his gentle mysticism is far removed from the fierce unapproachability of earlier electronic composers like Babbitt. Max Neuhaus is a "public," or "site," composer, interested in challenging conventional notions of where, how and why music should be heard. Walter Murch pushes our understanding of what a composer is to the limit, working in film and carrying on the 1950's French *musique concrète* tradition in the world of the modern sound studio.

None of the three "jazz" composers is part of the mainstream jazz tradition, which I think of as curiously akin to mainstream, historical classical music—full of activity but less creative than the really new forms. The Art Ensemble of Chicago, one of two groups in the book, is wildly eclectic, devoted to a rediscovery of African roots and overtly theatrical. Keith Jarrett struggles with intermittent success to blend jazz and classical styles, and embodies as purely romantic a sensibility as any in this book. Ornette Coleman, a jazz pioneer for thirty years, remains the crusty outsider for all his mainstream influence, and concretizes the ever shifting links between jazz and black popular music.

The final category is more diverse than any of the others. Eddie Palmieri, the leading American Latin composer and bandleader, works in a "folk" field largely unknown outside the Spanish-speaking world. Stephen Sondheim stands not only for Broadway today, but also for the whole tradition of the urban, non-rock popular song and even for American opera, which has fought its own battle over the decades between a European cultivated tradition and vernacular Americana. Neil Young and Talking Heads are both rock performers. But while Young is a folk musician with a country flavor who clings doggedly to the most radical simplicity, David Byrne and the Heads very deliberately push rock into the realm of art—one of the most vital forms of avant-garde "fusion" in America today.

What makes the critical function both just a little ludicrous and yet excuses it, too, is the knowledge that music proceeds serenely, quite apart from what critics write. Naturally, critics help shape posterity by influencing the immediate reception of new work, and no doubt a weak-willed composer can be dissuaded by harsh reviews. But one must have faith that a composer who is going to make important new music is not one who will lightly abandon that mission. As a person who makes it his business to keep his ears open, I can attest to the multiplicity of fine work being composed all over the stylistic spectrum. Such music is being made whether critics write about it or not, whether they praise it or damn it, and even whether they deign to recognize it as music at all. If this book is in any way a more accurate reflection of the realities of new American music today than some of the studies that have preceded it, it still remains just that—a reflection.

There are those who will never accept the notion that Neil Young can be discussed alongside Elliott Carter, or vice versa. But he *can* be; I do it, here. Ultimately, every writer has an imaginary readership. If the writer is to sustain a career, his imagination had better correspond at least loosely with reality. In my case, I sense a growing group of musicians, music-lovers and academics for whom the seemingly radical presuppositions that underlie this book are already taken for granted, at least subconsciously. Twentieth-century music throughout the world has suffered enormous shocks. Traditions have been disrupted and deflected, assumptions confounded, crises proclaimed. But for those optimists among us—more polemically, for those of us who actually *listen* to the full range of music in our time—this is a period of quite remarkable excitement. The excitement derives not just from the realities of music today, but even more from its potential. As a society built upon the very ideals of ecumenicalism and catholicity, as the leading technological and industrial nation of our time, and as the principal nexus between European high art and the musics of other classes and cultures, America stands at the forefront of the music of tomorrow. I've already heard some of that music, and I'm here to tell you it's terrific.

1

THE RISE OF AMERICAN ART MUSIC & THE IMPACT OF THE IMMIGRANT WAVE OF THE LATE 1930's

ERNST KRENEK

In 1945 Ernst Krenek, who was born in Vienna in 1900, became an American citizen. That same year he composed a choral piece called *The Santa Fe Timetable*, the text of which consists of the names of the railroad stations between Albuquerque and Los Angeles. While the concept was witty enough, it was not new; avant-gardists had been setting cute and curious things to music for decades. Indeed, one of Krenek's inspirations was a six-voice setting by Josquin Desprez of a section of the *Gospel According to St. Matthew* that is full of "begats."

The Santa Fe Timetable is part of a pair, meant as the "highly 'objective' documentary corollary," in Krenek's words, to the "subjective lyricism" of a piece composed the same year for voice and piano, *Ballad of the Railroads*. But what seems most striking about *The Santa Fe Timetable* today is its detachment from the colorful, intensely American landscape to which its title alludes. This is a dogged brand of strictly European, modernist, dissonant art music. Its effects are self-referential, non-evocative, abstract. As such, the work has a certain chilly allure. But of the breadth and expansiveness of the American Southwest, there is nothing.

Not that there necessarily *should* be; there is no law ordering American composers to sound American. But nonetheless it remains characteristic of Krenek's mature music that it is earnest, skillfully crafted and seriously intended, conceived for traditional forces and for elitist contemporary-music programs. Krenek makes no pretense of appealing to a popular audience, in this country or in Europe, where his music is performed more often than in his adopted land. In fact, his music seems hardly American at all.

Curiously, Krenek achieved his greatest fame in 1926 with a so-called jazz opera entitled *Jonny Spielt Auf,* which was produced in over one hundred European opera houses and seemed the last word in hip fashionableness. But it is not the "jazz" of *Jonny Spielt Auf* that establishes his claim to Americanism; today, this now totally forgotten opera recalls Puccini with a dash of timid modernism. Krenek himself moved on soon enough to the formal abstractions of serialism, his chosen idiom for the past half-century. He is included here because he is one of the last surviving composers who emigrated to this country in the late 1930's, a group that as a whole had a deep and complex impact on American music.

Ours is a culture built by immigrants. But it is impossible for even the most determinedly preserved ethnic subculture to survive here for long, untouched. There is something indigenously American, amalgam though it may be, that transforms what is brought here. The wave of emigrants from Central Europe in the late thirties was in one sense a blessing—a gift from Hitler. Some of the greatest composers of the century suddenly found themselves in America, and Los Angeles became for a brief moment the capital of the German intellectual world in exile. Krenek himself lives in Palm Springs to this day, although Southern California is now once again a lonely outpost for high culture, a breeding ground for American eccentrics.

Many of the immigrant composers of the 1930's taught, albeit in sometimes humiliating circumstances. Others worked in films or exercised a more general influence on the evolution of American music. In addition, there were conductors and solo performers, as well as a host of less prominent but highly skilled craftsmen who found their place in American orchestras or as teachers and who mightily upgraded the country's musical life.

Along with the benefits they brought, however, these musicians had a deleterious impact on the fragile evolution of a native American style, and especially on its Francophile mutation. American composers, and American artists in general, have long had to struggle with the advantages and disadvantages of their European heritage. This struggle has been particularly marked in the Northeast, where the principal national journals and academic institutions are located and where the "establishment" view of American culture is formed. Ralph Waldo Emerson's "The American Scholar" stands as one especially impassioned declaration of American cultural independence. But American politics and its economy turned out to be more easily liberated than its culture.

Prior to our own century, America contributed very little to the world's musical culture. Our "serious" composers were mostly pale imitations of the prevailing fashions of musical Europe. Ruddy musical pioneers—William Billings, Anthony Philip Heinrich—have been elevated to positions of prominence in revisionist histories of American music, but have not claimed a secure place in American concert halls, let alone in those of other countries. Louis Moreau Gottschalk might be an exception, but his international fame was more as a flamboyant, exotic virtuoso than as a serious composer.

Billings and Heinrich prefigured such grand eccentrics as Charles Ives, Charles Tomlinson Griffes, Carl Ruggles, Henry Cowell and John Cage. American composers have spoken most forcefully when they spoke as individuals, perhaps knowledgeable about European and establishment ways, perhaps not, but willing in either case to strike out on their own and chance the consequences. Just as Gottschalk was prized because of his strangeness, so, too, Europeans have responded to American music that is different from what they hear at home. This situation galls American composers who feel they have evolved strong personal variants of European styles, as they see European applause accorded to what they regard as bizarre and vulgar.

The real worth of Ives's music is still debated. But he is widely taken to represent the coming of age of American art music—the first composer to speak with a distinctly American voice and make the world listen. In the first four decades of this century, such voices became a chorus. Some of them were selfconscious about their Americanness, some of them exploitative, some of them negligible. But they all worked hard to establish an American style—symphonic, in the cases of Roy Harris, Aaron Copland, William Schuman and many others; experimental, in the line from Cowell to George Antheil to Cage to Lou Harrison; idiosyncratic, in the Gertrude Stein–Virgil Thomson collaborations.

What links much of this otherwise varied music is a sense of freedom from the weight of German tradition. It is sometimes difficult to remember, today, how large Germany loomed in American culture during the late nineteenth century. "The land of poets and thinkers" shaped our educational system, our philosophical and scientific ideas, and not least our music. Germans, Jewish and non-Jewish, conducted our orchestras and played in them, and young American composers went to Leipzig and Berlin to complete their studies. Just as he dominated Europe itself, Richard Wagner stood as the pre-eminent influence on younger composers in this country. Such a cultural weight might well have collapsed of its own accord, but World War I and its anti-German feelings hastened the process. As early as the late teens of this century, American composers were turning toward Paris, and by the early thirties Copland and Thomson had become the first members of that decades-long, remarkable pilgrimage to study there with Nadia Boulanger.

Yet this shift toward lightness, buoyancy and a popsy, deliberately anti-German simplicity did not mean a mere switch from German to French cultural imperialism. Several of these composers were inspired by France to reject Germany, and joined forces with others here who were determined to construct a native American style. With patriotism fueled by New Deal patronage and, curiously, by the folkish populism of the leftism endemic among intellectuals of that decade, the thirties saw a surge of selfconsciously American music unequaled in the entire previous history of the country, a surge that began to build in the twenties and washed forward into the forties.

It would be naïve to equate nationalism with esthetic worth, or to overvalue the music that came from this time. Some of it is surely undervalued today, and will be prized by future generations—the Stein-Thomson operas, many still-unknown Cowell pieces, Cage's early percussion and prepared-piano scores, some of the symphonic work of Copland and Schuman. It is true that many worthy scores by composers of this generation and its direct pupils have been temporarily forgotten in the subsequent fascination for rigorous serialism and wild-eyed experimentalism. But there was also a good deal of earnest naïveté in this music, especially with the once admired symphonies of Harris. Some of the populist rhetoric of the thirties was offensive to more refined sensibilities, whether they were influenced by Europe or not. It also blunted a more iconoclastic, less overtly nationalistic strain of earlier American experimentation.

But it was serialism more than populism that impeded the evolution of a truly American music. And it was the arrival of so many distinguished composers from Europe in the late thirties—indeed, nearly every principal figure in twentieth-century Central European musical modernism—that provided the catalyst for the post-war serialist reaction. Students of these men or composers inspired by their example emerged by the early fifties, full of ideas and a determination to see their music performed. They dismissed the Americanists patronizingly as primitive and the Francophiles as trivial. The evolution of what was perhaps the leading showcase for new music in the Northeast from the 1920's through the 1970's, the League of Composers/International Society for Contemporary Music concerts in New York, is an instructive example. The League derived from Copland's efforts to provide a forum for all good new music, but for American composers in particular. The American chapter of the ISCM was more overtly internationalist, but the ISCM had been founded in Salzburg in 1922 as a broadly catholic forum for all new music. By the fifties, the combined organization had been seized by Milton Babbitt and others of his views and turned into a forum for uncompromising serialism.

"Serialism" is a term for a variety of procedures that expand upon Schoenberg's original ideas of twelve-tone composition. Schoenberg rejected the basic organizational principle of Western music, the reliance on a home note or key, the development of tunes and harmonies within that key, and the modulation away from the home key and back to it. Composers had gradually eroded the security provided by that system with an ever richer chromaticism, so that by the teens of this century music seemed—even to the practitioners of such chromaticism, like Schoenberg himself—to be bereft of a firm formal underpinning. Schoenberg arranged the twelve notes of the chromatic scale in horizontal patterns, or "rows," and constructed his pieces from permutations of those patterns. This ensured a fashionable sonic abstraction while still reassuring composer and listener alike that order lurked beneath the seeming anarchism. His followers devised ever freer or more complex ways of varying the patterns, and eventually, with "total serialism," they extended the serial principle from notes to rhythm, dynamics and all the other "parameters" of music.

Krenek had settled on serialism as his compositional method before he arrived in this country in 1938, and has remained true to it thereafter—during his years of teaching at Vassar College and Hamline University in St. Paul, and as a Southern California free-lance composer with occasional academic connections since 1947. Like many other composers, he came to serialism after working in other idioms—first cautiously adopting some serial techniques, then embracing the system unreservedly. Like most serialists today, he is proud of the putative originality and independence with which he adopted Schoenberg's ideas. Theoretically and methodologically, not all his mature work is strictly serial. But what strikes one about this music is not its freshness of method but its staleness of effect.

There are bold, expressionistically dramatic moments in Krenek's scores—especially when, as in the mature operas or a big symphonic piece like *Horizon Circled* of 1967, he can indulge in the full color-istic range of the orchestra. But even then Krenek's imagination seems constrained by the tradition he has inherited. Most of his music is for conventional forces—symphonies, chamber orchestras, chamber ensembles, solo instruments, choruses. When he ventures into more unusual territory (a piece for solo accordion, for instance, or another for two pianos and electronic tape), the sound and idiom seem awkwardly adapted to such exotic means. Krenek's music is dry, static, shrill, abrupt, chromatic and pointillistic, full of skitter-ing little runs by solo instruments, extreme ranges of pitch and dynamics and predictable intimations of *Angst*. He speaks in a language derived from Schoenberg and Berg—and not only contributes little to that language, but speaks it less fluently than they do.

The very reasons he and other composers, starting with Schoenberg himself, turned to serial ideas in the first place are themselves worth considering. Serialism was once thought by conservatives to be the last word in virulent musical modernism. In part it was indeed a denial of a romantic expressive vocabulary that had become impossibly hackneyed. Yet its formulation and acceptance by a wide range of composers can also be seen, as Schoenberg himself sometimes saw it, as a conservative act, a response to the threatening implications of the harmonic system's chromatic dissolution. The "atonal" harmonic universe evolved by Schoenberg and other post-Wagnerian avant-gardists in the early years of this century seemed to have no rules, no points of reference. In fact, all sorts of unconscious structural ideas remained to provide coherence. But at the time, serialism seemed the only alternative to a steady descent into anarchy.

Their insecurities were only reinforced by the world around them. Carl E. Schorske, in his *Fin-de-Siècle Vienna*, has suggested that the political and social dissolution of the Habsburg Empire provided a catalyst for Viennese composers and intellectuals. Similar, if perhaps less overt, responses were taking place all over Europe, and World War I only dramatized the apparent need for a more durable order. Thus, Schoenberg's formulation of his twelve-tone method in 1924 represented a paradigmatic solution within the realm of music to the general process of disorder, collapse and attempted reconstruction.

In a 1964 essay entitled "A Composer's Influences," Krenek wrote that one reason he was attracted to serialism in the early thirties was that it seemed antithetical to Nazism: "The awakening of my interest in the twelve-tone technique, which was internally plausible as a result of both my exhaustion of the resources available from manipulating neo-classical and neo-romantic clichés, and my discovery of the challenges offered by the new technical procedures, coincided with my increasing disgust over the rise of totalitarianism. Seen in this light, my adoption of the musical technique that the tyrants hated most of all may be interpreted as an expression of protest and thus a result of their influence."

Krenek was an avid opponent of totalitarianism. Dictatorships of the right and the left have tried to suppress serialism. Yet there is a parallel between totalitarianism, as a rigid response to the dissolution of old values, and serialism, as a similar response to musical dissolution. In the same essay Krenek offers another non-musical explanation for his turn to serialism: he discovered it simultaneously with his new absorption in the doctrines of the Roman Catholic Church, in which he had been raised. Schoenberg, too, late in life, returned to religion—in his case, Judaism—in part as a reaction to the Holocaust but also, perhaps, as a reaffirmation of spiritual order.

Although Schoenberg sometimes dreamed of serialism as a reassertion of German musical hegemony, he more commonly thought of it as a purely formalistic ordering device, and most American serialists share that view. So do the Soviets, with their crude denunciations of "formalism." But just as with psychoanalysis, dismissed by its opponents as a web of metaphors conditioned by time and place, serialism can be considered narrowly Viennese and, by now, dated. And not just dated and extraneous to an American sensibility, but out of fashion. Serialism can be rightly proclaimed as the principal expression of musical modernism. In art and architecture as well as music, it has become recently modish to decry modernism, to dismiss its achievements as anachronistic failures. Yet one must not forget the excitement of the twenties, when the modernist innovations of the previous decades had their first real impact on society at large, and when the clumsy baggage of an outmoded romanticism seemed to have been triumphantly discarded. There was an emotional veracity to expressionist serialism, which so truly captured the torment and black excitement of that time. Today, many young post-modernists are rejecting serialism. They see it as a didactic stultification of human emotion, its once revolutionary expressive gestures frozen by overuse into cliché. But in Europe in the twenties and thirties, and in America in the fifties and early sixties, serialism seemed a way out of the fatuous rhetoric of the neo-romantics, the tub-thumping of the American symphonists and the boulevardier banality of the Francophiles.

It was no anomaly that Krenek won his first fame with the exploitation of American black pop and jazz, and then turned his back on those influences. Composers with far deeper roots in American popular idioms have likewise sought to express their "serious" selves through serialism and idioms borrowed from abroad— Mel Powell and Gunther Schuller, for example, who are both passionate and knowledgeable jazz lovers but whose formal compositions reflect that love all too rarely.

Krenek's involvement with America in the mid-twenties, while he was composing *Jonny Spielt Auf,* was hardly profound—as affirmed by the score itself, which, like Franz Schreker's once popular operas of the twenties, consists of tarted-up late romanticism with little hint of even Kurt Weill's *Threepenny Opera* Americanism, let alone real jazz. Even after Krenek moved to this country, his contact with American culture remained minimal. In this respect, he stands in sharp contrast to Weill, who had a similarly rigorous musical education—Krenek with Schreker, Weill with Busoni. Weill's absorption in American popular idioms, while always couched in a European sensibility, grew steadily, and with his own move to America, he turned out a body of work for the Broadway musical theater that will one day soon be more widely appreciated. Indeed, *Street Scene* is already recognized as one of the great American operas.

Krenek, by contrast, stayed aloof, always the European observer reporting on the quirks of the Americans for journals back "home." Deeply influenced by Theodor W. Adorno, whose Marxist analyses of music sociology were tempered by a deep distrust of commercialism and populism, Krenek had severe reservations about American democracy, especially as applied to music. "It has been said that God must have loved the common people because He made so many of them," he wrote in 1944. "A different opinion was expressed recently by an American writer, to the effect that God does not seem to have particularly loved the common people, or else He would not have made them so common. Amusing as it is, this quip contains a wholesome revolt against the all-too-readily accepted assumption that everything that appears in overwhelming majority is sanctified by its multitude."

Such sentiments are shared by American intellectuals who feel uncomfortable with their own culture. Indeed, artists recoiling from the philistinism of democracy have been common in both Europe and America for centuries, from Molière's *Le Bourgeois Gentil-homme* to Tocqueville to the romanticization of the artistic bohe-mian in the nineteenth century. America is the acme of industrial-ized democracy, the home of majority rule in art as in life. So American intellectuals, for all their residual patriotism, have often found their country's crudities abhorrent. H. L. Mencken's "booboisie" was only one expression of such disdain, and that from a particu-larly vital chronicler of American popular life. A more characteris-tic reaction, especially in the Northeast, has been a near-complete rejection of day-to-day American reality, and expatriation to Europe itself. For all its irony it is no accident that musical Americanists between the wars found their focus in Paris, not New York or San Francisco or Kansas City.

Serialists are not closet Nazis, nor do all northeastern American intellectuals despise America, nor does serialism doom composers to write bad music. Quite a lot of very bad music was composed by Americanists, Francophile or not, and there have been great American serial scores. But there is still something to the idea that countries, like individuals, have personalities, and that, whatever the formal methods employed for their expression, those person-alities should not be unduly suppressed. If there is a father to that idea, it was a German, Johann Gottfried von Herder. It was Herder who, in the late eighteenth century, most forcefully articulated the idea of a German cultural nationalism, as opposed to the then dominant Italian and French "international" fashions. For Herder, every people has an innate culture, expressed in vigorous if primi-tive form in its folk art, and a true artist will base his work on such foundations. Indeed, only if he does so can he hope for universal validity. That such ideas were eventually perverted by the Nazis should not discredit Herder completely. His theories or ideas like them were common parlance throughout Europe in the nineteenth century, espoused in Germany by the left as well as the right.

Compared with Stravinsky, Schoenberg and Hindemith, Ernst Krenek seems of distinctly lesser importance. Although he has his earnest champions among academics, former students, critics and a few performers, it seems likely that the judgment of posterity will echo his present obscurity. But Krenek is something more than just an individual composer. He is one of the last of a line of European immigrants who enriched our music but also suppressed the nascent evolution of a truly American musical culture. Perhaps such an American music could never have escaped parochialism without an infusion of the philosophical self-possession that so many of the Central European immigrants brought with them. But those same immigrants encouraged a pedantic, rootless academicism in a whole generation of American composers. It is only now that other styles are being heard once again, that Cowell's experimental spirit is reborn, and that the forgotten composers of the decades before serialism are being accorded the honor they deserve.

2

THE NORTHEASTERN ACADEMIC ESTABLISHMENT & THE ROMANCE OF SCIENCE

MILTON BABBITT

Considered all by himself, Milton Babbitt is an unquestionably important American composer. He has written some of the most austerely compelling music of our time. He helped pioneer electronic music in this country. He conceived new dimensions of musical theory that have had an enormous influence in America. He has taught a host of younger composers. He has contributed provocative and influential essays. And he has played an important role in our musical politics.

But even more than most of the composers in this book, he cannot be discussed in isolation. The reason is not merely that he epitomizes the entire Northeastern academic serial establishment, but that he has been so active and effective a leader and teacher of that establishment, and propagandist for it. The history of music is full of such leaders—composers who had important things to say who were then imitated weakly by a host of epigones.

Babbitt is perhaps the most complex composer ever. His works are so dense with ideas and realizations and permutations of ideas that, in the words of a fervent admirer, Benjamin Boretz, they "necessitate deep study of many scores for the acquisition of even a superficial sense of their musical scope." His theory has been labeled "total serialism," although that umbrella shelters a number of disparate practices. After World War II, inspired as much by Anton Webern as by his teacher, Schoenberg, European and

American composers began extending twelve-tone ideas to the other "parameters" of music. The early European leaders in this movement were Pierre Boulez and Karlheinz Stockhausen, and the summer new-music courses in the German city of Darmstadt became their ideological center. But Americans, and Babbitt in particular, can lay an equal claim to pioneering such extensions of serial ideas, and, indeed, the Americans carried this theorizing further than the Europeans—who began by the late sixties to dilute their rigor with Cageian chance devices (Boulez) or even to subordinate such intellection in the service of mysticism and ritual (Stockhausen).

Babbitt, who was born in Philadelphia in 1916 and raised in Jackson, Mississippi, began studying the violin and clarinet at the age of four, but evinced an early interest in mathematics, as well. His father was also a mathematician, and Babbitt's undergraduate years at New York University were divided between those two so often related disciplines. His principal composition teacher was Roger Sessions. "He represented, to me, the first American I had met who knew European contemporary music," Babbitt later recalled. After graduate study in music with Sessions, first privately and then at Princeton, he concentrated on mathematics during the war, but his first serious analytical studies of music appeared shortly thereafter. In 1948 he joined the Princeton music faculty, where he continued with his theoretical work, with composition and with the exploration of electronic music, helping to found the Columbia-Princeton Electronic Music Center in 1959. It was his presence at Princeton, along with that of Sessions, and his subsequent electronic experiments in cooperation with Columbia University composers, that led to the very notion of a "Columbia-Princeton school" of contemporary music—a term that has come, rightly or wrongly, to symbolize Northeastern academic musical rationalism. More recently, Babbitt has taught composition at the Juilliard School in New York.

Babbitt's music theory looms so large in his life's work that some of his closest associates have asserted, admiringly, that it represents a more important act of creation than his actual compositions; Boretz calls his "theoretical inventions . . . the principal substance of Babbitt's creative accomplishment." Those inventions, and, indeed, much of the technical analysis inspired by Babbitt that has routinely appeared in *Perspectives of New Music* and other journals associated with American academic serialism, is largely incomprehensible to anyone untrained in the higher reaches of contemporary mathematics. Those fearsome charts, those references to obscure recent advances in set theory, all are meaningless to the layman. And in this context, conventionally trained musicians are laymen themselves.

Babbitt's theoretical achievement was to bring the full resources of contemporary mathematics, philosophy, linguistics, psychology and acoustics to bear on a thoroughgoing reconsideration and extension of Schoenberg's theory. That meant the extrapolation of serial ideas into every aspect of music, not just pitch. It also meant the creation of a whole new language for musical analysis—it was Babbitt who introduced such terms as "pitch class" and "source set" into musical discourse.

But the reason Boretz and others place such stress on Babbitt's theory is not just its ingenuity in the abstract. Babbitt is a true avant-gardist in his confident willingness to jettison nearly all of the past. If, however, one strips music of the comforting presuppositions that an ongoing tradition entails—a set of expectations that composer and audience alike unconsciously share—then each new piece must create those presuppositions afresh, every time. Thus, for Babbitt, a work's theoretical underpinnings assume a far larger role than, say, the tonal system or sonata form did for an early-nineteenth-century composer. The theory and structure behind the aural surface of any single work must now take the place of an entire cultural context.

But while a cultural context is part of every person's heritage, an idiosyncratically conceived, abstrusely articulated theoretical system is not. When Babbitt himself attempts to put his ideas into words, and especially into a "program note" meant for a concert-goer, this distinction becomes painfully, amusingly clear. In an introduction to his *Aria da Capo*, for instance, he speaks earnestly of "models of similar, interval-preserving, registrally uninterpreted pitch-class and metrically-durationally uninterpreted time-point aggregate arrays." For another piece, called *Dual*, he takes a more accessible perspective: "[It] is just the progression from the local to the global in relational implications which should provide the listener with the means of achieving that cognition of cumulative containment and successive subsumption which human memory in general, and musical memory in particular, requires for a musical work to be entified, eventually, as a unified, closed totality—as an all of a piece of music." One way to look at such prose is that it is inept. Another, as the critic and composer Gregory Sandow has suggested, partly in jest, is that Babbitt is "just a little bit mad." Yet another is that he combines ivory-tower convolutions with a tweaking, donnish wit to a positively baroque degree.

When one turns to Babbitt's actual music, all that complexity is in full aural evidence—or at least the ear can recognize that there is plenty of complexity present, even if the exact nature of that complexity resists immediate understanding, let alone casual aural perception. Yet the surprising, rather wonderful thing is that, for all the dismissive distinctions made by Babbitt and his disciples between true music and "purely aural pleasure," Babbitt's own music *sounds* so good. By "good," I mean that it speaks to a sympathetic listener who has no prior understanding of its underlying structure. Certainly, the scores are disjunct and abstract, in a manner that makes the serialism of a composer like Krenek sound romantic. But they also suggest the instinctual musical mind of a true composer at work. The music projects clear differentiations between emotional moods, and a wide range of those moods, from the bleak loneliness and anger of his austere, powerfully emotional *Solo Requiem* to the vigorous passion and lyricism of the String Quartet No. 3 and the punning wit of his *All Set* for jazz ensemble.

To a large degree, Babbitt has transcended the tired Viennese-expressionistic clichés that color so many serial works, even those by Americans. His music suggests a Brave New World in every sense, a faith in technological progress and a fascination with the electronic and mechanistic sound effects that so seized the popular imagination of the thirties and fifties—a kinship that has led Sandow to link Babbitt with such other fifties phenomena as abstract expressionism, monster movies and rock & roll.

A work that handsomely combines all of Babbitt's diverse interests is *Philomel* (1964), a setting of a specially written poetic text by John Hollander about the maiden in classical mythology who is raped and ultimately transformed into a nightingale. Babbitt's setting is for soprano with recorded echoes and synthesized sound. Everything is as cool, otherworldly and precise as one might expect. But the very precision of the workmanship makes the extraordinarily compact lyricism stand out all the more. And Babbitt's sensuous, coloristic combinations of the various strands that comprise the piece, the eerieness of the echoes, the remarkable word-painting ("I am becoming my own song" is a refrain) and the final invocation of birdcalls are the product of a major twentieth-century composer.

But if his best music "works" so directly, what are we to make of the fierce unapproachability of his theory? Is the alluring aural surface merely inadvertent, the gift wrapping for the actual musical content? If so, it might seem that it was for music and theory like this that the dichotomy of "ear music" and "eye music" was coined. Actually, though, the very appeal of Babbitt's best music muddies the distinction. "Ear music," which sometimes has a pejorative ring to it, is music that the relatively uneducated ear alone can perceive and enjoy. "Eye music" is music of such complexity that the eye must first study the score before its mysteries can be perceived— music so dense that the ear alone could never hope to discern its secrets. Proponents of "ear music" argue that music should remain an aural art, and that any score that can only be enjoyed after thorough analytical study is a scholastic exercise. Those who prefer "eye music" respond that "ear music" has become simple-minded. For them, music is of the greatest interest when it is allied with an expansion of man's perceptual and intellectual capacities and, indeed, contributes to that expansion.

The relation between compositional theory and practice has always been complicated. Wagner is one of the most suggestive examples. For years, scholars took his theory as enunciated in *Opera and Drama* of 1851 as gospel, bending the scores that followed to fit the theory, and puzzling over the discrepancies. More recently, Wagner's later essays have been studied as clues to his gradual modification and, indeed, radical revision of his original theory of the "music drama" and the "total work of art." Wagner's theories now seem to have been rationalizations of ideas he had already arrived at intuitively in his composition. His theoretical writings retain their value, but less as abstract esthetic speculation than as guides to his own artistic practice.

With Babbitt, it is not always clear what the balance between intellectual adventure and compositional instinct really is. That so many of his scores, especially when they at last receive accurate and impassioned performances, "work" without prior knowledge suggests that the juices of inspiration still run strong in his veins. The same is true for the fierce, intense music of Charles Wuorinen and George Perle, both of whom have contributed learned theoretical studies and both of whom write music that can appeal to the non-specialist.

What seems equally clear, however, is that this theorizing and dogged, bar-by-bar analysis has become obsessive and "academic" in the most invidious sense. A number of the leading figures of this group have spoken out strongly against such pedantry—among them their dean, Roger Sessions. These critics are only following the lead of Schoenberg himself, who continually ridiculed admirers who could see the twelve-tone system only as an opportunity for row-counting.

More troubling are the implications of Babbitt's attitude toward his audience. In perhaps the most polemically noteworthy essay ever written by an American composer, "Who Cares If You Listen?," Babbitt passionately upheld the idea of music as pure research, and called upon interested members of any potential audience to follow him and his fellow composer-researchers, rather than to sit back and wait passively for compositional entertainment. This essay, written in 1958 for (and entitled by, to Babbitt's considerable chagrin) a popular journal, *High Fidelity,* incurred a horrified reaction from humanists. The notion of the composer as servant—whether in livery or in the democratic extension of that role from prince to wealthy merchant to impresario to the public itself—had become a deeply ingrained one; it still *is* deeply ingrained, for all the residual bravado of romanticism in our culture. And here was Babbitt coming right out and saying that it was the duty of the public to support and understand the composer, rather than the other way round.

Of course, Babbitt was saying a good deal more than that. His article is an inspirational plea that music be allowed to attain the heights of seriousness and complexity for which other "arts"—principally mathematics—have long been applauded. Babbitt cites an admiring 1957 *New York Times* report of a mathematical conference with a "scientific level so high that there are in the world only one hundred and twenty mathematicians specializing in the field who could contribute." In simplistic divisions of the human spirit between "the arts" and "the sciences," it can be forgotten how viscerally thrilling the methods and achievements of science can be, how art and science can intertwine, and how the higher reaches of science can become imbued with artistic, religious fervor. The dream of a musical style that would allow composers to join hands with theoretical mathematicians and physicists, a style that operates in a realm so exalted that only the select few can penetrate its secrets, is clearly a seductive one, at least for those who consider themselves members of the elect. We live in a democratic, pluralistic society. That means not that everyone must be the same, or conform to the dictates of the majority, but that we can tolerate and admire those elitists among us who choose to pursue narrower and, they think, more rarefied paths.

There are, however, troubling aspects to Babbitt's position. One is the very loss of certainty during this century among mathematicians and scientists themselves. Babbitt is too sophisticated not to allow a place in his theory for the unexpected. But if scientists are unable to provide a firm theoretical basis for their disciplines, then perhaps a musical esthetic can more confidently rest on instinct than Babbitt prefers to concede. And perhaps, too, it can be more comfortable about including communicativeness as a goal of music. In simpler times, music's roles as divertissement or functional religious inspiration were rarely questioned. Sacred music praised God—sometimes so freely that the priests fretted—and secular music praised man and his pleasures. Composers fulfilled the wishes of their time and society as expressed by their patrons.

In so doing, the greatest of them infused their music with individuality and genius.

Babbitt's purely scientific position is the furthest extension of the romantic ideal of the independent artist who flies free of the earth and its compromises. But those of us left behind must still function in the real world; composers must always have *some* kind of patron. By rejecting any debt to the public, a composer cuts himself off from his own culture, and tacitly accepts the patronage of the academy. For American intellectuals who fear their country and cling to a European or cosmopolitan ideal of pure art, that may seem no bad thing. But if our culture has something to offer in return—a vitality and energy and an exciting blend of disparate styles—then perhaps the composers are losing more than they imagine.

Besides, most of them are only as "free" as the constraints of their teaching schedules and tenure committees allow. Reliable statistics as to what percentage of American composers are academics are impossible to come by, simply because the definition of "composer" is so tenuous. But teaching is clearly the dominant means by which composers feed themselves in this country, and that circumstance has had a palpable effect on the kind of music they compose.

Self-expression up through the eighteenth century had to be filtered through the accepted modes of musical discourse. An original composer could still incur displeasure through his innovations or his personality—Mozart had his difficulties as well as his popular successes. But his was a far different situation from that of the quintessential romantic artist. Berlioz and Wagner may have starved or compromised by doing journalism or hack arrangements. But they remained in their hearts free men—even when, in Wagner's case, they conjured up an anachronistic rebirth of princely patronage.

In our own country and time, the situation has changed. Tax laws and the wider social demands on private foundations have reduced the largesse of the wealthy, who in any event feel more comfortable giving to institutions and performers than to composers. More crucially, today's composers, in the logical extension of

the romantic's demand for freedom ("who cares . . ."), have alienated not just their public but particularly the wealthier (and thus
generally more conservative) members of that public—their potential patrons. They are therefore almost forced, apart from peer-
dominated pittance grants from governmental agencies, to turn to
the academy for sustenance. In the academy, they find sympathy
for a linked set of ideas: musical composition as an arena for pure
research, an ever more complex musical syntax expanding our
perceptual limits, and the long-cherished notion of the inevitable
"lag" between present composition and future appreciation, pushed
now almost to infinity. But they also find what Babbitt himself has
called "the academic racket": a demanding teaching load, committee work and departmental politics. They are often isolated from
urban centers, and forced to conform to the stylistic prejudices of
the people who will ultimately decide if they are "serious" enough
to remain as tenured members of the music faculty.

American academic composers are not all serialists; other musical
styles exist within the academy, too. Especially between the coasts,
holdovers from the American symphonic tradition hold sway, some
of them concerned primarily with restocking the college choral and
band repertory. And in recent years, a growing number of post-
Cageian experimentalists have nested here and there, notably at
Wesleyan, Ann Arbor, Stanford, Oakland and La Jolla. Still, there
seems something peculiarly symbiotic about academic scholasti-
cism and the more trivial corners of the serial mind, and Babbitt
did more than his share to propagate a whole generation of dry-as-
dust, unthinking clones.

He did not do so unwittingly. Babbitt is a charismatic man, and
a sign of his strength of personality is the way he attracted some of
the most clever and articulate young composers and critics to
Princeton in the fifties, sixties and seventies. He and Sessions were
not the only bright lights in the department: Edward T. Cone was
there, too, and Earl Kim for a time. But although these men seek
now to de-emphasize the notion of a "Columbia-Princeton school,"
the fact remains that there was such an elite, and they led it.
Babbitt's polemics and proselytization were not confined to the
classroom. Along with Wuorinen and several others, he played an

active role in the performance of this music among new-music groups in New York and throughout the country, by means of a proliferating "good old boy" network of former students and colleagues. The ritual of the contemporary-music concert attended by a paltry crowd of professors and students, the students often compelled to attend as a course requirement, is a familiar one to any working reviewer. If only for these purely sociological reasons, the advent in the late sixties of serious non-academic composers who devised new forms of patronage and public represented a refreshing change in American new music.

Since the serial academics made little effort to appeal to the retrograde tastes of the traditional "classical-music lover," or were obsessed with electronics, they rarely sought or obtained the orchestral commissions that were routinely dispensed to the American symphonists. When they did compose orchestral scores, those scores were often of a difficulty that made their inclusion in the regular schedule of a symphony orchestra, hemmed in on all sides by unions and budgets, almost impossible. And if such a work *was* at last performed, it was often done ineptly, greeted tepidly and rarely repeated. The result has been a proliferation of smaller-scale works that could be performed by the ensembles of students and colleagues available in an academic environment—or in major centers like New York by such new-music specialists as Wuorinen's Group for Contemporary Music and Speculum Musicae. Just as with fragmented, small-scale pre-baroque groups that perforce specialize in chamber work, the public's understanding of the actual or potential expressive range of contemporary music is miniaturized.

If the polemics of the Columbia-Princeton school had been confined to the championing of its own music, no one could complain. But it is the nature of polemics to be *against* things as well as for them, and, indeed, it has been the natural tendency of all strong-minded composers throughout music history to disparage their rivals as well as advance their own cause. Still, the opacity and hostility of the Princeton circle to music it did not understand reached new heights, or depths. One instance among many was an article Cone wrote in 1977 for the *American Scholar* entitled "One Hundred Metronomes," a particularly silly and uncomprehending diatribe against experimental music in this country and in Europe. Cone doesn't understand, but it never occurred to him that that might be *his* fault.

It should be reiterated that this school of composers has produced significant music, and continues to produce it, even if some of its fiercer polemicists—Wuorinen, above all—are now espousing a greater catholicity. For good or ill, however, we seem now to be in the midst of a vehement reaction against the dominance of new-music programs, journals and theory by the Northeastern axis. Indeed, the reaction is so strong that Wuorinen's new catholicity begins to look defensive. The experimentalists are ever more active, and winning greater governmental and foundation support. The pop and jazz fusionists constitute a real school of their own. And some of the older symphonists like William Schuman and Ned Rorem are re-entering the polemical lists, joined by such composers as George Rochberg and David Del Tredici, who have abandoned serialism and turned, out of conviction or opportunism, to writing music audiences actually like.

At a party a few years ago, Babbitt was asked convivially which composer he would like to be, were he given his choice. His answer was Jerome Kern. That is not such a surprise. Between the end of World War II and before he joined the Princeton music faculty in 1948, Babbitt had a brief and unsuccessful career as a pop-song composer; he even wrote an entire musical comedy that failed. His expertise about pre-rock American popular song remains considerable, as does his record collection of such music.

He is not alone in keeping his passion for American popular culture rigidly separate from his "serious" work—separate even when he pays homage to it from afar, as in his punning *All Set* for jazz ensemble, which manages to be rather sweet in its simultaneous evocation of jazz and formal distance from it. Gunther Schuller and Mel Powell are other examples of this odd, sad bifurcation of sensibility. On his summer-showcase Tanglewood contemporary-music programs, Schuller takes a determinedly conservative, modernist line, ignoring not just jazz and serious rock but even much of the experimental tradition.

Our musical democracy is sufficiently diverse to encompass all kinds of music, from the most austere to the most vulgar and obvious. But one still wishes that musicians of talent like Babbitt and Schuller had found a way to make a more successful synthesis of their instincts. If Babbitt, for instance, could have combined the complexity and purity of his "serious" scores with the melodic freshness and easy appeal of the musical comedy. Or if Powell and Schuller could blend more consistently, naturally and unselfconsciously their detailed craft and skillful orchestration with the improvisatory freshness of jazz.

As it happens, there are younger composers today who are effecting just such cross-breeding—fusions that are organic rather than grafted. The work of these musicians does not invalidate the finest achievements of a man like Babbitt. But it does suggest that his music may remain the province of historical specialists in the further reaches of musical complexity. And while the musical dross of every age and style far outweighs the few works that last, it seems likely that the balance among American serialists is tilted rather too heavily toward the tedious.

The real answer to "Who Cares If You Listen?" is Milton Babbitt and his fellow composers: they would not have polemicized and taught and impresarioed and, indeed, composed so prolifically if they didn't. But for the mountain of unlistenable academic exercises they did so much to inspire, and for the now widespread belief among laymen that *all* new music is repellent pedantry, they have much to answer.

3

AMERICAN INTELLECTUAL COMPOSERS & THE "IDEAL PUBLIC"

ELLIOTT CARTER

If there is any kind of consensus as to America's "best" living composer, it is Elliott Carter. Of course, the adjudication of "best" is so subjective that nobody can actually stake the claim. Still, among critics, fellow musicians, the musical community abroad (especially in Britain) and perhaps even, by now, the general public, Carter has attained a reputation no other composer can challenge. In 1979 Andrew Porter, who speaks for the Anglo-American establishment as well as anyone, thought it "at least likely that if there were to be an international poll to nominate 'the greatest living composer' Carter's name would lead all the rest."

Carter has achieved this reputation through the quality of his music first of all, and because it appeals to a group of highly active, energetic performing virtuosos who have propagated it. His personality also plays a part—crusty and puckish, the living image of what a great composer *should* look like. And he has won his eminence without becoming part of the American academic world; he remains a free artist, responding to commissions and making music on his own terms.

Born in 1908, he has had a fascinating stylistic evolution. Carter started as a Francophile neo-classicist, even though now he attributes the French bias of his youth more to the circumstances of world affairs in the thirties than to any innate leanings on his part. I have already touched on the manner in which young American composers after World War I, sated with Teutonicism, sought out France as an antidote. Almost by accident, they discovered in Paris a heretofore obscure French pedagogue named Nadia Boulanger, who became the doyenne for several generations of American composers, starting with Aaron Copland and Virgil Thomson. Carter himself studied with her between 1932 and 1935, and the line continued at least as far as the mid-1960's, with Philip Glass. What American composers got from Boulanger was an impeccable grounding in musical basics—ear training, rock-solid musical literacy, differentiation and refinement of styles. Her training may have been maternally domineering at times, and some of the composers rebelled. But if they stuck it out, she gave them a technical and stylistic foundation they could build on any way they liked.

For all his subsequent originality within clearly defined limits, Carter was in his youth no pathbreaker. The American Francophiles favored music that was neo-classical in form, traditional in harmony and straightforward in expression—and, as such, conservative in relation to the philosophical convolutions and quasi-scientific abstractions across the Rhine, which became the inspiration for Milton Babbitt and the young American serialists who emerged after the Second World War. Carter's early music evinced a certain originality, but it was couched in received idioms. For a time, he even allied himself with the then prevalent populism of the thirties, out of a "natural desire to write something many people could presumably grasp and enjoy easily at a time of social emergency," as he recalled. In the late thirties and early forties he composed stage works—incidental music and ballets—and choral pieces, two forms he has given up since, as well as orchestral scores and songs in greater profusion than he has sustained in recent decades. It was only in his forties that he took the first steps toward his mature style, in his First String Quartet of 1951.

The First Quartet was composed in the Arizona desert, where he had gone to escape the pressures of life in New York and to reconsider his music. The quartet marks his break with his past, and with the divided allegiances that had confused his music until then—his diverse debts to his teachers, traditions, public and inner convictions. From then on, the last of these was to claim his principal loyalty. In this score, he decided, he would give full vent to his tendencies toward "advanced" composition. As is not uncommon with Carter, the overall plan was suggested by another art—the contrast of "real" and "dream" time in Cocteau's film *Le Sang d'un poète*. The quartet also includes quotations from Ives and his friend Conlon Nancarrow, the reclusive master of the avant-garde player piano who has lived in Mexico since 1940. Carter achieved his desired effects, and satisfied his need for a personal idiom, with a texture made up of what he calls "many-layered contrasts of character"—contrapuntal ideas carried into every aspect of musical thought and worked out with abrupt and focused exactness.

That First Quartet and all his music since, an evolution he has summarized in an essay called "Music and the Time Screen," concerned themselves above all else with tempo and rhythm. He devised the term "metric modulation" to describe the process by which his music shifts rhythmic gears like the modulation from one key to another in tonal harmony. The theory was inspired by jazz and formulated in conjunction with Nancarrow. "The effect I am interested in producing," Carter explained, "is one of perceived large-scale rhythmic tension, sometimes involving the anticipation of the impending final coincidence of all the disparate rhythmic layers at some key moment." He has also concerned himself with the precise and original deployment of orchestral color, with steadily more ingenious and idiosyncratic formal procedures, with a newly complex polyphony—"simultaneous streams of different things going on together"—and with a subtle parallelism between music and literary texts.

The result has been a mature output of originality, individual strength and knotty fascination. He might be called an associate member of the Columbia-Princeton club, one who leavens the extreme rationalism and tensely controlled precision of the fifties and sixties with the neo-classical and Americanist styles of his youth. Looked at another way, he has adapted the ethos of serialist rationalism to the crabbed, indomitable spirit of such New England transcendental composers as Ruggles and—without his boisterous vitality—Ives.

Carter works slowly, accepting only a few of the many commissions that are pressed upon him. His catalogue since the early fifties consists mostly of chamber and orchestral scores, with the chamber work predominating. In 1975 he returned to vocal writing—a wise decision, one might think, given his evident predilection for a certain sort of American poetry (Whitman, Crane, Elizabeth Bishop, John Ashbery), although the instrumental angularity of his recent vocal writing suggests he is still searching for a way to write for the voice.

Noticeably missing from his output are experimental idioms, electronics, recent stage works or any sort of opera. Quite apart from the conservatism of American opera companies and audiences, and the difficulty he would have trying to fill up a whole evening, the very demonstrativeness of the stage would seem foreign to the guarded privacy of his personality. Carter has never been a selfconscious avant-gardist, however, in the sense of pursuing any of the latest trends. Indeed, in his commitment to conventional instruments and notation and his unwillingness to leap into serialism, electronics or experimentation, he must be called a traditionalist.

It is the sheer density of texture in Carter's later work that first strikes one. A score like the String Quartet No. 3 of 1971 unfolds with myriad busy details, yet if the performance is right in letter and spirit, those details fuse into a genuinely communicative experience. Carter has far transcended the homogeneity of the classical and romantic quartets. For him, each instrument is an individual character, and the texture, for all its fevered activity, is always sufficiently transparent that the ear can follow each separate line. This is not a music for relaxation, for the balm of a restful flow of sound. Instead, it demands the most intense concentration. But it also encourages such concentration, and rewards it. And the very existence of hyper-active minutiae brings a breathless excitement characteristic of the unfolding of a particularly bracing baroque piece. There·is a full range of emotional moods here, but Carter refuses to allow a single emotion to establish itself luxuriously. Moods fly by, breathless and tense, jostling for attention.

Although Carter may deliberately eschew the formalistic complexity of Babbitt, he offers an ample complexity of his own—often using systems and modes of musical discourse invented for that one score. In a work like his Third Quartet, isolated moments retain and recall his past, and the past of American art music. But if there remains a nostalgic flavoring of Francophile Americanism here, it has been shaped decisively by the Germanic, serial Zeitgeist. "My music," Carter said recently, "does have a strong bias towards systematizing."

This complexity places extreme demands on its executants. Performers since at least the time of Beethoven have struggled with the seemingly superhuman difficulty of the best new music. Soloists and orchestras may protest, and sometimes succeed in toning down such scores, as with Joachim's bowdlerization of the Tchaikovsky Violin Concerto. Yet composers continue to write music of ever greater complexity. They do so in part because the task poses them an interesting challenge. As the level of instrumental accomplishment improves—and it *has* so improved, steadily, over the decades—they sense the opportunity to realize heretofore unrealizable ambitions. And with the fulfillment of that opportunity, they are inspired to still more "impossible" feats. At the same time, as instrumentalists master new techniques and formerly fearsome scores, they, too, seek out new difficulties. The existence of a band of new-music virtuosos like Speculum Musicae in New York serves as a tempting competitive challenge to a composer, and it is a challenge men like Carter welcome.

But there are dangers in these ever more difficult pieces. While chamber groups such as Speculum may seek them out, symphony orchestras will not: their musicians may have improved, too, but their rehearsal time is still circumscribed by their union contracts and the need to prepare at least one new program every week. A score such as Carter's *Symphony of Three Orchestras* of 1976 offers a far wider range of color and texture than a string quartet. But even in a presumably well-intentioned and scrupulous performance like that recorded by Pierre Boulez and the New York Philharmonic, the numerous moments of inexactitude and slack tension suggest the problems inherent in all orchestral performances of works this complex.

Thus a dangerous division opens up between highbrow chamber music and middlebrow orchestral concerts—a division some would argue has existed ever since Beethoven's late string quartets, but needn't be encouraged further. Composers can become obsessed with virtuosity, just as readily as performers. It may seem odd to think of Elliott Carter side by side with Paganini. But both men betray a similar love of display for its own sake.

How much complexity can an audience be expected to perceive? Carter has spoken out forthrightly against Babbitt's defiant indifference to the general public, and in favor of "ear music." "It's obvious," he once remarked, "that the real order and meaning of music is the one the listener *hears* with his ears. Whatever occult mathematical orders may exist on paper are not necessarily relevant to this in the least. Total serialism invades every dimension of the musical rhetoric and predictably produces disastrous results, from any artistic standpoint, in the vast majority of cases."

Still, there can be no denying that for the comfortable middlebrow who likes mostly Mozart, Babbitt and Carter sound about equally complex and off-putting. This brings us again to the supposed "lag" between the work of an innovative composer and its eventual reception by a wider audience—and its eventual performance by musicians practiced enough to do it justice. In one of the best-known and most amusing books about music in recent years, Nicolas Slonimsky in his *Lexicon of Musical Invective* assembled a litany of critical misjudgments—vituperative or calmly reasoned dismissals of works that have since come to be regarded as indisputable masterpieces. This historical scenario conveniently ignores the many works recognized as masterpieces today that were prized from the start by patrons, critics and public alike. But the theory retains an understandable appeal to a contemporary composer who feels himself cruelly ignored.

Carter writes for an "ideal listener," a "possible public" rather than the "existing public"; his training, he said, gave him "the idea of what a public could be." This not only reveals a more conventionally humanistic and communicative sensibility than Babbitt's, but perhaps also a more calculated attitude toward worldly success. Carter is surely correct that in the future his music will be more expertly played and more widely admired. Indeed, compared with just a few years ago, the future for him has already arrived, in both the quality of the performances he receives and the degree of his critical, if not yet public, approbation.

Yet the obsessive knottiness of his music suggests something more troubling. That is the too ready equation in our culture between complexity and excellence, and between pedigree and artistic worth. Among our academics and lovers of Europe, among those who worry that American culture is but a poor transplant of the European original, there is an instinctive veneration of tradition and busy ingenuity, and a concomitant distrust of the simple. These inclinations are an intellectualized extension of the virtuoso's love for showy display. In the absence of a sure personal feeling for what is artistically meaningful, listener, performer and composer all regress to the ornate and pedantic exposition of craft.

This prejudice exists in the other arts, if not in such an extreme form, and wherever it exists, it saps vitality. Despite those who decry American painting of the post-war period, such painting is an internationally admired phenomenon. Much of it is at least ostensibly simple: the complexity comes with the conceptualization and perception. There are few who would dismiss traditional Japanese culture as simplistic. Yet its purity of expression derives from its austerity. As Ned Rorem, that defiantly Francophile composer, put it in a 1982 program note: "Today, even in France (indeed, especially in France), there is a drive to equate Serious with Complex. And what is serious? Are Wilde and Chaplin and Copland serious, or the ultra-simple Mondrian or Erik Satie? Is Schoenberg more serious than Ravel by virtue of being harder to grasp—of having a 'system'? Surface is as telling as depth, the casual as touching as the Big Statement."

Although Carter studied non-Western cultures as a youth, he is now uncomfortable with traditional and ritualistic forms: he once wittily remarked that "Gods and spirits are very conservative in their tastes." What he failed to add was that a conservative tradition in one culture may be turned to radical ends in another culture. And that a study of a culture like the Japanese can cast light on our own esthetic presuppositions. Recently Carter complained jokingly, but bitterly, too, that most of his Juilliard composition students wanted to write minimal music. Perhaps that is just a fashion of the moment. But perhaps it represents something deeper, a decisive swing away from the very fetishism of complexity which has defined modernist composition, and which constitutes the basis of Carter's esthetic.

If Carter feels abandoned by the younger generation of his own establishment world, that will only reinforce his already deeply felt isolation from the hostile environment of American culture. He regrets the absence of an elite that has the "power to give a single cultural style to American society," as in aristocratic Europe. He regrets the "deep pessimism of so many American writers," and how composers here today "are worried about whether or how long serious music can persist, since at the present moment the extraordinarily rapid expansion of the 'popularity' of 'popular' music apparently threatens to sweep away the actual values and pleasures, as well as the resultant prestige, that a small group derives from serious music." He complains that "the artistic horizon of the American composer is not expanded by life in a society that is unable to furnish him with artistic and intellectual ideas and critiques of sufficient depth, clarity and quality to be of much use."

Such sentiments might seem to place Carter in the line of the sometimes embittered, sometimes extravagantly optimistic American outsiders, at one with Whitman, Ruggles and Ives. Indeed, as a young man Carter was befriended by the aging Ives, and one should not forget his kinship with Nancarrow. Carter's status as an American loner is reinforced, too, by the determined way he has constructed his own musical idiom, one that defies and stands apart from the competing fashions of the day.

Yet if there is any synchronism between art and life, then Carter's calculated music implies a calculated personality. There is a whiff of careerism about Carter, although perhaps no more so than with any ambitious composer. He once noted that when he composed his String Quartet No. 1, he was convinced the public would reject it, and was both surprised and delighted when it became his most widely praised piece to date. Maybe boldness and iconoclasm provide their own rewards, and composers should simply not try to court success. But Carter's reaction to the quartet's reception also indicates that he cared rather deeply about the public in the first place. In retrospect, considered as a whole and compared with contemporary experimental idioms, his mature work sounds almost as if it has been carefully staked out with an eye to what the public might eventually accept—bold but not *too* bold; difficult but still conceived for traditional instruments in traditional concert formats.

The existence of a lag between many great composers and subsequent public acceptance hardly means that any music the public rejects is guaranteed of immortality. There are connoisseurs of indisputable taste who are deeply moved by Carter's music. There are others who are left indifferent by it. I myself sit uneasily on the fence. Most of Carter's work, even that of his maturity, has failed to seize my affection as other music has done. But the best of it—the lapidary evocation of Hart Crane in the woodwinds and the trumpet solo at the beginning of the *Symphony of Three Orchestras,* for instance, or the sheer nervous ferocity of the Third Quartet—has an irresistible greatness. One should probably have enough faith in the "lag" to assume that more of his work will have that same impact in time.

Carter once wrote, "I soon began to realize that whatever American character my music had would be the character of myself making music. I came to realize that America is itself being created right here before us, moment by moment, combining its sometimes perplexing unwillingness to consider the past with its good-natured generosity and idealistic hope for the future. To chart a cultural development here, it seemed to me, was a waste of time, while what was and is important is to make the present, with all its connections to the past and anticipations of the future, exist more powerfully than either of these."

A better testimony to the individuality and idiosyncratic vitality of the greatest American composers could hardly be written. The irony is that it was written by a man who has not always been able to express such a Whitmanesque affinity for the moment. Carter in his music and his life seems more frequently to be caught between the grand elitist tradition of European art music, the ruder strength of the American character and his own sense of isolation—itself sometimes proudly hermetic and sometimes wistfully supplicatory toward the here and now.

At the end of "Music and the Time Screen," Carter evinces a pained doubt that his self-analysis will be taken in the proper spirit. His words are likely, he realizes, to be made canonical and repeated unthinkingly in classrooms for years to come. But those words, he counsels us, are "the outer shell, the wrapping of the music. The reason for writing it—for developing it in the way described, for weighing every note, chord, rhythm in the light of their expressive intention and their living, spontaneous interrelationships, and the judging of it all, almost unconsciously, against a private standard of what gives me genuine sensuous pleasure, of what seems fascinating, interesting, imaginative, moving, and of urgent importance— cannot be put into words."

Of course it can't. But maybe, just maybe, it is the very contradictions in his work and personality that have inspired those decisions. For me, Carter's achievement, for all its demonstrable magnitude, seems curiously constrained, flawed by a lack of inner clarity and expressive directness. Dialecticians may think otherwise. And posterity, after all, will be the judge.

4

THE AMERICAN EXPERIMENTAL TRADITION & ITS GODFATHER

JOHN CAGE

Krenek, Babbitt and Carter all belong in one way or another to the established mainstream of Western art music. Each is an individual, yet each has tried to make a music of the twentieth century that represented some sort of extension of that mainstream. Even Babbitt, the pure researcher, remains part of the tradition. So does John Cage, I suppose, or so it will seem from the perspective of a musicologist two hundred years from now; historians have a way of identifying causal links that are invisible at the time the causation is supposed to be taking place. Cage may think of himself as a complete iconoclast; he is certainly so perceived by those who find his music and his ideas hateful or absurd. But his inspiration can even now be seen as a form of renewal.

For present-day experimental music, Cage is a father figure, an icon. His influence is cited without question even by his opponents. There are those who wish the whole "far out" musical scene would just disappear. They think of it as an excrescence, a bizarre error, just as they—and some experimentalists, too—dismiss serialism as a Viennese eccentricity that got out of hand. There are traditionalists who condemn both camps, and rightly see a similarity between the systematic abstraction of a Babbitt, with his convoluted set theories, and Cage, with his dice and the *I Ching*. But all of them recognize in Cage the leader of a musical movement that has had an enormous impact, in this country especially.

Before we consider Cage himself, however, it might be useful to remember that he had his antecedents. That is not to take away from his so earnestly sought-after originality. But it does set the record straight. If American art music—music that really spoke with this country's voice and was heard by the world—was largely the product of eccentric loners, historians can still look back at those loners and cite their similarities of method and style. Even those who had active early lives in major capitals—Ruggles in New York, for instance—eventually withdrew to isolated locations; others were shaped early by such isolation even if they ultimately gravitated to the capitals. Their favorite retreats are New England and California. Both have traditions of cosmopolitanism and tolerate— some might say foster—eccentricity. New England produced the earlier masters, Ives himself and Ruggles, above all. California can claim Cage, a product of Los Angeles who passed through Seattle before coming finally to New York, but also Cowell, Lou Harrison, Dane Rudhyar, Harry Partch, Terry Riley and Pauline Oliveros.

All of these composers can be faulted for their idiosyncrasies. They did not care much about what past composers had done, nor did most of them have much direct influence on the future— meaning younger composers who emulated them. Few bothered to perfect a diverse and sophisticated technique. They chose instead to master only what served their expressive purposes, although in turn their visions may have been constrained by technical weakness. It seems sometimes that we have been a musical nation of Mussorgskys, with precious few Rimsky-Korsakovs to fix things up. America has lacked, for worse but perhaps also for better, just what Carter says it lacks: intellectual resonance among peers, to provide enlightened criticism and appreciation.

On the other hand, better Mussorgsky than Rimsky; better raw genius than craftsmanship. The virtues of these loners are the virtues of America itself—a willingness to chance the new, to strike out fearlessly, to plunge into experiences of which Europeans or teachers or parents might disapprove. These composers cultivated musical traditions from beyond Europe. They reveled in new scientific developments, exploring their potential and letting their discoveries alter their assumptions about what music was in the first place. They flatly refused to be bound by any textbook definition of what music was or what a composer should do.

I speak of these composers as loners, yet they came out of a tradition of American experimentalism that flourished in the twenties and thirties, before it was deflected by the populist surge of the mid-late thirties and suppressed by the American serialists of the late fifties and sixties. The godfather of this first wave of experimentation, and the man to whom Cage owes an enormous and freely admitted debt, was Henry Cowell.

Cowell's impact on American musical life was blunted by the sexual prejudices of his time. In 1936 he was convicted of "statutory charges involving an unnamed seventeen-year-old boy," in the words of the *San Francisco Chronicle,* and spent four years in San Quentin; upon his release, he still lived under a cloud of disapproval, although he was pardoned in 1942. Cowell's music remains sadly neglected, but it is clear that he will eventually take his place as one of the great American composers. Anyone curious as to what he accomplished need only seek out a New World Records disc of his *Quartet Romantic.* This is a piece of such difficulty that it could only be properly performed by musicians wearing headphones so they could pace themselves against electronically precise "click tracks." Yet Cowell's complexity never makes a statement of itself. This is music of direct accessibility, for all its many secrets. In later years, he sought to link his experimental ideas with Western folk music and the musical traditions of the world as a whole, and in so doing he was once again a pioneer.

Apart from his music, which was rarely played after he himself stopped promoting it, Cowell inspired other composers through his writings in the *Musical Quarterly* and with his New Music Edition publishing firm, which Cage later called "independent and therefore not politically strong." "Anything that was vividly experimental was discouraged by the League of Composers and the ISCM," Cage added. Above all, there was Cowell's book, *New Musical Resources,* in which he boldly predicted an enormous number of musical advances that subsequently became everyday assumptions among younger composers, from tone clusters to chance music. The book was published in 1930, but Cowell had begun writing it as early as 1916, when he was nineteen years old. Among the many who attested to its influence was Conlon Nancarrow.

Today, people think of "modern American music" in terms of its latter-day manifestations. It is easy to forget that between the wars there was an active American new-music scene, and not just in New York. The acme of the League of Composers and the ISCM, along with the Copland-Sessions concerts of the late twenties and early thirties and such conductors as Serge Koussevitzky and Dimitri Mitropoulos, constituted a scene perhaps not so active as today's, but arguably even more creative. Besides, in those days the contemporary American composer still spoke to his fellow musicians and intellectuals in a way that happens too infrequently now.

So Cage, who was born in 1912, did not emerge unaccountably from the waves. He came out of a tradition, actually studying with Cowell and with Schoenberg in Los Angeles, although he was a rambunctious pupil, more interested in rhythm than harmony. He made his first mark while still on the West Coast with percussion pieces of a sort pioneered by Edgard Varèse and Cowell and also propagated by such diverse composers as Harrison and Carlos Chávez. Then came his move to New York in 1942, the beginning of his decades-long association with Merce Cunningham, and his mature work.

As with Cowell, Cage's theory, encouragement of younger composers and personality have served even more than his music to define his influence. With Cowell, there is still hope that his catalogue as a whole may reveal a consistency that the few pieces known so far suggest. With Cage, some of the carefully crafted music from the thirties to the early fifties remains underperformed, and may well be revived. But by and large Cage has not lacked for performances; what there is we have heard, and any change in posterity's judgment will come from a change in attitude, not from a rediscovery of the work itself.

Cage's music has undergone shifts of style and emphasis, as with almost all composers. In his case, though, the shifts have been radical ones, complete transformations of method, performing forces and sheer sound. What has remained constant is his questing spirit of adventure, his determination to seem fresh and even outrageous, and his meditative epistemology.

The most striking pieces from his early years, the 1930's and 1940's, are those for percussion and prepared piano. The percussion scores still sound highly attractive in their rhythmic invention. Cage was not alone in the exploration of such effects, and not the first. But the pieces are playable and enjoyable, full of exuberant racket and a feathery delicacy. They demonstrate a palpable love for sonority and rhythm, and they are frequently programmed to this day.

When it comes to rhythmic sophistication, even imperialist defenders of Western art music—those who still see all other traditions, including popular and folk musics within the West itself, as "primitive"—must concede that the West has been backward. There are good reasons for that, primarily the need for a steady beat in order for several players to articulate vertical chords. As orchestras expanded in the nineteenth century, this need for synchronization grew more acute. The rhythms of the Balinese gamelan are also simple by comparison to those of Indian or African music, for the same reason. Were a composer to notate one hundred individual orchestral parts with the rhythmic complexity of an Indian raga exposition, the result could only be chaos.

There were other sacrifices made for ensemble precision in the West, principally in the realm of microtonal subtlety. Those subtleties lived on in the lieder recital and in the ornamentation of variable-pitch instruments like the violin. But the impetus has been away from intimate niceties and toward big, bold, simplistic blocks of sound, with subtlety achieved through the precisely ordered combination of individual parts, each played by a musician severely limited in personal expressive autonomy. Hence the neuroses of orchestral musicians today, trained as soloists but forced to function as cogs in an anachronistic musical machine.

Cage's music for prepared piano was an extension of his percussion pieces. The prepared piano, which Cowell invented and Cage perfected, involves the alteration of the sound of a piano by "treating" the hammers and inserting various materials between the strings, as well as plucking and striking those strings directly by hand. These works have a wonderful charm as a sort of Rube Goldbergian gamelan. With their quirky sing-song step and delicate timbral effects, they are likely to be played long after Cage's other music has receded to the library shelves. Their composition occupied Cage off and on until 1954.

There was no sudden leap from these primarily rhythmic works into the free-form variety of his mature output. The transition included a number of works for conventional forces that reflect an Oriental philosophical influence not yet extended into the actual method of composition. Scores such as *The Seasons*, a ballet for chamber orchestra (1947), and String Quartet (1950), both of which portray the cycles of nature from an Oriental perspective, have a quiet, meditational aura, yet remain the products of a conventionally trained Western composer.

But by the early fifties, Cage had begun to jettison all that. Since then, the range of his work has been huge, expanding music into new areas or betraying it altogether, depending on one's point of view. There are graphic scores—experiments in notation that seek to inspire rather than command a player, and hence attract theatrically oriented performers like Bertram Turetzky, the double-bass virtuoso, or Max Neuhaus, when he was still a percussionist, to create along with Cage. There are overt conceptual pieces, works in which the philosophical underpinnings are clearly more significant than any mere sound. The apex of that genre was *4'33"* (1952), "tacet for any instrument or instruments," in which the performer sits before an instrument playing nothing, and thereby invites the audience to contemplate the diversity of supposed silence. Often, in recent decades, Cage has also made use of chance procedures, most frequently involving the *I Ching*, to help determine specific compositional choices.

For a time, he was actively concerned with electronics, an interest that had been preceded by his use of mechanical sound variables, as in his *Imaginary Landscape No. 1* of 1939, which includes a part for variable-speed turntable. The electronic works, often collaborations, range from studies for synthesizers to pieces that more or less rigorously rely on computers. They are often more easily discussed under another heading, that of the "happening," or random free-for-all. On a small scale or in the most rambunctiously grandiose terms imaginable, Cage (with an assist from Ives) pioneered what might be called the circus concert, in which lots of people do lots of different things at once, all in the service of a joyous cacophony. Examples include *Atlas eclipticalis* (1961), for "any ensemble from eighty-six instruments," *Variations IV* (1963), for "any number of players, any means," and *HPSCHD* (1967–9), for one to seven harpsichords and one to fifty-one computer-generated tapes, the complete version of which has filled up indoor sports arenas for hours on end. More recently, Cage has concentrated on austere solo collections, *Etudes australes* for piano and the *Freeman Etudes* for violin, which refine randomness to an almost celestially pure boredom.

Music and esthetic philosophy are hardly his only concerns. The graphic scores were just the first step in a steady extension of his creative ideas into the realm of the visual. More recently, inspired by poets like Clark Coolidge and Jackson Mac Low, who applied his compositional methods to words, he has become a more active poet. But his many talks and lectures, which have been collected into a steady stream of books since *Silence* of 1961, amount to their own form of aural artwork, as the recorded version of some of them, *Indeterminacy*, proves so well. Finally, he has long been a fervent mycologist, pursuing his fungi with a benign intensity that is itself esthetic.

All this work shares a willingness to explore nearly anything. But not all of it, especially the music of the past twenty-five years, has been very interesting to *hear:* neither "ear music" nor "eye music" but, perhaps, "head music," in that it seemed most interesting as ideas for pieces rather than as pieces *per se.* The very nature of Cage's esthetic discounts the importance of finished craftsmanship and a focused point of view. It is up to the audience to provide that point of view, and there can be little doubt that audiences have derived more all-purpose intellectual sustenance from the contemplation of Cage's work than from that of most serial academics.

Still, Cage shows a disturbing indifference to how his music actually sounds, which in turn suggests a curious parallelism to Babbitt and his lesser disciples, in other respects so completely his opposites. This similarity has to do with a systematic pursuit of abstraction. Both Babbitt and Cage reject the comfortable familiarities of tonal music. For both, abstraction can help jostle and expand a listener's consciousness and perceptual powers. Both men's work can sometimes be perceived as fields of pure abstraction, akin to the seemingly random patterning of Jackson Pollock and other New York abstract expressionists. Babbitt goes about his abstraction through the higher realm of set theory. Cage throws dice, consults the *I Ching* and lays translucent music paper across star maps—although in his very early work he too experimented with mathematical formulas. Each achieves a disjunct flow of sound that disorients and, often, bores listeners. Indeed, from that perspective, Cage is the purer of the two, being the more boring.

But unlike Babbitt, Cage is very much concerned with the perceptual relationship between composer, piece and audience. For him, music is never just sound; it is an invitation to alter one's way of perceiving the world. And it is through his prose, where he can make explicit the "didactic element in my work," as he puts it, that Cage has had his greatest influence. The message emerges in spite of, or perhaps because of, the way he attempts to confound normal denotative explications by techniques similar to those he applies to music: cut-ups, rearrangements of arbitrary patterns, etc. Composer after composer has cited a reading of Cage's first prose collection, *Silence,* as seminal for the realization that there were other possibilities out there, waiting to be tried—other ways of doing things than had been taught at the conservatory, or even ways of composing music without formal training at all.

Silence, which collects many of Cage's writings from 1939 through 1961, is a curious document to read today. Cage is no more a polished prose stylist than he is a craftsman as a composer. Ideas abound, but so do contradictions and inelegancies and semi-literacy. James Joyce is a writer Cage much admires, to the point of basing his *Roaratorio* (1980) on *Finnegans Wake.* But Cage's attempts at a stream-of-conscious flow of word-plays and allusions hardly match the poetic clarity of Joyce.

There is still much to ponder here, however, and much inspiration if one is ready for it, as a whole generation of young American experimentalists in the sixties clearly was. The message is quiescent, Zen-inspired, nature-worshiping, anarchic and optimistic. Some selected quotations, strung together with the randomness Cage himself so much admires: "New music: new listening." "Silence becomes something else—not silence at all, but sounds, the ambient sounds." "Any attempt to exclude the 'irrational' is irrational. Any composing strategy which is wholly 'rational' is irrational in the extreme."

"We must bring about a music which is like furniture—a music, that is, which will be part of the noises of the environment." "In Zen they say: If something is boring after two minutes, try it for four. If still boring, try it for eight, sixteen, thirty-two, and so on. Eventually one discovers that it's not boring at all but very interesting." "The novelty of our work derives from our having moved away from simply private human concerns towards the world of nature and society of which all of us are a part. Our intention is to affirm this life, not to bring order out of chaos, not to suggest improvements in creation, but simply to wake up to the very life we're living, which is so excellent once one gets one's mind and one's desires out of its way and lets it act of its own accord."

"Responsibility to oneself; and the highest form of it is irresponsibility to oneself which is to say the calm acceptance of whatever responsibility to others and things comes along." "There is all the time in the world for studying music, but for living there is scarcely any time at all." "If one feels protective about the word 'music,' protect it and find another word for all the rest that enters through the ears." "Here we are. Let us say Yes to our presence together in Chaos." "The day in the woods I took a compass was the day I got lost for sure." "The truth is we don't know what we're doing and that is how we manage to do it when it's lively. I believe what we're doing is exploring a field, that the field is limitless and without qualitative differentiation but with multiplicity of differences, that our business has changed from judgment to awareness." "The field is not just a field of music, and the acceptance is not just of the sounds that had been considered useless, ugly and wrong, but it is a field of human awareness, and the acceptance ultimately is of oneself as present mysteriously, impermanently, on this limitless occasion."

"What we had in mind was something like those Japanese gardens with a few stones in them." "What do we like? We do not like to be pushed around emotionally." "I quoted: 'The purpose of music is to sober and quiet the mind, thus making it susceptible to divine influences.'" "I'm losing my ability to make connections because the ones I do make so belittle the natural complexity." "We are not trying to put our emotion into someone else. That way you 'rouse rabbles'; it seems on the surface human, but it animalizes." "Now structure is not put into a work, but comes up in the person who perceives it in himself. There is therefore no problem of understanding but the possibility of awareness."

These remarks, echoed by others not just in this book but in Cage's subsequent collections, suggest the impact on his thinking of Oriental mysticism—and his role, along with others, in its dissemination to America as a whole. Zen Buddhism was his first inspiration; in the late forties and early fifties, Cage attended lectures by Daisetz Suzuki, who was the principal conduit for Zen not only to him but to Allen Ginsberg and the Beats. Beyond Zen there is Indian religious thought and medieval Western mysticism, especially Meister Eckhart. For Cage, the primary task is a meditational acceptance of nature, rather than an aggressive imposition of individual consciousness onto nature, society and one's fellow man. This quietly contradicts Western man's Faustian ego, defining itself against the cosmos. The attendant notion of an art stripped of needless rhetoric and reduced to its spare essentials is not new— as demonstrated by the Bauhaus, neo-classicism and serialism, all of which defined the fashion in the twenties for a "new objectivity." Still, Cage's Orientalized interpretation of this minimalist urge was indeed new.

Orientalism itself has had a long impact on Western music, from at least the time of the "Turkish" craze for drums, triangles, cymbals and vaguely Middle Eastern modalities in the Vienna of the mid-late eighteenth century (e.g., Mozart's overture to *The*

Abduction from the Seraglio). Composers' fascination with world music expanded in exact proportion to Western imperialist discovery and domination. Erik Satie, who stands as Cage's principal influence among Western composers, was himself profoundly affected by the interest in things Oriental that suffused Paris around the turn of the century. Oriental timbres and coloristic exoticism became part of the composer's stock in trade. There was a whole fad for operas set in exotic locales, of which *Aida* and *Madama Butterfly* were but the culmination, and folk tunes from one's own country became a similar resource.

Cage's Orientalism was different, and more pervasive, a direct manifestation of the powerful religious undercurrent that has defined American culture from the beginning. To be sure, some of the prepared-piano pieces recall a gamelan. But most of Cage's music has nothing to do with any Oriental style. Instead, he sought his basic inspiration from Oriental philosophy and religion, and let the new personality that emerged shape his music.

His insistence that it was the listener who "created" a musical experience also had a profound impact. A creative listener can apply his creativity just as well to a Beethoven symphony as to one of Cage's tapestries of boredom. Yet Beethoven, in his very insistence on telling us something, makes a listener's self-assertion more difficult. Of course, too, that quiescence of compositional attitude, that passivity in the face of mediocrity or outright fraudulence, allows a lot of "bad" music to be composed and performed. For Cage, the gains in stimulated creativity for composer and listener alike far outweigh the losses. And the very idea that perception can be heightened by meditative concentration is surely nobler than the idea of perception being *forced* into growth through a confrontation with difficulty—the puritanical premise of Babbitt's esthetic.

Above all, Cage's message to younger composers was that they had permission to do any damn fool thing they wanted to. Some responded by doing damn fool things. But Cage allowed an indigenously American sense of humor and eccentric personal liberation to flower, and helped create a whole subculture of American new music that fostered such eccentricity. For the first time, American loners had a context in which to work, a support system of sympathetic peers, the kind of resonance Carter so covets for his own very different music.

Cage himself, for all his ostensible passivity, has been active in the creation of that support system, principally through the patronage he could dispense as Cunningham's music director. A number of fairly prominent composers worked steadily with him, above all David Tudor, Earle Brown, Christian Wolff and Morton Feldman, Feldman being the most impressive of the four. Cage also managed to provide performance opportunities for almost the entire range of New York–based experimentalists in the late seventies with the ongoing studio performances the Cunningham company gave in its Westbeth rehearsal space.

I ended my discussion of Elliott Carter with the suggestion that his proclamations of isolation might mask a shrewder careerism. The same charge has been leveled at Cage by Virgil Thomson in his essay "Cage and the Collage of Noises." Thomson dismisses Cage's music and ideas as a "one-way tunnel leading only to the gadget-fair." He speaks of Cage as a "professional celebrity," of his "always pushing," of his music being "emotionally shallow," of its "puny and inconsequential sound," of his "monorail mind and his turbine-engined, irreversible locomotive of a career." Thomson's Cage is a long way from Buddhistic quiescence.

Cage is hurt by such criticisms; he once co-wrote a biography of Thomson, but has broken off the friendship now. And he heatedly protests against the idea that his true influence will be felt in his esthetics, rather than his art. "I don't think what my critics have said is true," he argues. "I think the ideas are important but the music is important, too."

But perhaps there is something that transcends both esthetics and music. "Personality is a flimsy thing on which to build an art," Cage once wrote. Yet he himself seems to make his most direct and appealing impact through his own personality: the all-American grin, the ruggedly handsome yet childlike face, the calm, sly wit of his public narrations. Finally, as with Carter, it seems only marginally noteworthy that a man would want to advance his career: that, too, is the American way. Nor is it unprecedented for a composer to advocate Oriental meditation and self-abnegation and still possess a gargantuan ego: Richard Wagner did the same, a century ago. Were Cage merely a meditator, his religiosity would be of concern only to himself. That might be better for his soul than the tug and hustle of a composer's career. But Cage's enormous influence on American music has surely been beneficent. And any lingering tensions between the man and his work may ultimately serve creative ends not just for him, but for us, as well.

5

ROMANTIC DEFIANCE,
ENLIGHTENED PATRONAGE
& MISANTHROPY IN THE MIDWEST

RALPH SHAPEY

Any composer, carefully considered, laps messily beyond the categorical boundaries analysts set for him. Ralph Shapey, however, overlaps more boundaries than most. On one level, he has through his teacher, Stefan Wolpe, a direct lineage from Schoenberg. He might thus be considered an example of the penetration of serialism into American music. Or, along with Wolpe, he might be seen as a leading instance of a composer *refusing* to be bound by serialism's more formalistic implications. Instead of pushing serialism to its logical extremes, as did Babbitt, Shapey drew back and, like others of his generation (he was born in 1921), worked out a highly personal adaptation of Schoenberg's ideas.

But to discuss Shapey in terms of his serially inspired pitch-choices is to set ludicrous limits on both the man and his music. He is yet another loner, so embittered that for a while, between 1969 and 1976, he discouraged all performances of his music, and even pretended he had stopped composing altogether. His outsider status holds true even if, for nineteen years, he chose to fight for recognition in New York City, with only partial success. In 1964 he moved to Chicago, where he illustrates the fate of composers between the coasts. He is also an academic, since he teaches at the University of Chicago, thus demonstrating how the academic network encourages a dissemination of talent around the country. Yet all the while he has retained the characteristics of a New York composer of the fifties, marked by an association with the "New York school" of painting.

Shapey might have been expected to have enjoyed a guaranteed entrée into the New York establishment through Wolpe. Wolpe was born in Berlin in 1902, left Germany in 1933 for Vienna and, a year later, for Palestine, and finally came to this country in 1938. As a young man, he studied with Busoni and Hermann Scherchen and was associated with Paul Klee and others in the Bauhaus, and he undertook further studies with Webern in the thirties. As Krenek had done, Wolpe went through several styles before settling on his final idiom. In the late twenties, like Hindemith and Weill, he simplified his procedures to make his music more accessible. He composed jazzish pieces, participated in Dada experiments and, in Palestine, developed an interest in Jewish music. But ultimately, with the onset of Nazism and under the influence of Webern, he returned to a more abstract and purely esthetic notion of art.

Wolpe's mature style, which he practiced in New York until his death in 1972, has been described by Eric Salzman as "a kind of flashing, fantasy serialism." Like Luigi Dallapiccola and unlike too many American serialists, Wolpe was able to transcend the daunting methodology of serialism and express himself as composers traditionally had done. But he did so without any sacrifice of complexity or rigor, and thus directly inspired the circle of New York composers that gathered around Charles Wuorinen and Harvey Sollberger and their Group for Contemporary Music.

Shapey followed his teacher in composing music that is idiosyncratically serial in means but "generally romantic in gesture," as one critic said of Wolpe's music. Shapey was once called a "radical traditionalist." It is a term he is proud of, and it means first of all that he works with standard classical-music forces—solo instruments, chamber groups, orchestras, choruses—and no electronics or overt experimentation. Although his harmonic idiom is more pungent than that of a nineteenth-century composer (or a modern-day nineteenth-century nostalgist), his sense of large-scale form recalls the romantic era. Not for Shapey the abrupt and spare pointillism of so many Webern-inspired serialists. His string quartets are long, his symphonies have a symphonic sweep, his oratorios sprawl luxuriously yet build to grand and searing climaxes.

Shapey's music is constructed with big, bold, opposing blocks of sound that clash and resolve contrapuntally. The counterpoint is between sound masses rather than sinuous lines. "I think about setting masses against other masses," he explained shortly before his sixtieth birthday. "I'm interested in the relationships between things. Even if an object doesn't change, if you place that object against some other object, there is, I believe, a kind of subtle change. This is not to say that I compose with philosophical ideas in mind. Pure music cannot be philosophical. But the philosophical ideas are part of my inspiration, if I may call it that. Part of myself, as a human being. They are not an afterthought; they are part of the Gestalt. Right, wrong or otherwise, this is Ralph Shapey."

The very existence of those sound masses, and the audible tension they generate, place Shapey's music a good distance from the static, determinedly abstract, unvariegated sound-fields of the more didactic American serialists. For so many of the more abstract composers, serialism is a means of ensuring a neutral randomness; their music sounds clinical, stripped of emotion or commitment. Shapey uses dissonance in the old-fashioned way, as an expression of tension and even anger. This is music with sweep, drive and passion. It is also music with an overt kinship to the other arts and to philosophical and scientific theory, as the allusion to Einstein's relativity suggests. While he lived in New York between 1945 and 1964, Shapey was closer socially to abstract expressionist painters than to his fellow composers. The structurally complex, bold and impassioned work of such men as Franz Kline and Willem de Kooning (who was also close to Wolpe) inspired his music more than that of Schoenberg's and Wolpe's drier disciples. Later, he liked to speak of his composition's kinship to sculpture, in its tactile immediacy.

Shapey's affinity to artists and poets is itself of interest. Too many twentieth-century composers have lost such links—or, if they have maintained them, it has been with safer, less commanding figures. Perhaps advanced composers are correct—that there is a necessary lag between serious original music and its public appreciation. Shapey himself agrees: "Great music is not for the masses," he said in 1977. "Not that they can't take to it. You, I, they, we all have a right to it, but we must come to it. It is not supposed to come to us." Yet while the general public may not be expected to respond immediately to new work, other artists should be. Artists share assumptions about innovative approaches that transcend the boundaries of a given art form. If a musical style does not appeal to like-minded painters, poets and dancers, it is probably hermetic. Not "too" hermetic; there should be no such proscription in a free society. But if music does not reach out to a community of artists, as it did in Paris in the nineteenth century and the 1920's, or as it does in New York's SoHo today, it verges on sterility.

Shapey has a rough, sensuous love of sound. In that regard, he has clear bonds with two other major twentieth-century composers, Varèse and Olivier Messiaen. Both were French, although Varèse came to America and lived here almost uninterruptedly from 1915 until his death in 1965, exerting a significant influence on the evolution of experimental music in New York during the twenties. But Shapey's sonorities never slide into coloristic display, as did so many of the *Klangfarbenschule* ("sound-color school") compositions of Europe in the sixties. Shapey's ideas are always bound together by audible form, which allows him to indulge in stylistic diversity, including allusions to jazz and other popular idioms, without cheapening his music or blurring its focus.

Beyond sound itself, Shapey's romanticism expresses itself in his grandiose notions of what his pieces are about. Many composers resist writing program notes out of the same distrust of words that animates their suspicion of critics. Often, they don't want to bother with real technical analysis because they don't think a lay audience could understand it. Or they may really believe in "ear music" and feel that an audience worrying about whether it is hearing everything it is supposed to hear will miss the music's more elemental message. Shapey will have none of this. In his public pronouncements, he spends little space on technical minutiae. Instead, he indulges in the cosmic, quasi-poetic verbiage that distinguished the musical self-descriptions of romantics from Wagner through Ives and Ruggles. His notes for an orchestral piece called *Rituals,* for instance, run in part like this: "A great work of Art is a work which transcends the immediate moment into a world of Infinity; complete and infinite within itself; of inevitability and of Oneness; and a series of such moments must result in a dynamic unforgettable experience."

Asked once if great art "afforded us a form of religious communication," Shapey answered, "If you want to call it religious, OK, call it religious, because for me, yes, *great art is a miracle.* Now if you've experienced these things, whether it's with art, religion— you call it religious experience. I'm talking about an experience in which, for that moment, you have lost control of your basic life, and lived in a different time-element, a different sphere. You receive something so marvelous that you cannot define it. You want it again—despite an element of fear, you remember it as a moment beyond yourself! It's one of the most marvelous experiences of your life. If you've experienced that, you know what I'm talking about. I believe great art can do that to you. I've experienced it. If you haven't, I'm sorry."

Such a sensibility, unsurprisingly, produces music that appeals to the uninitiated. In my experience, Shapey's work is almost always greeted with an enthusiasm rare for classical contemporary scores, be the audience new-music hard-liners or symphony subscribers who can't wait to get to the *Emperor* Concerto after the intermission. Shapey says that following a Chicago Symphony performance of one of his pieces, Jean Martinon, the orchestra's music director, came backstage and exclaimed, "I can't believe it. The ladies are loving it. They are giving it a standing ovation."

All of this might read like a litany of success, except for one small detail: Shapey feels he has been cruelly ignored by a hostile, philistine world. He has some reasons for feeling that way. It was only recently that he obtained a publisher. The 1981 performance of *Rituals* by the American Composers Orchestra was the first New York performance of any of his orchestral scores. He has never won the Pulitzer Prize, which has been awarded to several less worthy composers. And there was his now notorious "strike" between 1969 and 1976.

Many of Shapey's complaints make sense. All sorts of honorable people fail to win Pulitzers, but they remain America's foremost compositional accolade, and it clearly galls Shapey to see his inferiors exalted. His recent acquisition of a publisher, Presser, does not excuse the industry's failure before that—although it is difficult to believe the rank hostility with which Shapey says other publishers rejected him. "We have no time for geniuses," he says Peters told him. Or, from Boosey & Hawkes: "When you're dead and buried, Ralph." Even Presser's appearance on the scene does not entirely mollify Shapey. He complains—and in this he speaks for many composers, however much he overlooks economic realities as he does so—that in almost every case Presser has chosen to photocopy his manuscript rather than engraving it in the old, time-honored way. Not all composers are elegant musical calligraphers, and Shapey resents the dissemination of his own clear but scrawling notation when other composers get what he considers to be more professional treatment.

Shapey is a vocal opponent of the fixation on performers and star conductors at the expense of composers. This was a problem for composers even before they started writing music that laymen found offensive. Actually, of course, many composers' most important new work was rejected at first; the "lag" theory again. What seized people's attention in the eighteenth and nineteenth centuries was the flamboyant castrato, the glamorous prima donna, the demonic fiddler, the thundering piano virtuoso. Each of those (except the castrato) still enjoys the public's favor, but above them all stands the jet-setting star conductor. When one is dashing about, it simplifies matters to carry along a narrow repertory that can be repeated from city to city. To please both musicians and budget-conscious boards, it is wise to concentrate on familiar or simple pieces that do not require excessive rehearsal. In this, the conductors are happily abetted by the unions, whose contractual stipulations often preclude the allotment of extra rehearsal time for complex new pieces. In his complaints, Shapey has right on his side. He also manages to offend the conductors who might otherwise play his music—however badly.

Shapey has a feisty, unforgiving, self-righteous personality. His

misanthropy is ever present, sometimes luridly colorful and sometimes rather sad: "The old masters were part of their society. You
might say it was a very special society, and it was: It was the elite
of their day. But we don't have any elite today. Unless you want to
call the intellectuals the elite. But intellectuals, if they are the elite,
are just as bad as the rest of the human race, because they have to
have their rear ends tickled all the time. They're so sophisticated.
I'm not interested in tickling them with a feather; I'd rather jam a
hot rod into them!"

It is Shapey's "strike" that provides the most insight into his
personality, which seems a not unappealing combination of self-
pity, anger, theatrics and passion. Shapey never went so far as to
burn his scores or to sue performers like Paul Zukofsky, the violinist, who ignored his ban. He even continued to compose, furtively.
But this was still a dramatic protest against what he felt to be the
slighting of the contemporary composer in general—he has long
championed the work of others, by leading an annual series of
new-music concerts with his University of Chicago Contemporary
Chamber Players—and of himself in particular.

It would be easy to say that he was his own worst enemy—
that, had he only been reasonably politic, he would have had a
more immediate success. But that is not his way, and it has not
been the way of many significant composers of the past—Berlioz,
for instance, or even Beethoven. And it has not been the way of
many of America's most interesting if sometimes eccentric composers,
the men I have referred to as loners. Even when they spent their
youth fighting to get their music and other interesting new music
of their day performed, as did Ruggles in New York in the twenties,
they subsequently withdrew, either geographically or spiritually,
into resentment and pride.

But if a composer wants performances and approbation, he
must learn to wheel and deal. Or at least to avoid overt offense.
Shapey managed to organize a number of performances of his own
music while he lived in New York, and he continues to do so today
in Chicago. But he never ingratiated himself with a group of young
performers that felt like championing his music consistently and
persistently. Perhaps that was because he was *too* romantic in a

time that preferred the cool exactitudes of abstraction. He feels it was because he couldn't or wouldn't play the game. "I have never been and never will learn to be charming, a flatterer, political," he said. "I do not belong to any of the 'clubs' or 'established cliques,' I have not studied at any of the universities, I did not go to the 'right' teachers." "If you don't belong to a clique in New York, you're in trouble," he complained on another occasion. "I studied with Wolpe, but I never even belonged to *his* clique." As usual, he is over-dramatizing; Wolpe was, after all, very much one of the "right" teachers. It will be interesting to see, when Shapey finally is awarded his Pulitzer, whether he will permit himself to accept it. He might turn it down melodramatically, as "bones thrown to a dog," as he once characterized his previous honors.

Shapey emerged from his self-imposed isolation largely through the promptings of Paul Fromm, the Chicago-based new-music patron who supported *Perspectives of New Music* for years and who pays for the "Fromm Week" of new-music concerts every summer at Tanglewood. "Paul Fromm continually talked to me about it," Shapey recalls. "He reminded me that I told my own students that a work is not fully born until it is performed." Fromm's function in American mid-century new music should not go unremarked. His own tastes reflect perhaps too narrowly the Central European milieu of his youth; in that sense, he has helped impose immigrant tastes onto the American mainstream. But Fromm is too benign and open-minded to merit such a nefarious image. He genuinely wishes to foster quality whatever its source, and even withdrew his support from *Perspectives* when he came to feel that it reflected too polemically the total-serialist point of view. The Fromm Week at Tanglewood is another rather narrow view of new music, however much it likes to congratulate itself on its catholicity. But it is becoming more diverse, and Fromm's loyalty to Gunther Schuller, who actually programs the Fromm concerts, is touching.

Fromm's patronage points up the lack of similar new-music support born of personal taste and individual initiative. Another noble example of such patronage is Betty Freeman, a far less well-known woman who divides her time between Beverly Hills and Turin and who has in her discreet way supported any number of

experimental composers by sudden checks in the mail, some solic-
ited and some not. And the contributions of the de Menil family
to all areas of new American art should not go unmentioned.

The alternatives in American arts patronage, aside from the
academy itself, have been corporations, private foundations or state
and federal government. Corporations prefer big, obvious, middlebrow performances of the classics—or, in the realm of the contemporary, modishly splashy mall sculptures and board-room paintings. The National Endowment for the Arts, even before the Reagan
years, favored institutions over people. Several of the private foundations were more open and adaptable, and the New York State
Council on the Arts has had a generally admirable record; indeed,
its support has helped ensure New York's status as the center for
new arts in this country.

All these organizations, private or public, rely on committees.
There can be advantages to committees, especially if the alternative
is pork-barrel favoritism. The ability of the New York State Council
to resist political pressure and to base its awards on the recommen-
dations of artists' panels is particularly laudable. Yet Fromm, Freeman and the de Menils suggest an appealing alternative, one that
should co-exist with the foundations and councils and to which
other rich people of opinionated taste should contribute. It is relatively easy to "patronize" the visual arts. All you have to do is invest
in an artist by buying some art and hope your investment appreci-
ates; if it doesn't, you have a tax write-off. Music is not so tangible,
and so an investment in composers must come from purer motives.
That is not to say a blind, self-punishing sense of duty. Private
music patrons seem genuinely to love the music they support.
Beyond any sense of pleasure they may derive from assuring music's
future and helping people of talent, they are excited about what
they pay for. That is as it should be. And if, as it seems, composers
are beginning to write music that people have at least a chance of
liking, the prospects for more enlightened private patrons, people
who are not tied to any committee and can operate on the basis of
instinctual preference, are good indeed.

Shapey looks back on his move to Chicago in 1964 as a blessing. It has allowed him to live at a human level, given him time to

compose, provided him the means for an accomplished chamber ensemble to perform his own music and that of others. But his removal from the New York scene, despite his disappointments there, made it more difficult for him to win quick recognition. And even though he says Middle Western composers still regard him—rightly, in terms of style and attitude—as a New Yorker, his move points up the dilemmas of composers outside New York. Chicago may be the slightly defensive "second city," but as a center for new music, it lags behind not only New York but also San Francisco, Los Angeles, Boston and even San Diego.

That New York is the country's cultural capital is no news, nor are complaints against its dominance. The National Endowment during the Carter administration tried to decentralize American culture by fostering regional centers. This populist impetus certainly had an impact on opera, in the blossoming of vital companies all over the land. With composition, the results were less dramatic. That is partly because the universities remain the central source of support for most American composers, and are less susceptible to sudden influence from a new federal administration.

Composers need a capital for two reasons. First, the interchange between like-minded musicians, sympathetic artists in other fields and constant critical response quickens the mind and heightens one's sense of self. Second, the very presence of the national media in New York makes it possible for a composer to win immediate recognition, which in turn can have repercussions on commissions and grants. By moving to Chicago, Shapey reinforced his self-image as an ignored outsider. He made his move for the same underlying reasons that Ruggles retreated to Vermont and Nancarrow moved to Mexico City. Yet, curiously, for all the grief it has caused him, that may have been the step that ensured the vigorous individuality of his music. For there is a danger in capitals, as well: a too ready absorption in the trends of the moment, a deflection of one's sense of self through excessive feedback, a sapping of creative energy through hectic hyperactivity, day after day.

As it is, Ralph Shapey remains a vigorous and active composer, perhaps even one with his greatest work before him: at this writing, bolstered by a lavish five-year grant, he is composing a full-scale grand opera about which he remains secretive. He may be bitterly unhappy about his lack of worldly fame. But maybe, just maybe, in refusing to complete the Faustian bargain that staying in New York might have entailed, he will win himself a more honorable judgment from posterity.

6

THE RETURN OF TONALITY, THE ORCHESTRAL AUDIENCE & THE DANGER OF SUCCESS

DAVID DEL TREDICI

Whatever one may think of the ultra-rationalist rigor of Babbitt and his cohorts, there is a general consensus now that total serialism has peaked. In the area of mainstream classical new music, the kind of avant-gardism that feels a direct linear kinship with the past, we are in a new era. But confusion remains as to the nature of that new era. For some, it is defined by an opening up to audiences and to human emotion, motivated either by composers' noble inner compulsion or by their craven, careerist retreat. For others, it is marked by a new concern for orchestral color or ritual or by a return to tonality, in deliberately archaic or brand-new forms. Others look fondly to the distant past—a "return to romanticism." Still others define the new, more popular styles in relation to the immediate past—to their own renunciation, regretful or defiant, of serialism. Others simply refuse to concern themselves with the past at all, or steadfastly maintain their ignorance of it: composers compose, after all; not many are trained as musicologists or academic analysts.

Composers could be chosen to illustrate all these variants, and in the next chapter I shall deal with one, Frederic Rzewski, who in part exemplifies the "return to romanticism." But in this chapter I want to consider a man who incorporates most of these considerations into one, still-evolving career. David Del Tredici was trained in serial procedures at Princeton, yet as of this writing he is fixated on broadly tonal, tunefully popular settings of portions of Lewis Carroll's *Alice* stories. His pieces in this new style, particularly *Final Alice* of 1976, have won him considerable acclaim, including a Pulitzer Prize. Thomas Willis of the *Chicago Tribune* called the response after the premiere of *Final Alice* "the most enthusiastic reception of a new work that I have ever heard at a symphony concert," and the recording of the same score by Sir Georg Solti and the Chicago Symphony actually topped a 1981 classical best-seller chart one week. In short, he is a serious composer who has won the kind of attention from conductors and audiences that such composers are supposedly incapable of.

Yet Del Tredici's success has been clouded with confusions and contradictions. He found himself abandoning serialism without being at all sure he was doing the right thing. His use of tonality, however unusual and original, incurred the antagonism of his former serialist colleagues. His success has been limited by the organization and attitudes of contemporary American symphonic life: even with his applause and his record sales, he has not attained the frequency of performances that a similarly honored, accessible composer a century ago would have expected automatically. He has thus been compelled to rethink in a sometimes painful way the very question of precisely whom it is he composes his music for in the first place.

Del Tredici's early biography follows the prescribed pattern for a bright young serial academic. Born in 1937 in Cloverdale, California, north of San Francisco, he attended the University of California at Berkeley and had early ambitions as a concert pianist. In 1958 he encountered Darius Milhaud at Aspen, where he was studying for the summer, and it was Milhaud who was the decisive influence on his shift to composition. After a year at Princeton in 1959–60, he worked privately in New York with Robert Helps, returning to Princeton in 1963–4. His teachers there were not the rigorous Babbitt or the nearly as fierce computer composer James K. Randall, but Sessions and the gentler Earl Kim.

Del Tredici's music in the sixties followed the pattern, too. It was stern and serious, atonal and disjunct in a way that did honor to his teachers' ideas of what modern music should be. But even then it showed welcome glimmers of personality. And he was never a strict serialist, for all the fashionable chromatic abstraction of his idiom. As he put it in 1980, "I tried to be a twelve-tone composer. But I would get through the first twelve notes and then my ear would want *another* note. I used serial techniques, but I always liked to have some overriding expressive element."

The *Alice* series began in 1968, and the transition from knotty expressionism to sunny tonality was not abrupt. The first pieces were full of dissonant patches, a "scrim of wrong notes" over a tonal underpinning. The big breakthrough did not come until *Final Alice,* an hour-long piece composed as part of a round-robin series of Bicentennial commissions by six major orchestras, supported by the National Endowment for the Arts; each orchestra premiered its own commission and played all the others, as well. *Final Alice* is a sixty-five-minute cantata for an amplified soprano singer-narrator, a "folk group" of soprano saxophones, mandolin, banjo and accordion and a gigantic, Straussian orchestra. The text is a setting of episodes from the last two chapters of *Alice's Adventures in Wonderland,* with an apotheosis from *Through the Looking Glass* and additional texts from a Victorian poem by William Mee called "Alice Gray" (which Carroll parodied) and other poems "that touch on the affectionate relationship between Lewis Carroll and Alice Liddell—the real-life Alice," as Del Tredici puts it. The intention, he goes on, is to "tell two stories at once"—that of the Wonderland trial and Alice's awakening, mixed in with an "implied love story, which I wish to bring closer to the surface—not so close as to disturb the story, but close enough to leave a recognition."

There is no chorus here, and the soprano soloist, singing and speaking, takes all the dramatic parts. But this seems an almost arbitrary, self-limiting device. As Del Tredici concedes, "*Final Alice* teeters between the two worlds of opera and symphonic music." In fact, one suspects, had not Del Tredici simply felt more comfortable with orchestras and orchestral commissions, he might have cast his inspiration as an opera.

The musical language of *Final Alice* is very different from the austere syntax of the typical modern symphonic score, the sort that alienates orchestral audiences today. There are real tunes here, clothed in conventional harmonies (D major, B major, all the old, cozy keys). Whenever dissonance is introduced—and it appears continuously in only one section—it serves a traditional dramatic purpose, to depict chaos and confusion.

My allusion to Richard Strauss was not casual. With their wide leaps and lack of a lyrical line, most serial scores are extremely ungrateful for the singing voice. Del Tredici's soaring writing for the soprano overtly emulates Strauss. He justifies his orchestra's Straussian size, too, with his piquant coloristic and pictorial effects. The Strauss connection extends to the very end, with the sort of self-referential in-joke Strauss loved so well—here a thirteen-time repetition of a three-note figure, as in *tredici* ("thirteen" in Italian).

Unfortunately, the orchestral effects are sometimes so massive that they threaten to overwhelm the soprano. For that reason, Del Tredici amplifies his soloist, but the amplification often sounds unpleasant in live performance—in part because classical music has not had as much practice as rock in the techniques of amplification. Thus, the recording of *Final Alice,* in which balances have been adjusted so that the soprano sounds "natural," is a better way to encounter the work, even though one scene and one aria have been cut to fit the single disc.

Straussian though it may be, this music could hardly be mistaken for *Don Quixote.* Del Tredici stakes his claim to modernity first through his very decision to write such unashamed tonality: by now, consonance itself sounds strange and fresh. In addition, his almost obsessive repetition of a few tunes and variants of them casts an hypnotic spell very different from the theme and counter-theme, contrapuntal development and resolution of the typical nineteenth-century orchestral piece. And the use of the "folk group" and other popsy touches lend the enterprise an insouciant contemporary spirit.

In his brilliantly sure deployment of the full-scale modern symphony orchestra, Del Tredici remains very much aware of the difficulties that have plagued composers like Carter, who suffer as orchestras with limited rehearsal time and indifferent conductors butcher their carefully conceived complexities. Del Tredici is not alone in this concern for what an orchestra can actually be expected to play: John Corigliano, another composer of facile, fascinatingly eclectic contemporary orchestral music that players and the public genuinely like, worries about the very same thing. Del Tredici tries to slip some complexity for the connoisseur into his seeming simplicity—"I *do* like all those complicated underpinnings," he says. "They lend a richness to the expressive gesture." But he also strives to keep his notation as direct as possible, especially in rhythmic matters. "You can't write for that fifty hours of rehearsal in the sky," he argues. "What you get is three or four hours at the most. And since my pieces are getting longer and longer, there's almost no rehearsal time at all. Rhythm is where you have to make the most simplifications. A lot of notation is vanity. To simplify my notation but maintain all my rhythmic quirks was really a kind of creative challenge."

Del Tredici's shift of style began when he became fixated on Lewis Carroll. One might therefore ask whether it was the *Alice* texts that suggested a new idiom to him, or whether his own artistic evolution led him subconsciously to Carroll. Before the *Alice* pieces, he was fascinated to a less extreme degree with James Joyce, and Joyce and a modified serial chromaticism seemed to work well together. Now he is talking about William Burroughs, and wonders if that might not lead to an altogether different idiom.

If Del Tredici is led by his texts, one should not assume that he is weak-willed. There are those who contend that Hugo Wolf was the greatest of all lieder composers precisely because he allowed his musical facility, which seemed of a lesser order when it came to abstract music, to adapt itself to whatever text was at hand. In fact, it can be argued that a recourse to text-setting is one way out of problems posed by purely musical considerations. Could Wagner have pushed music into the unsettled, yearning chromaticism of *Tristan und Isolde* without the inspiration of his own text? Or could Schoenberg, still unsure of the principles of the twelve-tone system, have felt so free with the shifting "atonality" of *Erwartung* without a text as a compass?

Music does not evolve simplistically in a straight line; it is not a neat series of "problems" which, once resolved, are no longer worthy of consideration. When Wagner showed that it was possible to postpone almost indefinitely the resolution to the tonic, it became a sign of timidity to write harmonically straightforward music. Composers today are seeking various ways to escape the trap of a too rigid linearity, the seemingly inexorable slide into dissonance in which any tonality sounds retrogressive. Starting as far back as the neo-classicists between the wars, composers began to plunder the past, to elevate long outmoded ideas to a fresh contemporaneity. The result has been a calculated eclecticism which progressives—among whom the serialists have been the most polemical—condemned outright. That disdain was the source of the controversy between Stravinsky, who led the Paris neo-classicists in the twenties, and Schoenberg. And therein lies the drama of Stravinsky's turn to serialism late in life, after Schoenberg's death.

Chief among the artifacts of the past that composers have picked up, polished and put to new uses has been tonality—the very basis of Western music. Schoenberg himself said that there were lots of good pieces still to be written in C major. Yet the stricter serialists demurred, as if any tonal behavior was a betrayal of the serialist principle. Composers like Del Tredici, who had had all the correct serial training and had then renounced the faith, were singled out for especially ferocious condemnation.

There are those who have argued all along that systematic musical abstraction contravenes the laws of nature. This isn't quite so crackpot as it sounds. Ernest Ansermet and Leonard Bernstein adduced the very nature of the overtone series, with its gradually less consonant overtones ascending upward into inaudibility, as proof of the inherent consonance of nature—the "harmony of the spheres." If they are right, then the return of so many composers today to tonality—and the fascination with the physics of sound on the part of so many minimalists, which goes so far that some of them, like La Monte Young, are content to contemplate a perfectly tuned fifth for "eternity"—can be considered a return to sanity after decades of perversion.

It is possible to welcome the return of tonality without the invocation of such cosmic verities, however. Tonality and various kinds of "atonality" should be able to co-exist, side by side—indeed, George Rochberg has suggested that the contrast of tonality and atonality is today's equivalent to the older juxtaposition of major

and minor. The very acceptance of an historically minded eclecticism among today's composers presupposes their recognition of a
variety of traditions that sustain contemporary "new music." There
is no unanimity even within the classical tradition that serialism
represented the only logical next step for the late romantic composer;
there are plenty of late romantic composers carrying on undaunted
even today in the United Kingdom, Scandinavia, the Soviet Union
and the United States. If a composer still feels that a style or a
device is capable of fresh usage, then that style or device is still
alive for him. And if a composer comes back to such a style having
long abandoned it, the sense of freshness may be even more vital.
"For me," Del Tredici says, "tonality was actually a daring discovery.
I grew up in a climate in which, for a composer, only dissonance
and atonality were acceptable. Right now, tonality is exciting for
me. I think I invented it. In a sense, I have. When you're a composer,
you've got to feel that, on some level, you're doing something for
the first time. Maybe no one will agree, but *you* must feel that
way."

Aside from classical music, composers are now drawing upon
other traditions—jazz, popular music and a whole world of non-
Western musics. Third-world music may not always be "tonal" in
the strict Western sense, but for the most part it rests firmly on a
home note, building upward from there in intervals based on the
overtone series. Composers who allow themselves to be influenced
by such traditions may write music that sounds comfortably "tonal"
to the lay public, yet retains its vitality and originality. But the
originality may be expressed in different ways than a direct expansion of chromatic possibilities. That is one reason why both serialists and traditionalists resist the music of such composers as Steve
Reich and Philip Glass. Their music is harmonically static, and is
thus perceived as simplistic. But it has rhythmic complexities and
meditative implications that its opponents discount impatiently if
they hear them at all.

It wasn't just tonality that characterized the accessibility of the
new mainstream classical music of the late seventies. It was a
renewed interest in musical color and in extra-musical ritual and
mystery, a reversion to the color mysticism of Scriabin and Kandin-

sky in Russia and Munich before World War I. Color and ritual might not seem directly related, but they apparently still are, both in this country and in Europe, where many of these concerns were first re-expressed in the sixties. Sound-color was the principal interest of the so-called *Klangfarbenschule,* which united the flamboyant sound experiments of the Poles of the sixties—Witold Lutoslawski, Henryk Górecki, Krzysztof Penderecki, Grazyna Bacewicz—with Iannis Xenakis's idiosyncratic musical and scientific mysticism in France and the work of such German-based composers as György Ligeti and Mauricio Kagel. Lapsed serialists like Stockhausen and Luciano Berio demonstrated a fresh interest in sound-color, too, although Berio is really a determined eclectic and Stockhausen is now best known as the leading European ritualist.

In America, the principal exponent of both sound-color and musical mysticism has been George Crumb, whose work preceded the recent efforts of Del Tredici, Rochberg and others by a good ten years. Crumb was the American composer of the 1960's who appeared most likely to unite the warring camps of the conservative critics, fierce serialists and wild-eyed experimentalists. His elegantly notated, ritually inspired, exotically colored scores seemed a fresh beginning for a serious new music that could appeal beyond the narrowest of peer groups. But Crumb hasn't sustained that reputation, and today his music sounds gimmicky and limited. The rituals were always a little silly—earnest academics wearing party masks and parading about solemnly while whacking percussion. And the actual sound of his music, while still capable of winning admiration for the delicate acuity of Crumb's ear, seems a loose and unfocused reduction of the more vigorous sound-colorism of Europe.

Del Tredici's *Alice* pieces also suggest that composers are now incorporating elements of popular music with a newly organic felicity. "Serious" composers have made use of popular music for a long time; some of the great medieval and Renaissance masses are based on popular songs of the day. But this new kind of usage is different—a giddy potpourri of disparate elements. Ives is the real progenitor here. Berio, while he taught at the Juilliard School, became especially interested in the idea, and in his *Sinfonia* of 1968 he worked it out with a typically European precision—pleasing, but very different from the rougher exuberance of an Ives or a Cage. Del Tredici's pop appropriations sound stiff in the pieces of the late sixties and early seventies, as awkward and unsuccessful as most third-stream jazz works. But by *Final Alice* he had achieved a happier fusion, a serious symphonic score that breathes the spirit of popular song without the constraints of its formal simplicity.

But even to mention "popular" music here suggests that these *Alice* pieces are indeed popular. In concert, they have generally proven so, or at least not so unpopular as yet another doggedly dissonant prestigious premiere that is shelved with relief by all concerned after its first performance. And the record did sell briskly when it came out. But once *Final Alice* had made its round of obligatory first performances, and apart from a few premieres of the subsequent works in the series and one more scheduled recording, Del Tredici has hardly received many more performances than Carter. If this is "selling out," the price has not been very high.

The fact is that orchestras, their music directors, their boards and their audiences seem deeply confused as to just what they want in the way of new music. Often the players resent anything out of the ordinary. The conductors are too busy polishing their narrow repertory of classics and trendy exotica to bother with new music, especially new music of American or local origin. In any case, since most of the major music directors are European and spend the bulk of the year outside the country, they hardly have time to cultivate local composers. Those composers, in turn, are busily lobbying to get their pieces played. So that when an orchestra *does* finally capitulate out of a misguided sense of duty, the chosen piece is quite likely to be a poor one by the most accomplished local careerist.

There is also a tendency to avoid contemporary works unless they are prestigious premieres or proven triumphs. If the St. Louis Symphony has already given a first performance, then the Boston Symphony is less likely to repeat it than to undertake a first performance of its own. A commissioned world premiere will reap more prestige, unless a new work has already established its credentials with enormous éclat all around the country and the world.

In a situation where hardly anyone in a position of responsibility—and that usually includes the local music critic—really knows or cares much about new music, indifference, haphazardly selected pieces and rough performances abound. Scores are chosen in response to pressure: to mollify the local musical community, to satisfy some vaguely perceived obligation to the new, to balance racial or sexual quotas, to fulfill a grant obligation or to make the orchestra look good in the eyes of potential governmental or foundation panels. The reason pieces *should* be chosen—because somebody cares passionately for them and wants them to be heard—is all too rarely a factor. People in this country are desperately unsure of their capacity for esthetic judgment. They are fearful of looking ridiculous if some "authority" proclaims them "wrong." The sad reality, that authorities have had a dubious record of success themselves in recent decades, has not yet filtered down to the public at large.

A notable exception to this gloom is the San Francisco Symphony (which, coincidentally, commissioned Del Tredici to open its new Louise M. Davies Symphony Hall in the fall of 1980 with an *Alice* piece called *Happy Voices*). Edo de Waart, the orchestra's Dutch music director, has been enlightened enough to share the responsibility for programming with Michael Steinberg, once one of the country's best music critics, at the *Boston Globe*, and John Adams, a composer who teaches at the San Francisco Conservatory, to advise him on experimental music. The result has been not only a particularly intelligent selection of new and not so new pieces of contemporary music for the regular subscription programs, but also a symphony-sponsored new-music series run by Adams.

This European notion of the *Dramaturg*, a scholarly expert who advises artistic directors on repertory and niceties of performance practice, and who also writes program notes and develops the organization's educational policies, can be of real value here. *Dramaturgs* are best known in opera companies, where they help the stage director and designer with new productions. In American opera companies, let alone symphonies, there is rarely such a figure. Steinberg has shown, first and partially with the Boston Symphony and now more fully in San Francisco, how valuable such an addition to an orchestra's staff can be.

Quite apart from the orchestras' own administrative confusions, the verdict is still out on the quality of Del Tredici's music, which provides another explanation for the resistance he has encountered. The conductor Erich Leinsdorf played *Final Alice* but then dismissed it as "in my personal opinion totally without merit, parlaying the major-sixth chord into a fifty-eight-minute work, not counting a seven-minute cut." One does get a little surfeited with the main tune before any of these pieces is finished. But for many the sheer repetition ultimately establishes the requisite mood of wondering enchantment. Del Tredici must also contend with jealousy for the success he has had; Crumb encountered the same problem. Given the insecurities of conductors and boards of directors, it is easy enough for a backstage whisper campaign to undercut any composer's reputation—to suggest, in Del Tredici's case, that he is a superficial opportunist.

Just for whom, then, *is* he writing this music? It is a truism that composers cannot be considered real artists unless they adhere unswervingly to their inner instincts, shunning the seduction of the crass outer world. This conceit fails to correspond with either the great popular art of today—films, rock—or even much of the great classical music of the past. Mozart may have hated the Archbishop of Salzburg, but he managed to compose music that satisfied his patron and himself. Sometimes the sheer tension between an unsympathetic patron and an artist can stimulate creativity, however unpleasant it may seem at the time—as if the patron becomes the surrogate for the more nebulous pressures of the society at large. Today, too often, the patrons of classical music—the panels and foundations and councils—seem indifferently tolerant of what they get. That is why private patrons like Fromm and Freeman can prove so valuable. They reward composers who please them, and provide a specific standard of taste against which a composer can measure his own inspiration. He may choose to reject the patron, his taste and his money. But at least there is a point of reference.

"The public" is a chancy abstraction for any composer, elitist or commercial. At least in popular music and jazz, people can express their preferences tangibly by buying tickets or records. Even there, however, middlemen intrude, and in classical music, the problem is even more severe. Shapey, for instance, has had notable public successes, but they have won him precious few orchestral performances. Yet to abandon the goal of reaching some kind of broader public is to betray a lack of faith in one's society, and to isolate oneself from it. That may seem an apolitical act, but it is actually a tacit concession to the status quo, and hence an intensely conservative political position.

Corigliano shares with Del Tredici a deep distrust of romantic pride and its latter-day manifestation in serial elitism. "It's a view of the artist as misunderstood genius alone in his temple, composing music no one understands for the benefit of posterity," he complains. "Audiences pay money to see or hear something that will move them, excite them, interest them or in some form involve them. If a composer has something important to say, it is his obligation to find a way of saying it that fulfills these basic requirements without compromising his standards in any way. Audiences are made to feel guilty if they don't appreciate what they hear. The burden on composers to write masterpieces is astronomical. This obligation to be profound and eternal with every utterance makes music such a grimly serious business."

The principal bearers of this pressure are a composer's peers. Babbitt, in "Who Cares If You Listen?," was willing to discount the lay audience, but retained the right to communicate to his equals—fellow composers, students and interested professionals, however few. Unless a composer has an iron will and a determined confidence in his own isolation, he is likely to be susceptible to such pressure. Hence Del Tredici's poignance when he discusses his doubts as he got deeper and deeper into the tonal world of *Final Alice*.

"About halfway through the piece, I thought, 'Oh my God, if I just leave it like this, my colleagues will think I'm crazy,'" he recalled. "But then I thought, 'What else can I do? If nothing else occurs to me, I can't go against my instincts.' But I was *terrified* my colleagues would think I was an idiot. People think now that I wanted to be tonal and have a big audience. But that was just not true. I *didn't* want to be tonal. My world was my colleagues—my composing friends. The success of *Final Alice* was very defining as to who my real friends were. I think many composers regard success as a threat. It's really better, they think, if *nobody* has any success, to be all in one boat.

"Composers now are beginning to realize that if a piece excites an audience, *that doesn't mean it's terrible*. For my generation, it is considered vulgar to have an audience really, *really* like a piece on a first hearing. But why are we writing music except to move people and to be expressive? To have what has moved us move somebody else? Everything is reversed today. If a piece appeals immediately, sensuously, if an audience likes it: all those are 'bad things.' It is really very *Alice in Wonderland*."

7

THE ROMANTIC REVIVAL & THE DILEMMA OF THE POLITICAL COMPOSER

FREDERIC RZEWSKI

If David Del Tredici has retreated from academic serialism, then Frederic Rzewski has made a similar retreat from Cage's anarchism, and from the experimental-music scene Cage fathered. But Rzewski has done far more than that, and not just the very diversity of styles he has explored. He has modified Cage's ideas to the point of rejection, and has also "returned to romanticism"—although with very different intentions and implications than either Harold C. Schonberg's nostalgia or George Rochberg's aural super-realism. Above all, Rzewski is attempting to lead a rebirth of the long-dormant political spirit of American classical avant-gardism. Everything considered, he raises so many issues that the fact that his actual music is only intermittently interesting becomes almost secondary.

Rzewski was born in Westfield, Massachusetts, in 1938, attended Harvard College and did graduate work at Princeton. He studied music there, along with philosophy and Greek literature, but his musical studies were focused on Wagner rather than on composition. Since 1960 he has helped support himself as a pianist specializing in new music. Although he spent a considerable amount of time in New York in the early-mid seventies, he has since the sixties lived mostly in Rome, part of a small but lively group of young American avant-garde composers. In 1966 he helped found a live electronic-music performance group called Musica Elettronica Viva.

In the course of a still young compositional career, Rzewski seems to have tried almost every available avant-garde idiom, from serialism to aleatoric Cageianism to experimental happenings to electronics to minimalism to structuralism to late romanticism. But since the early seventies his overriding interests have been political, and they have helped bend his mature style toward accessibility and tonality.

The first stirrings of this latest idiom can be heard on an Opus One disc that also includes a perky, non-political jazz-gamelan piece entitled *Les Moutons de Panurge* from 1969. The rest of the disc consists of *Coming Together* and *Attica*, both from 1972 and both inspired by the prisoner uprising at the New York state prison at Attica in September 1971, suppressed on the orders of the then governor, Nelson A. Rockefeller.

These two pieces reveal an obvious debt to late-sixties New York downtown avant-gardism. In both cases, Rzewski sets up a stirring, driving instrumental base for the recitations of Steven Ben Israel, an actor from the Living Theater, who repeats or intones political texts by participants in the Attica uprising. The pieces are particularly compelling examples of what might be called motoric minimalism—repetitive music enlivened by the energies of jazz. But they make no pretense of speaking to any audience other than one already open to avant-garde idioms. They are political in the same sense as Steve Reich's tape-loop composition of 1966, *Come Out,* which takes a recorded phrase from a black injured by the police and builds a mystical extravaganza on top of it. Both composers are inspired by topical events, but make use of an idiom that speaks to a far different social and racial group than the victims of the oppression that is being protested.

As if he recognized that discrepancy, Rzewski in his more recent music has included overt popular, accessible and tonal elements. He has been influenced by such avant-garde, politically oriented jazz musicians as Anthony Braxton and Steve Lacy, as well as by Weill and Hanns Eisler and the political folk-song movement of the South American left. Examples of this idiom include the *Four Pieces* for piano (1977), *Song and Dance* for the chamber group Speculum Musicae (1977) and *Four North American Ballads* for piano (1979). But its best known manifestation was a set of thirty-six variations for solo piano (1975) on the Chilean song "*¡El Pueblo Unido Jamás Será Vencido!*" or "*The People United Will Never Be Defeated!*" The song was composed by Sergio Ortega and the now expatriate Chilean leftist folk group Quilapayún, and has become the international musical symbol not just of the spirit of the aborted Allende regime, but of leftist anti-imperialism everywhere. Rzewski's piece of the same name is a grand, fifty-minute set of thirty-six variations of the thirty-six-bar theme. The numerical relationships are exact: six groups of six variations, with the sixth variation in each section summing up its five predecessors, the sixth section recapitulating the previous five, and the sixth variation of the sixth section (i.e., the thirty-sixth variation) serving as the grand finale. "The movement of the whole piece," writes Christian Wolff, the former Cageian who is now himself a political composer, "is towards a new unity—an image of popular unity—made up of related but diverse, developing elements (not to be confused with uniformity), coordinated and achieved by a blend of irresistible logic and spontaneous expression."

Wolff is certainly correct about the lack of uniformity. The overall idiom suggests romantic piano writing, with an idiomatic felicity in that writing that has warmed the hearts of piano buffs and provides some rattling virtuoso passages. But this is not just a romantic resurrection. There are variations that recall serialist rationalism and experimentation, too, as well as bits of performer choice (including some sweet and poignant moments when the pianist whistles), citations of other political songs both composed and folkish, and a tense overall energy reminiscent of Bach and his baroque variation forms.

Eclecticism, meaning a radical shift of idiom from piece to piece or even within a given piece, is ever more common in contemporary music. Its very prevalence flouts the notion of a single, agreed-upon style, and reinforces the historicism that has pervaded Western culture for a century or more. Yet most composers who practice eclecticism do so with an underlying personal style. Even a man like Stockhausen, who has moved from total serialism to electronics to chance to ritual, has his own Teutonically commanding personality to unify his work. Rzewski has not given evidence of such a strength of personality, and so his extreme stylistic diversity might be interpreted as a lack of compositional sureness, a failure of confidence in *any* of his chosen idioms. Still, he has won his greatest fame with music that sounds like nine-teenth-century virtuoso piano music—like the piano variations of Brahms, for instance. In so doing, he has become a leading symbol of the "return to romanticism," the style whose principal exponent is George Rochberg.

Rochberg is a controversial case. A strict serialist for many years, he abandoned that style in the seventies and returned to romanticism as completely as he could, turning out a series of works that could almost be mistaken for discoveries from the past. Often, in fact, as in his String Quartet No. 3, Rochberg mixes composers within the same piece, offering a Beethovenian fast movement and a Mahlerian slow movement.

There is an ideology behind all this. "I am turning away from what I consider the cultural pathology of my own time," he wrote, "toward what can only be called a *possibility*: that music can be renewed by regaining contact with the tradition and means of the past." In a paper read at a conservatively oriented new-music conference sponsored in early 1981 by New York's 92nd Street Young Men's–Young Women's Hebrew Association, Rochberg eagerly embraced the suddenly fashionable notion that modernism has failed. He undercut his own case by confusing rationalist and experimental avant-gardism without any explanation of their dissimilarities, blithely attacking "modernism" for both sensation-alism and hyper-intellectualism. Still, his defense of tonality, eclec-ticism and the place of emotion in music was a spirited one. "If it appears that a large part of the music of the twentieth century was a *music of forgetting*," he argued, "the music of the end of the century and beyond must become a music of remembering." Roch-berg interprets his own words with complete literalness: for him, "remembering" means remembering how to write music exactly like composers long dead, and reminding audiences that their music still exists as a living force. They hardly need much reminding, however, since such music makes up the bulk of symphonic, chamber and recital programs already.

In a spoken aside—the whole talk was an expansion of detailed written notes that were handed to the audience in advance—Rochberg suggested that the history of music has alternated between periods of complexity and simplicity, each provoking a reaction to the other, and welcomed the advent of a simpler period. The exact connection to his own music, which is crafted in a painstaking and complex way, is unclear. And while his words might seem to serve as a fine credo for a renewed interest in popular music and the recent vogue for minimalism, Rochberg seems to consider minimalism as but another of the "sensationalist" experiments now being superseded.

As an exercise in logic, Rochberg's speech left something to be desired. As an articulation of his own intentions—the principal value of most composers' theoretical writings—it made considerable sense. Certainly, audiences are responding to his "romantic" pieces. And as manifestations of conceptual art, they have their curious merits. No matter how determinedly Rochberg and Rzewski may try to write in the style of Beethoven or Brahms, they cannot do so precisely, nor can we hear their efforts the way those composers' original audiences did. Every man is unique; time has passed for them and us, and therefore the effort to recapture the past only points in a rather poignant way to the impossibility of that effort.

Any attempt to go backward is partly progressive for that very reason. The early serialists' complaints against the neo-classicists foundered because they failed to appreciate this paradox. The attempt to recapture the past, in a piece like Stravinsky's reworking of the past in *Pulcinella,* can quicken our appreciation of both past and present. It is not that present-day composers are blindly regressing to time-tested ways that "worked"—although Rochberg sometimes sounds as if that is his very intention. Instead, the composer sets up a counterpoint between times, and makes an art out of the tension that results.

Whether Rochberg achieves enough tension is debatable. Whether Rzewski achieves it is even more doubtful, but at this point in his career the provision of esthetic pleasure for highbrows is not his stated intention. If Rochberg is working in esthetic terms, Rzewski's terms are political. He "returns to romanticism" because his audience has never much developed past romanticism in its musical tastes, and he is trying to slip them a political pill in the sugar coating of a musical style they will find palatable.

Rzewski calls his new esthetic "realism," as in "socialist realism," although he has sometimes seemed to avoid that specific term, no doubt for fear of appearing unduly provocative. Realism for Rzewski means, among other things, "a conscious employment of techniques which are designed to establish communication, rather than to alienate an audience." Varying circumstances entail different audiences, and that variability in turn justifies compositional eclecticism: "There are all kinds of different techniques which you can employ for different kinds of situations," he said in 1976. "Personally, I don't think that I've ever developed what you might call a 'style.' Every music that I do seems to be very different than the thing that came before. You cannot rely on one historical tradition any more."

The largely romantic *Pueblo Unido* variations are meant for traditional concertgoers, people who dote on "classical music" as defined in terms of the standard repertory. Rzewski has spoken admiringly of the Italian Communist Party's "electoral strategy, which is to win over as many of the petit bourgeoisie people as possible through the use of culture." Why, one might wonder, is the lower middle class so important for the world revolution? Because, in America especially, such people "constitute a large element of this country," and because "the future of world politics may depend on which direction this class of people decides to take in the next ten years."

Rzewski makes a distinction between his own intentions and Beethoven's libertarian idealism—or, by extension, Verdi's nationalist fervor or Wagner's socialism and, later, world-redeeming mysticism. All three nineteenth-century composers believed in the universality of art, in its potential to better man's place on earth—or, increasingly in Wagner's case, his place in the cosmos. Such faith presupposed some congruity between a composer's musical style and what people wanted to hear. In Beethoven's case, the disjunction between his highest instincts and his populism helps explain the disparity between the austere late string quartets and the ebullient choral conclusion to *Fidelio* or the tub-thumping "Ode to Joy" finale of the Ninth Symphony. Verdi was a born populist, at least until he was in his eighties, with the intricacies of *Falstaff*. And Wagner, for all the richness of his music, never lost the popular touch. Even when he was denounced by conservative critics as an extreme avant-gardist, he knew the people would respond to his music dramas, and they did.

Marxist class analysis has shaken our confidence in such universality; Rzewski may think he is fulfilling a useful function by narrowing his aim to the lower middle class. But really, today, universality may actually be more real than it once was: as a by-product of improved standards of living, general education and mass communications, the old class demarcations have, on some levels at least, eroded into a society with shared values that extend over the entire class spectrum. Thus, composers have the potential—or, it might be argued, the obligation—to reach that larger mass audience. Marxist composers especially must decide whether the lower classes are the standard-bearers of the popular spirit or corruptions of the prevailing bourgeois ethos. The result of their indecision has been a profound crisis for "serious" artists with generous social inclinations. At the same time that classical composers, recoiling from the philistinism of the marketplace and the horrors of our century, have retreated into an ever more arcane complexity, an audience with ever more basic tastes has grown up beneath them.

The United States has rarely fostered explicitly political composers—serious composers ready to address that dilemma—nor has the United Kingdom. There was a flurry of such activity in the thirties, during the wave of leftist populism that swept all the arts, often led by men who, like Rzewski, had spent considerable time abroad. Virgil Thomson, although he was always too personal and urbane to be considered a simple populist, wrote in a folkish idiom that sometimes—in his film scores and lesser instrumental pieces—did sound simplistic. Aaron Copland developed a popular variant of his own idiom, by which he is best known today. Roy Harris's symphonies, now so rarely performed, were classic examples of a quasi-Soviet popular style adapted to American tunes and tastes. Marc Blitzstein tried to emulate the directness and political impact of the Brecht-Weill collaborations. Weill himself was in America by this time. But, freed from Brecht's influence, he turned to the more comfortably middle-class musical, and to liberal ideals removed from those of the more dogmatic populists and the increasingly rigid, Soviet-dominated American Communist Party.

There are various reasons for the lack of overt political activity by American and British artists. Perhaps, one might innocently suggest, people were just happier in these two capitalist democracies than they were elsewhere. Certainly the spread of empire in Britain and the conquest of the continent in America occupied people's energies. The successive waves of immigrants into this country, for all their initial squalor, became relatively content soon enough, especially when they remembered the privations they had left behind. The relative paucity of government support in this country also contributed to our essentially non-political art. In Europe, first the kings and then the state created a funded establishment culture. But this meant that those left out had a clear enemy against which to strike. Today, that tradition of protest has become so ingrained that the opposition itself, even the bitter and terrorist kind, is sometimes funded by the government. In Britain and especially in this country, artists owed their patronage to conservative individuals until a very few years ago.

The more general impotence sensed by so many American artists—the kind Carter complains about—also serves to undercut political art. Artists feel isolated from the actual working of the country, from its vast size and its fixation on money and war, however much they may be caught up in an idealized vision of its spirit. They feel detached from any sense of artistic community, and the sheer size of the United States reinforces their sense of powerlessness. They are not alone in feeling this way; it is the rare citizen or even politician who feels he has made a tangible impact on the country as a whole.

In Europe, where artists have long been more politically inclined, the widening gulf between avant-gardism and popular taste led to various desperate attempts to reverse the process of artistic intellectualization and to reach out to the middle and working classes both. The best-known examples occurred in Germany during the Weimar Republic. Weill simplified his style, partly under the influence of Bertolt Brecht. Hindemith wrote *Gebrauchsmusik* for amateurs to play. Even such composers as the young Stefan Wolpe wrote music for the common man. And Hanns Eisler and Paul Dessau continued the Weill tradition in East Germany after the war.

As an American living in Rome and interacting with the small but significant European-based American musical community, Rzewski is reviving a tradition that flourished in the thirties, of the American composer who is not really an expatriate or an exile, but who looks at his country through European eyes. In his case, that means not just a greater political orientation than is common here, but a predilection to view the problem of political art music from the perspective of the Frankfurt school. The principal esthetician of that school was Theodor W. Adorno, whose extensive writings on the sociology of music are still too little known here. Adorno and Herbert Marcuse, who represented a somewhat less austere variant of this thinking in America during the sixties, worked to develop a coherent Marxist esthetic that would embrace the proletariat and the avant-garde. But both fell afoul of the same dilemma that had thwarted similar efforts in Berlin during the twenties. The workers don't *want* to listen to highbrow avant-gardism, no matter how sincerely leftist a composer may believe himself to be. Given a choice—and they were, at Otto Klemperer's experimental Kroll Opera in Berlin between 1927 and 1931—workers will take *La Bohème* over *Erwartung* any time. Even *The Threepenny Opera* was more a *succès d'estime* among intellectuals and middle-class trendies than it was a hit with the workers.

For Adorno and his epigones among American intellectuals, popular music—in other words, rock, but also light pop, jazz, country, soul, funk and all the various hybrids—is fatally compromised as a true expression of the folk spirit, let alone as art, by its commercialism. Adorno, who formulated his views before the real advent of rock, held a view common among classical and jazz fans, that pop music is popular only because it is massively propagated on the radio. To some extent, certainly, radio exposure determines taste, and now that rock itself has developed its own split between commercial and non-commercial styles, devotees of commercially marginal new-wave rock are advancing the same view—that the domination of the American sales charts by soft rock and other familiar styles is the "fault" of radio and the record companies. But in the end, such a view seems to misunderstand profoundly the nature of popular taste. People have always shown a penchant for simple, clear, tuneful music. Capitalism may distort, but it also reflects, more accurately than leftist idealists wish to admit.

Rzewski shares Adorno's views on popular music. "If all you are offered for sale in the stores is shit," he once said, "you get addicted to shit." Although he admires jazz, and feels no American composer who isn't "deaf" can ignore it, he apparently does not feel comfortable himself in adopting a jazz idiom, nor has he found a style of his own that partakes consistently of its spirit. Instead, he subverts his esthetic inclinations to his political opinions, and concentrates on winning over the lower middle class, because that is what he can do best.

But even petty-bourgeois audiences can sense when they are being patronized. Worse, such calculating patronization saps esthetic validity. On the whole, for all its evident skill, Rzewski's political art is an art of condescension. And of folly. The late Cornelius Cardew, who was a more radically Marxist, less musically gifted British counterpart to Rzewski, demonstrated this paradox more overtly. Neither he nor Rzewski nor Christian Wolff has, to my knowledge, made much of an impact on the working classes, or on the third-world masses, or on China, or whomever it is they are ostensibly celebrating in their music. Nor have they made much headway with intellectuals, since their experimental, neo-romantic or neo-popular idioms are not really as interesting as real experimentation, romanticism or pop. And despite an occasional flurry of press attention, they haven't even done much to sway the petty bourgeoisie in any perceivable direction.

In Britain, Adorno to the contrary, the genuine political music of the time is made by rock, reggae and ska bands: the Specials' "Ghost Town" became the anthem of the riots during the summer of 1981. It is one sign of life in the British Communist Party that it has been alert enough to secure rock bands for Party social functions. These bands speak the musical language of the people who are actually being oppressed. Yet the best of them speak with their own voices, too, ones not crippled by the artificiality that comes from patronization.

In America, there hasn't been much politicizing of note from our popular musicians recently, apart from Jackson Browne's antinuclear benefits or Charlie Daniels's jingoistic "In America." But in the sixties, there was a good deal of it. Bob Dylan is the best-known example; his was a musical poetry that did indeed speak to people. Again, it spoke most forcefully to college students; Dylan was never the biggest seller of his time. Still, he had a mass audience that felt moved to political action by his music.

Whether politically motivated or not, stylistic fusions do not seem to work very well unless there is an element of unselfconsciousness about them. A trained composer like Rzewski finds it difficult to write beneath himself, or to find an audience when he does so. In the same way, classical composers—even those deeply knowledgeable about jazz like Schuller himself—made a mess of "third stream" music because they were not really comfortable as classicists with the jazz tradition. And too many jazz musicians who try to "sell out" with jazz-rock lack the requisite popular touch. Rzewski's political convictions indicate a strong moral sense, and he has great musical talent, too—one reason he is so stylistically restless may be his too easy mastery of everything he attempts. When he relaxes and simply lets himself be led by his musical materials (even when the choice of those materials may have been politically inspired), he can write music that is genuinely gripping from a purely esthetic standpoint, as in the *Four North American Ballads*, with their stirring evocations of American folk song.

But before we can expect an American musical style that is at once political and esthetically true, a composer must emerge who feels truly comfortable writing music that appeals to people. Condescending for political reasons is just as deleterious to inspiration as selling out for commercial reasons. The serious political composer of the future must work securely within an idiom that people want and then stretch out and transform that idiom into art—as the best popular and jazz composers have already done. Bob Dylan's "Blowin' in the Wind" or one of Bruce Springsteen's autobiographical laments says more about everyday life in this country than Frederic Rzewski will probably ever know. And says it more "artistically," as well.

8

POST-CAGEIAN EXPERIMENTATION & NEW KINDS OF COLLABORATION

ROBERT ASHLEY

A retreat from an extreme position is one thing; evolution beyond it is another. Those who have gone on from Babbitt and Cage may also have "retreated," like Del Tredici and Rzewski, in that they have chosen not to push extreme theoretical positions into the realm of pure abstraction. But their work is better considered an advance, a constructive exploration of musical ideas made possible by the sometimes destructive liberation effected by their predecessors.

Robert Ashley, who was born in Ann Arbor, Michigan, in 1930, was never part of Cage's inner circle, although Gordon Mumma and others of Ashley's close associates were. But from the late fifties, Ashley has been a leader of American experimental music, first in Ann Arbor, later at Mills College in Oakland, California, and now in Manhattan. All along, his career helps cast light on the circumstances of new music in different parts of the country. Although his interests have shifted and the sound of his music has changed, a core of concerns has defined his work: "conceptual art," electronic music, minimalism and a new kind of musical theater involving a reconsideration of the collaborative process that has heretofore defined "opera." Above all, Ashley has proven, along with a host of other colleagues and collaborators, that it is not only possible but fruitful to carry on the American experimental tradition of Cowell and Cage.

How useful is it to try to define "experimental music" or "new music," as opposed to mainstream classical avant-gardism? Sometimes such definitions bog down in angry polemics and illogical distinctions, as Michael Nyman proved in his *Experimental Music,* which remains the only book so far that attempts to define and discuss the subject comprehensively. The sponsors of the now annual New Music America festivals have also struggled to define the term, if only so they can figure out whom to exclude. These festivals are supposedly all-inclusive, theoretically open to Babbitt, Wuorinen and any of the other Northeastern hard-liners. Yet those composers have not so far participated, and nobody seems to have made a very strenuous effort to invite them.

The best definition brings us back to the Ives-Cowell-Cage tradition: American composers operating in blissful ignorance of or defiant opposition to their European heritage. Mystics and irrationalists—even when they are operating in areas of considerable technological sophistication. Limited interest in highly developed musical virtuosity, and a general preference for consonance—though not necessarily tonality—over dissonance. Often absorbed in the Orient, for specifically musical or broadly philosophical inspiration, and in various forms of jazz and popular music. Concerned with reconceiving the relationship between artist and audience—working to develop a listener's powers of sensation and esthetic empathy. Interested in all artforms, often practicing other arts themselves and welcoming artists from other media as composers.

The performers in the New Music America festivals, or at such downtown New York performance spaces as the Kitchen or Roulette, do not all conform to every one of these characteristics. Indeed, disagreements about what this tradition actually entails can provoke lively arguments, as a series of panel discussions that I organized in conjunction with the first New Music America festival in New York in 1979 indicated sometimes rather too vividly. There have even been complaints about the seemingly bland term "new music" itself. Critics point out the debts to Cowell over fifty years ago, and the varieties of other music that are also new but stylistically uncongenial with this group of composers.

Another way of defining this school is to include in it everyone frozen out of the contemporary classical-music concert scene in the Northeast and around the country—any and all musicians who think of themselves as artists but who are not considered "serious" enough by the establishment. This distinction involves not only esthetics but cliques. The Northeastern contemporary-music forums are mostly for professors and their students. The "new music" composers are also friendly with one another, and as more of them have found academic perches, they have begun to develop their own master-student relationships. These friendships and professional obligations are especially strong in the generation born around 1930. Their bonds have been documented rather wonderfully by Ashley himself, in a series of videotaped interviews with and performances by seven (eight in the book version) composers called *Music with Roots in the Aether*. Ashley also provides a particularly good example of the master-student syndrome, in the circle of younger composers that grew around him at Mills College, many of whom now perform regularly in New York.

For all his soft-spoken diffidence, Ashley has always been a catalyst. During the three stages of his mature life—Ann Arbor, Oakland and New York—he has fostered extensive collaborative ventures. In a sense, it was his first, Midwestern phase that was most heroic, if only because he had less to work with when he started. The Midwest had enjoyed an earlier period of experimentation with John J. Becker in Minnesota and Illinois in the thirties and forties, but that activity had died down after World War II. More recently, Shapey has been active in Chicago, but he is no experimentalist. And although he gathered some disciples around him at the university there, he has not so much engendered a Midwestern renaissance as fortified an outpost for his own idiosyncratic variant of New York serialism.

Ashley went to college at the University of Michigan, and after a stint at the Manhattan School of Music he returned to Ann Arbor in the late fifties. From 1958 to 1966 he and Mumma ran the Cooperative Studio for Electronic Music there, and after a variety of other electronic experiments and mixed-media events, he founded the ONCE group in 1963—which had grown out of the ONCE festivals starting in 1961. This soon became the principal Midwestern center for "happenings," multi-media experiments and avant-garde "operas." In 1966 he helped found the Sonic Arts Union, another collaborative that included himself, Mumma, Alvin Lucier and David Behrman.

In Ann Arbor during the sixties, Ashley was at the center of a burgeoning scene, although that scene has not sustained itself since his departure. The activities of the ONCE group, which drew national and international attention, were extravagant, idealistic, outrageous and, at their best, as effective as sixties experimental music ever managed to be.

A fundamental inspiration for that scene, and essential to any understanding of twentieth-century American experimental music, was a fascination with the very nature of sound. Between 1960 and 1961, while still in his formative years, Ashley worked as a research assistant in acoustics at the University of Michigan. The study of acoustics—of the essence of sound, the ways we perceive it and its relation to "music"—has been central to this whole group of composers. Roger Reynolds even wrote a big, thought-provoking, rather incoherent book on the subject (and many others, besides) called *Mind Models*.

This interest is part of the broader questioning by many diverse contemporary composers of the very nature of music and of its role in society. Composers are no longer content to accept the assumptions about these matters that have become embedded in Western culture over the past few centuries. Just as sociologists and cultural anthropologists are reformulating the nature of society, so these composers, often inspired by the different musical structures and social forms they encounter in distant cultures, want to explore every aspect of their art. Often their music-making serves merely to demonstrate their researches. Sometimes, as in the case of Alvin Lucier, the results from a strictly esthetic standpoint can be dauntingly spare and didactic. But the passion of the intention remains impressive.

Aside from his acoustical and electronic work, Ashley was obsessed in this early period with finding formal equivalents for the spontaneity he had heard in jazz. "I learned music from listening to jazz," he recalled. "But I realized at a certain moment of my life—when I was in my early twenties—that music was not as abstract as I had imagined. In order to play jazz, one had to be able to speak the language of the people who play jazz. And that meant from the start, almost exclusively, that you had to be black. In other words, the stories that were told by jazz music were stories that I didn't grow up with; they weren't my stories. I went through exactly the same experience with European music. At a certain point I realized that neither was I European—and especially not European from the nineteenth century. That ended that.

"My early pieces basically were all ways of trying to understand so-called jazz techniques, or the techniques that came out of thinking about jazz and spontaneity, and how those techniques could be applied to stories that I understood—my stories. I was trying to figure out how to make procedures that would invoke spontaneity."

Ashley moved to California to become director of the Mills College Center for Contemporary Music in 1969. The center had been founded in San Francisco in the early sixties and was the real fount of this sort of experimental music in the country. Operated in conjunction with Ann (now Anna) Halprin, the choreographer and dancer, and with KPFA, the venturesome flagship of the Pacifica chain of listener-supported FM radio stations, the center became the most visible focus for a wide range of composers. The list is impressive. It includes not only such men as Terry Riley, Steve Reich and Morton Subotnick, but also a number of composers who moved on to Reynolds's Center for Music Experiment and Related Research at the University of California at San Diego, near La Jolla—Robert Erickson, Pauline Oliveros and several more.

Thus, when Ashley arrived in California, it was as a visitor from afar who had been invited to revive a scene that was already losing some of its luster to such better-funded alternatives as the University of California at San Diego. Part of the problem was the indifferent, not to say hostile, attitude of some of the musical press in the San Francisco area. Newspaper critics like to downplay the extent of their power. Otherwise they might feel constrained by the attention paid to their pronouncements. But critics *are* powerful. Their encouragement can build audiences, support grant applications and secure tenured appointments at universities. It can also soothe and bolster fragile egos, and generate a sense of excitement about new music. Many of the important San Francisco critics during the late sixties and seventies had little taste for experimental music, which was of course their privilege. But a few also chose to mock it obtusely, and their attitude helped cripple a once vibrant local musical community.

Ashley's lifelong work has been the evolution of new forms of mixed media—or opera. When he was still in Michigan, he actively approximated operatic forms with his happenings and theatricalized concerts. One example of his work from the sixties is a piece entitled "She Was a Visitor," recorded on Odyssey Records. The conception might sound schematic, with a speaker intoning the phrase "she was a visitor" over and over, matter-of-factly. There is a chorus, divided into groups, each with a leader. The leaders select phonemes freely from the spoken phrase and relay them to their groups of singers, who then sustain them quietly for the length of a breath. The score also makes provision for audience participation (like many pieces from this tradition, the technique is simple and accessible); the choral sound can be further deployed through clusters of loudspeakers around the hall or above the audience's heads. The result is a rapt cloud of choral humming, fragmented by the spatial dispersion and by the lags built into the process of the group-leaders relaying their intentions to their singers. The effect is both precise and eerily mysterious. "She Was a Visitor" is, in turn, part of a longer "opera" called *That Morning Thing,* which Ashley managed to mount during his Mills years.

Other recorded examples of his work from the sixties and early seventies include *Purposeful Lady Slow Afternoon* from his time with the Sonic Arts Union, and *In Sara, Mencken, Christ and Beethoven There Were Men and Women* (1972). In both, as in his later work, the basic form is narration supported by instrumental or electronic music. In the former piece, the text, recited by a woman, is an erotic melodrama of forced oral sex, to the accompaniment of electronic effects that sound like chimes and a Tibetan horn (sex and violence are never far beneath the surface with Ashley). In the latter, Ashley himself speedily reads a frenetic, jumbled text over a busy electronic backdrop.

Since his move to New York, his major project has been a

"video opera," *Perfect Lives (Private Parts),* pieces of which emerged on records, in concert and on television for several years. It was finally presented complete in live performance in 1981, and in its final video form in 1983. *Perfect Lives* is a summation of everything Ashley has been working on for years, with the addition of a newly intensified interest in video and the experimental art-rock that has flourished in New York since the late sixties.

The piece is based on Ashley's own poetic narration, his own "stories," hovering tremulously between measured speech and song, a stream-of-conscious monologue that at times opens up to embrace several characters but is really a projection of Ashley's multifaceted sensibility. There is an ostensible seven-part plot featuring the narrator, "the world's greatest piano player," a girl named Isolde and her brother, who become involved in a bank robbery that is more metaphorical than real. This tale is not so much enacted as recalled in fragmentary fashion, a characteristic manifestation of post-narrative theater, and the settings are hardly realistic. "R," the narrator, is the central figure. The piano player confines himself to playing piano, and Isolde and her brother "D" are more visual than vocal presences. Ashley recounts everything in a seemingly calm and reasonable monotone, but there is something disturbing about his voice—its shakiness, emotionality and barely repressed violence— that hints at far deeper feelings. Very occasionally the calm patter of words erupts into conventionally musical formulations, rhythmic cadences that don't actually lapse into song but clearly transcend speech. The "formal model" for the overall structure of the narration, he has said, is the Tibetan *Book of the Dead.*

Beneath the text is instrumental and sometimes quasi-choral music, composed as much by the collaborators as by the titular "composer." Those collaborators include a pianist named Robert Sheff, who calls himself Blue Gene Tyranny, and an art-rock bandleader, Peter Gordon, both of whom worked with Ashley in California, plus a glamorous singer and performance artist, Jill Kroesen, as Isolde, and David Van Tieghem, a percussionist, as "D." Their music is alternately mellow and cocktailish, dreamily romantic, bland background rustle and sharply punctuated minimalist rock. The instrumentation is that of a jazz or rock band—acoustic and

electric keyboards, electric guitars, saxophones, percussion. Sometimes the texture is spare and distant; sometimes it is full of a
bustling, insistent energy.

This is as much as one gets on the parts that have emerged so
far on records. But as a "video opera," *Perfect Lives* exists on additional levels. In some live performances—by their very nature only
partial realizations of the dramatic concept—Ashley has presented
himself like some minimalist lecturer, reciting his texts from a
lectern set among coolly dispassionate graphics, with the musicians
discreetly to one side. In the video segments, directed by John
Sanborn, the texture is altogether busier, full of a sometimes
dizzying mélange of video tricks, multiple images, rapid cross-
cutting, color alteration and dissolves. The overall impact is far
more complex than what might be suggested by the outwardly
bland simplicity of the text and the sometimes deliberate triviality
of the music. Everything contributes to the whole, and is given
new meaning by that whole—just as Wagner first conceived his
"total works of art" as organisms that superseded each component
and imbued all of them with life.

Perfect Lives has not been Ashley's only project in recent years.
He has attempted to document on video and in print the experimental work of his fellow composers, and to keep his own past
achievements alive in performances and on records. He has also
continued his experiments with the nature of speech and sound, as
in an LP called *Automatic Writing*, which is full of what might be
called avant-garde pillow talk: hushed, broken, erotic voices (some
in French, from his wife, Mimi Johnson), with electronics and
filtering by the composer.

Ashley emerged from minimalism, but works like *Perfect Lives*
and *Automatic Writing* are only problematically minimalist. The
purest form of minimalism derives from Cage, with his *4'33"* of
silence, in which an audience in a formal concert setting is invited
to contemplate ambient sound. Or perhaps the purest form was
some of La Monte Young's experiments in the sixties—the "eternal"
electronically generated note of A, or simply ascending scale patterns repeated over and over with lush instrumentation in a dim,
hieratic environment. Or, with the addition of strict structure and

repetition, the harmonically static, sparse early pieces of Steve Reich and Philip Glass—single lines or rhythmic patterns unfolding inexorably.

Compared to any of these, *Perfect Lives* is positively maximal, with its overlapping parts and sometimes dizzying textures. But compared to a late-romantic symphony, or even to a busy serial score, it is minimal indeed. One has to have an appetite for hypnotic repetition to enjoy this music—a willingness to give oneself over to the flow of Ashley's invention. There is considerable repetition in the harmonies and rhythms, and a deliberately monochromatic tone to the narration.

All of this grew out of earlier work that was decidedly minimal—pieces like "She Was a Visitor" that consist of nothing but barely audible speech and steady washes of sound. Such seeming austerity was akin to similar minimalism in the painting, sculpture and poetry of the sixties. Ashley's early works of this sort were also examples of "conceptual art." Nearly all art and music of the past was created in a cultural environment in which artist and audience enjoyed a shared understanding of the purpose of art: the artist meant to praise God or please his patron or celebrate sensual love. The *idea* of the *Mona Lisa* is of lesser interest to most people than the finished reality of the painting and the mysteries that arise from its contemplation. Conceptual artists wish to elevate the "what if" of the artist's initial musings to the same level as the finished work—or beyond. La Monte Young, again, was a pioneer, along with Cage. A typical Young piece of this sort, from 1960, was notated thus, in its entirety: "This piece is little whirlpools out in the middle of the ocean."

Ideas of this sort are easy to misunderstand—or to mock. And Ashley's work raises a related issue that continually bothers laymen about experimental art. That is the extent to which such artists deliberately provoke an audience, or deliberately bore it. If an audience member is bored or annoyed, isn't he being a dupe not to give vent to his frustration? One reads about grand donnybrooks at premieres of the past; *The Rite of Spring* is the best known. Why don't audiences today rise up in righteous indignation? Even Nicolas Slonimsky, who chronicled critical foolishness in his *Lexicon of Musical Invective*, complains now about the bland tolerance of the critics of our time. Aren't composers *asking* their listeners to protest, and disappointed at their passivity?

Ashley, for one, was very definitely out to shock, especially during the ONCE performances, and there is still a sometimes disturbing, self-destructive undercurrent in his work. To open the 1979 New Music America festival at the Kitchen, he unearthed a 1964 piece called *The Wolfman*, which consisted of him shouting with maximum amplification against a deafening electronic roar. It may have been meant as an expression of primal rage. It also seemed designed to enrage the audience.

Artists are usually *not* asking for violent protest, however: they want to go about their business and please people. That there aren't more violent protests is in part because of the docility of American audiences, and in part because we have all been brainwashed by the "lag" theory and books like Slonimsky's; nobody wants to look a fool in the eyes of posterity. Most contemporary-music concerts, especially the academic-serial variety, are so genteel and tepid that anyone with enough energy to stage a violent protest would not bother to attend in the first place. At rock concerts, the volume is so loud that anger from a mere unamplified human throat would be pitifully ineffectual. But new-music concerts, at which an artist is trying his best to delight and enrapture, can still arouse passionate protests.

Ashley's austere speech experiments in the early seventies, with no traditionally "musical" elements at all, raise yet another issue, an issue that Cage already posed explicitly in his writings and implicitly in his compositions. That is the limits of the term "music." Cage sought to avoid the issue by suggesting that those who considered any of his pieces not music simply think up another designation. In a statement to support grant applications for *Perfect Lives* (Ashley's writings are few and mostly aphoristic), he writes that "there is a hard line between speaking and singing, hard to find, but hard, nevertheless, imposed from somewhere." In the wake of Cage's and Ashley's speech experiments, a whole school of "text-sound" composers has come into being, some of them poets with an inclination for chanting, others composers with a fascination for words. Some recite in so artful and formalized a manner that it is easy to call what they do music. Others place the primary emphasis on their words' denotative or connotative meaning, rather than their sound. For a while Ashley seemed to fall on the speech side of his "hard line"; with *Perfect Lives,* to the extent that one can make the distinction at all, he is back into song. Perhaps the best course is to follow Cage's advice, and relax.

The last, and perhaps most fascinating, of the questions raised by Ashley's work is the way in which he conceives of collaboration. All forms of musical theater—indeed, of music itself, unless we are talking of a solo piece performed by the composer, and even then somebody else usually made his instrument—are by nature collaborative. But the conventional function for an opera composer has been to provide the music. Sometimes the text, too, or the stage direction, or the conducting, but above all the music.

The multi-media experimental world of the sixties from which Ashley emerged was imbued with communitarian idealism. For him, the very nature of collaboration is loose and ambiguous. "The nature of the collaboration in every aspect of the composition of *Perfect Lives (Private Parts)* is that I could not do it alone," he wrote in his grant statement. "It is *required* that *Perfect Lives (Private Parts)* represent as many voices as it can sustain. They are independent and simultaneous. The technique requires them to be synchronous. Otherwise, they are separate, private parts (joke). The hierarchy of those parts, the priority of their appearance, comes from complicated, practical causes; obviously, there needn't (or shouldn't) be a hierarchy, as such. The idea is old fashioned and suggests 'accompaniment.' I find the idea of a single vision, the idea of the 'auteur,' incompatible with the demands of maintaining a mode of actuality. A technique of profound collaboration is essential."

In other words, he didn't write the music, or at least a lot of it. This will offend traditionalists, and lead them to discount *Perfect Lives* as an opera. Ashley composes instead what the composer and critic Charles Shere has called the "greater music" of the opera's overall form and linguistic structure. He oversees the actual music, and contributes actively to it: it wouldn't be the same without him; he is the most important single collaborator. Indeed, one might argue, as Shere has, that Ashley's very personality, expressed through his roles as "librettist" and narrator/"singer," ensures that this "opera" is shaped in an essentially musical fashion.

But even if he didn't compose all the music in a conventional manner, what else are we to call a work like this but "opera"? The word "opera" is the plural of "opus," which means "work" in Latin; neither form implies the predominance of music. More extreme examples of contemporary "operas" created by non-composers are some of the grandiose stage pieces of Robert Wilson. *Einstein on the Beach* was created in collaboration with a recognized composer, Philip Glass, but in other major works before and after *Einstein,* Wilson assembled the same elements—mysterious dialogue, ritu-alistic stage action, sumptuous settings, glacial pace—and accom-panied them all with a curious collage of thin little original compo-sitions, taped excerpts from hither and yon and anything else he and his musician-assistants could come up with. The music was hardly primary, yet these works are still best encountered in an opera house, and they are certainly multi-media experiences of a grandly operatic nature.

Because of the moribund conservatism of its patronage and audiences, traditional opera today is even more sterile than instru-mental classical music. Frozen out of regular opera houses, exper-imental composers with an instinct for musical theater turned to different forms—the whole mélange of mixed-media events, happenings, video and varied collaborative ventures of the sixties and seventies. Some of these artists operated under the aegis of the theater (Wilson), some as dancers (Meredith Monk), some in art galleries (most of the happenings of the sixties and "performance art" of the seventies). Glass, for one, says his idea of opera "doesn't recognize a grandfather of tradition. We're mostly working pretty close to our shoes." The true antecedents of Glass's opera are, instead, "a non-narrative theater that comes from the worlds of painting and dance."

Most of these multi-media artists accompanied their innovations with rhetoric to the effect that the old institutions and ways of looking at opera were dead, and that they were doing precisely what they wanted to do. Now, however, whether mellowed by age or seduced by belated opportunity, many have jumped at the chance to work in a conventional operatic environment. Ashley is too defiantly weird, perhaps, ever to feel at home in a situation like that. Always the pioneer, he may one day realize his dream of *Perfect Lives* on international satellite television, circumventing opera houses altogether. But he may also be forced to watch as others, more adaptable, reap the rewards of his mixed-media experimentation.

9

THE ORIENT,
THE VISUAL ARTS & THE
EVOLUTION OF MINIMALISM

PHILIP GLASS

Not so long ago, Philip Glass and his ensemble still played most of their New York concerts downtown, almost surreptitiously. One night in the spring of 1973, the site was the large, high-windowed SoHo loft of the sculptor Donald Judd. The only piece on the program was *Music with Changing Parts*. At ninety minutes, it was enough.

Glass's music epitomized a rather wonderful moment in New York avant-garde history, and it still breathes that spirit today. The early seventies was a time of individual accomplishment after societal upheaval, tempering the optimism of the sixties with a new, craftsmanlike care. Innovations still seemed possible, and the barriers between "serious" and popular art looked like they were crumbling. For all its conceptual ingenuity and technical skill, Glass's music had won an audience because people *liked* it. "People," in this case, meant anyone with an openness to the arts of the day, and a feeling for the vitality of the city and of the country's best popular music.

Glass's ensemble that night played with the spirit and precision that only years together can bring. The music danced and pulsed with a special life, its motoric rhythms, burbling, highly amplified figurations and mournful sustained notes booming out through the huge black windows and filling up the bleak industrial neighborhood. It was so loud that the dancers Douglas Dunn and Sara

Rudner, who were strolling down Wooster Street, sat on a stoop and enjoyed the concert together from afar. A pack of teenagers kept up an ecstatic dance of their own. And across the street, silhouetted high up in a window, 'a lone saxophone player improvised in silent accompaniment like some faded postcard of fifties Greenwich Village Bohemia. It was a good night to be in New York City.

Today, nothing and everything have changed. Nothing, in that Glass's music is still recognizably his own. His evolution has been fascinating but consistent, extending Cage's anarchism in a way that might seem to contradict it completely. Everything, because Glass's audience isn't just a few SoHo artists anymore. In terms of recent attention by the mass media, and with audiences stretching from art museums to concert halls to opera houses to rock clubs, Philip Glass has become about the best-known "serious" composer of his generation.

Best known does not mean best loved by contemporary-music traditionalists. David Del Tredici's career indicates the jealousies that can arise even with his far more limited kind of success. Glass and his "school" of composition, which also includes such other leading minimalist-structuralist-trance composers as Terry Riley and Steve Reich, constitute the most controversial new-music style in recent decades. It is prized by its admirers for reuniting serious music with interested, emotionally committed young audiences. It is damned by its enemies as so lacking in complexity and emotional range that it can hardly be called "serious" at all.

Although he is regarded now as an iconoclast, Glass's early history was an entirely conventional one for a traditionally minded young American composer. Born in Baltimore in 1937, he studied flute at the Peabody Conservatory and was a prodigy in more than music. He graduated at the age of nineteen from the University of Chicago, went on to the Juilliard School for a Master's in composition with Vincent Persichetti and William Bergsma, and worked at the Aspen Festival with Milhaud—around the same time as Del Tredici—and later, in Paris, with Nadia Boulanger. Glass spent a year in Pittsburgh as a Ford Foundation fellow, as part of a program in which promising young composers were placed in residence around the country. His music from that period—band marches, overtures for school and community orchestras and the like— belonged unashamedly to the non-serial, American-symphonist school, although like almost every young composer Glass had also tried his hand at serialism.

This predictable destiny was altered forever in the mid-sixties, during Glass's rather rambunctious tenure with Boulanger. She made him go back to the basics, as she did all her students, and while Glass valued the experience in some ways, he bridled at the discipline. In addition to what he considered Boulanger's pedantry, nearly all the contemporary music to be heard in Paris then was at Pierre Boulez's Domaine Musical series—which Glass has since described as "a wasteland, dominated by these maniacs, these creeps, who were trying to make everyone write this crazy creepy music."

He was thus primed for a violent reaction into simplicity, and the moment came when he was employed to work with Ravi Shankar, the Indian sitarist, on an archetypically sixties hippie film by Conrad Rooks called *Chappaqua*. Glass's job was to take Shankar's raga improvisations and notate them so that Western musicians could play them on the soundtrack. Glass set about this task without much prior knowledge of Indian music, and tried to figure out as he went along just how it "worked." His conclusions proved erroneous as ethnomusicology. But they were the seeds of his own mature style.

What Glass responded to was not the microtonal subtlety of Indian music—"my strong point was not that kind of precise hearing of microintervals"—but its rhythmic structure. He perceived that structure as additive and subtractive, the building up of chains of modular rhythmic patterns out of smaller units of two and three notes. As a result, he scrapped his previous catalogue—some twenty pieces in his conventionally modernist style had actually been published—and turned instead to defiantly simple strings of notes full of a jumping rhythmic life, with pitch choices simple and almost arbitrary. Not surprisingly, nearly everyone he showed them to in Paris hated them. It was only after he had returned to New York that he slowly began to find allies, and the beginnings of a career.

This phenomenon of innovation born of imitative misunderstanding is not quite so silly as it sounds. Many of the new styles in rock music, for instance, have derived from failed attempts at imitation, another example of the benefits of an imperfect technique. A teenager will try to duplicate a record on his electric guitar. Through misunderstanding or technical failings, he will not succeed. But the resultant sounds will fascinate him, and he will be on the way to the evolution of a new style. Of course, innate originality helps; another theory holds that a true original's imitations must always fail for the very reason that the new cannot be denied.

Although Glass's music then and now sounds nothing like Indian music, the very fact that it was Shankar and Indian music that triggered his mature musical thinking is yet another indication of the impact of Oriental ideas on vanguard American composers, and a rather more complex one than, say, the efforts by Colin McPhee or Lou Harrison to recreate the sounds of Oriental music with Western instruments or to compose a cosmopolitan music for Eastern instruments. As with Cage, the influence was more one of philosophical attitude. Although he doesn't like to discuss it publicly, Glass has been a Tibetan Buddhist for years. And an important inspiration for his operas is the Kathakali dance-dramas of Southern India; he has visited the principal center of such drama in the Indian state of Kerala several times.

The way this Oriental influence most decisively expressed itself in American music of the sixties and seventies was in a newly meditational mode of perception. Western art music has been built on tension and release, which would be unthinkable without the tonal system, with its balance between consonance and dissonance and its excursions away from and back to a home key. Such music involves considerable variation of dynamics, and rhythmic ideas that, while fairly primitive, still build to an ever more rapid climax. The meditational approach is more quiescent. The listener settles into the flow of a piece rather than tensely awaiting its denouement; a parallel between traditional masculine and feminine love-making suggests itself. Someone accustomed to conventional Western classical music may find this new meditational music uneventful, simplistic and dull; the new listener—and many Orientals—find classical music noisy, clumsy and brash.

It is no accident that the rise of Western interest in Oriental meditation, music and life coincided with the increased use of marijuana and hashish. That is not to say that such music had to be made or enjoyed while stoned, although that certainly happened, on both sides of the footlights. Glass himself speaks eloquently about the parallelism between some kinds of music, drugs and religion, yet stresses that they do not depend on one another. For him, they all partake of "a non-ordinariness with certain other experiences." His music, he feels, differs from conventional classical music in that it is "non-narrative"; since it exists in "another time system," it shares attributes with trance states, religious ecstasy and drug experiences without being synonymous with them or dependent upon them. What he says is clearly true, but that does not obviate the fact that marijuana, even for those who ultimately don't much enjoy the drug, can be revelatory—*was* revelatory, for a whole generation of Americans in the sixties. That revelation, that new way of hearing things, can be recalled without recourse to a joint, and, indeed, profoundly affected the way we made, heard and judged all music.

Glass's early Paris pieces of 1965, those based on strictly additive principles, were composed for the American avant-garde theater troupe Mabou Mines. They were built on what he called "repetitive structures with very reduced pitch relationships, a steady eighth-note beat and a static dynamic level." When he returned to New York, after studies with the tabla player Allah Rakha and the first of many trips to India, he continued with this pared-down, minimalist music. The rapt and simple pieces of this period consisted of single lines of equal notes, played on a keyboard or violin. The effect may seem impossibly schematic in description. The actual results, for those who were sympathetic, were charged with hypnotic mysticism and rhythmic life: people listened to these pieces purl rapidly past and were enraptured by their sheer kinetic purity.

Such music may, as he now insists, have been original for him, but it was not unprecedented. The grandfather of this style was La Monte Young, who began as an experimental jazz musician and subsequently pioneered a hieratic minimalism without the rhythmic impetus others later brought to it. The father was Terry Riley, the composer of *In C*, although Glass never fully explored that score's communitarian, participatory implications. Reich, who had worked with Riley on *In C* in San Francisco, returned to New York shortly before Glass got back there from Paris. Reich had ideas that were very similar to Glass's at the beginning. The two talked about music a lot in the late sixties, and played in each other's ensembles. After 1970, when both were in competition for the same grants and performance opportunities and were invoked interchangeably in the press, they developed a fierce rivalry, which has since been muted by manners and ameliorated by their divergent stylistic directions.

Glass's musical evolution to the opera *Einstein on the Beach* in 1976 was steady and logical, although some of his stylistic innovations seemed disruptive or even retrogressive at the time. He soon combined his additive procedures with cyclical ideas, setting different additive combinations in rhythmic counterpoint against cyclical patterns. His music gradually assumed a greater density of texture, both in the number of players on a given line in unison or parallel motion, and in the introduction of rudimentary counterpoint. This was the period in which his ensemble was coming together, so that the outer "skin" of the music took on the character of whoever was playing it at the time. By the early seventies, the basic instrumentation was two or three electric pianos and organs, several amplified winds and a wordless, instrumental female soprano—along with a sound designer and mixer who was considered a member of the group.

The harmonic language of these pieces was static—one key for the entirety of a long section—and it was this refusal to come to terms with either conventional tonality or its serial extension that more than anything else enraged the contemporary-music establishment, accustomed as it was to equating technical complexity with artistic worth. Such harmonic contrast as there was in Glass's music existed at the seams between sections, when the whole ensemble laboriously shifted gears. Gradually, Glass found himself paying increasing attention to those seams, and slowly began to introduce modulations within sections; the key moment came in 1974, with Parts Eleven and Twelve of *Music in Twelve Parts,* which suddenly erupted into functional, root-movement harmony—in other words, full-fledged tonality. From there, the way was open to the large-scale tonal organization conducive to opera.

Reich, in the meantime, pursued his own development to greater harmonic and textural complexity. His music is woodier, softer, more rippling and gentle. While Glass was seeking grander effects through rock amplification and the theater, Reich enlisted ever larger ensembles, to the point that he is now writing for symphony orchestra. Glass has come to the symphony, too, in the form of the opera pit band. But by now, once one overlooks the outer similarities, their styles are as different as the two men always claimed they were.

Stately or agitated repetition has been heard before in Western music. The passacaglia and chaconne, in which the same "tune" is repeated over and over in the bass or elsewhere, more or less audibly, is one example. "Gimmick" pieces like Wagner's *Das Rheingold* prelude or Ravel's *Bolero* anticipate Glass's style even more directly, as do Carl Orff's still too little-known settings of Greek tragedies for gamelan-like percussion orchestra. Yet the new style is still really new, with its jumping energy and shifting colors.

For the real antecedents of this music, one must look not to previous examples in the West or the Orient. The direct precursors were the painting and sculpture fashionable in New York during the sixties. If Shapey and even Babbitt suggest an affinity with New York abstract expressionism of the fifties, Glass and Reich can claim kinship with another "New York school"—that of sixties minimalism. The plethora of sixties paintings with analytically reductive, repetitive structures and simple, even childlike formal elements all fed into a common pool of inspiration in lower Manhattan. In a sense, it is more fruitful to consider the general ambience of New York's artistic community, led by painting and then by vanguard dance, than to seek out specific visual-aural parallels. Glass, for instance, has long been friendly with the sculptor Richard Serra; he once worked as Serra's assistant, and they have nearby land in Nova Scotia, where Glass does most of his composing. Similarly, the painter Sol LeWitt has been a longtime friend and collaborator, designing some of Glass's album covers and working with him and Lucinda Childs on a piece called *Dance* in 1980. And it was no accident that Donald Judd hosted that 1973 *Music with Changing Parts* concert.

The painting connection extended beyond esthetic inspiration. While the world of uptown contemporary music defiantly ignored this new downtown music, the art galleries and museums welcomed it. "I gravitated towards artists because they were always more open than musicians, and I liked looking at what they did," Glass told Ashley. "They were more interested, really, in what I was doing." Well into the seventies, it was the Whitney and Guggenheim museums and a variety of downtown galleries and artists' lofts that provided the principal base for this music. It was championed not by music critics (a few exceptions aside) but by art critics, and the feature spreads in *Artforum* came long before those in *Musical Quarterly*—which as of this writing has still not devoted an article to Glass. Indeed, the hostility to Riley, Reich and Glass from conservatives and uptown avant-gardists alike may be the best testimony to the vitality of their music.

Although the connections between this school of composers—and it really *is* a school, with all manner of spin-offs both in classical music and in rock—and visual artists are obvious, such affinities extend into all areas of the downtown SoHo arts community. In Glass's case, not only is his music used by every other loft dancer one encounters, but he himself served as music director and composer for Mabou Mines, of which his first wife, JoAnne Akalaitis, was and is a member. The dance connection was even more direct in Reich's case. For a time, he lived with Laura Dean, who choreographed a number of works to his music and later took to composing Reichian scores herself.

The musical world's first interest in Glass and Reich came from Europe. During the seventies, they and many other New York avant-garde performing groups, including new-jazz musicians, toured France, Germany and Holland regularly, playing at state radio stations, art galleries and concert halls. This has been adduced by disgruntled American composers of greater domestic reputation as further proof of Europe's incorrigible trendiness; the French also doted on Jerry Lewis. But the enthusiasms of a few fashionable French were only a small part of the intensity and seriousness of Europe's reaction to this music. Reich and Glass may possibly have been first perceived as novelties, but Europeans soon found their music not only representative of America in a way that other American art music was not, but worthy of admiration in the abstract. Glass's growing European reputation was solidified by the tour of *Einstein on the Beach* in 1976. Robert Wilson, who collaborated with Glass on *Einstein,* already had a cult reputation in France, from which Glass benefited. Following the end of the tour and some bad feelings between the two men that precluded, for a while, further collaboration between them, Glass received a commission from the Royal Netherlands Opera for an opera by himself alone. By "alone" one means he was the determinant force, although Constance DeJong, a longtime friend, helped him assemble the text and received credit as librettist. That opera was *Satyagraha,* a series of tableaux on the life of the young Gandhi in Africa. First performed in Rotterdam in the fall of 1980, it toured Holland and was presented in upstate New York and Brooklyn in the summer and fall of 1981.

Opera was not so foreign to Glass's sensibility as one might imagine. He had worked in long time-spans before, with the four-hour *Music in Twelve Parts.* Mabou Mines had accustomed him to the stage. Wilson's esthetic, with its hypnotic stage pictures and glacial movement punctuated by abrupt *coups de théâtre,* had many points of contact with his. And Glass, ever mindful of the economic aspect of a composer's career, realized that operatic commissions were his surest guarantee of financial stability.

Einstein and *Satyagraha* are very different, but again represent a logical evolution in Glass's development. *Einstein* is for the ensemble and untrained singers. Their text consists of solfège syllables and numbers that limn the rhythmic structure of the music: Boulanger's influence on Glass returns over and over again. The music often recalls Glass's pre-operatic instrumental idiom, especially in the dances, and serves throughout as accompaniment to Wilson's remarkable stage pictures. *Satyagraha* owes much to Wilson's dramaturgy. But this was a work commissioned by a functioning opera company—as opposed to the specially formed, lower-Manhattan touring company that performed *Einstein*. There is a real symphony orchestra in the pit, and a real cast of operatic singers and chorus on stage. The action is not realistic; Glass's sympathy with "non-narrative" theater precludes that. But the *sound* of the music conforms with surprising ease to the classical tradition. It is on the one hand an orchestrated (and deftly so) version of Glass's ensemble style; on the other hand, it recalls Fauré and Bruckner in its sensuous, stately, untroubled unfolding. Glass's ensemble music is hard-edged and insistent; *Satyagraha* is soft, flowing and meditative, as befits its subject.

The success of these two operas—the Achim Freyer production of *Satyagraha* in Stuttgart in the fall of 1981 earned respectful reviews from even the orthodox modernist critics—has ensured Glass as lively a future in opera as he chooses. Dennis Russell Davies, the American music director in Stuttgart, commissioned another opera from Glass, based on Immanuel Velikovsky's *Oedipus and Akhnaton,* and the city of Amsterdam has asked for yet another opera after that.

In the midst of all this, as if to prove that he could maintain his diversity, Glass and his ensemble—which will not have a part in these full-scale operas—played more and more in rock clubs, and Glass even co-produced, along with his longtime sound technician, Kurt Munkacsi, two RCA albums of a minimalist-structuralist rock band called Polyrock. For Glass, the New York rock clubs in the late seventies constituted "the most important and vital new music scene today, more challenging and innovative than what I was hearing coming out of the schools or from people imitating me. I find their approach to their music serious, lively, risky; these guys are doing all the things that artists are supposed to be doing."

Is Glass's newfound operatic opulence and cult rock stardom part of the Cage tradition? The answer depends on how one interprets Cage's influence. If we measure that influence by the number of composers whose music *sounds* like his, then his impact has been small. If we interpret his writings to mean that formal music should disappear and we all, "composers" and listeners alike, should become equals, then he has been a failure, too. But if Cage's influence was primarily one of liberation, a permission to explore, then Glass owes him an enormous debt, as do many other composers. It is a debt they own up to: *Silence* was a crucial text in Glass's transformation from dutiful young American composer to what he is today. Cage let conventionally trained composers tear down or ignore the "rules"; he let them experiment without fear of condemnation. "I admired his ability to stand on his own feet," Glass told Ashley. "You know there is this maverick tradition in America that's very strong. It's in Ives, Ruggles, Cage, Partch, Moondog, all of these weird guys. That's my tradition."

In the mid-sixties, Glass went back to the basics and built up a personal style from there. In retrospect, we can note similarities to earlier forms of music, to non-Western music, to SoHo composers and to painting and dance. But the actual piece-by-piece evolution was Glass's own, in a way that composers who deal in received idioms—*knowing* deep inside that they have an absolute freedom to experiment, yet repressing that knowledge—cannot match.

In creating his own style, Glass illuminated still further the relation between musical simplicity and complexity. Traditional composers complain that his music is insultingly simplistic. Of course it is, if the criterion is a complexity that only a peer can penetrate. But if the goal is a music with structure and integrity and conceptual fascination that simultaneously excites and moves an audience, then music which fails to do that has fallen short. On its own terms, Glass's music has complexities its critics rarely consider. Rhythmic units fly by with such a speed that it takes a player considerable concentration not to get lost. Lines sometimes overlap in ways that are difficult to perform or perceive. And when played with great speed and the high volume Glass favors, exotic acoustical phenomena emerge—"beats" and combination tones—to lend the music an unexpected textural richness.

Over the course of the past fifteen years, Glass has built an audience that for diversity and sheer numbers surpasses that of any "serious" composer today. In so doing, he discovered something rock musicians have known all along. When you attract a following that loves your past work, and expects more of the same, you encounter pressure *not* to change your style. A composer like Rzewski can shift facilely from idiom to idiom because, to be blunt, nobody cares what he does, least of all "the people." But Glass and the rock bands have *fans,* and those fans get disgruntled when they feel "betrayed." Were Glass suddenly, on a whim, to write a serial piece, it would be regarded as an aberration by his admirers. There are already those who cherish the early, austere pieces, who found *Einstein* too busy and fussy, and who feel that in *Satyagraha* he softened his style beyond salvation. Such pressure can function as invidiously as the strictly commercial pressure to duplicate a hit song—which is merely the leverage of fans' expectations translated into a direct threat not to buy anything unorthodox. It also parallels the pressure applied to academic composers by their teachers and peers, who understandably prefer approaches similar to their own.

The pressure can come from within, as well. Glass finally decided to introduce harmonic modulation into his music because he resented his own instincts telling him he could not. "I decided to change the rules," he recalled. "I noticed that I had been operating under a lot of rules that had become automatic, and that there were things that weren't possible to do in my music because I had made them forbidden. I said, 'Why can't I do it?' 'Well, there's this rule.' 'Rule!!? Who's making the rules? *I'm* making the rules.' And that was the end of the rule."

Whether the pressure comes from the public, one's peers or one's self, the strong will resist and the weak will capitulate. Despite the complaints of those disappointed with *Satyagraha,* Glass has in essence, for all his evolution within his own terms, stuck with the style that defined his maturity. One can only hope that was because it best expressed what he wanted to say, rather than because it was what his career demanded. But a steady evolution has helped define his public image and lend coherence to his work in a way that vacillating eclectics can never achieve.

During his many years of marginal economic existence, Glass worked as a furniture-mover, plumber and taxi-driver; a few weeks after the glamorous *Einstein* premiere at the Metropolitan Opera House in 1976, he was back behind the wheel of a cab. But he was able to avoid the academy and to keep his odd jobs at a minimum by touring with his own performing ensemble. He also refused to let his music be published, in order to ensure exclusive performance rights for his own group. More and more composers have taken to starting ensembles of their own—Reich and Wuorinen in New York, Shapey in Chicago, Peter Maxwell Davies in London and Pierre Boulez in Paris. Glass and Reich played only their own music, while the others diversified. In all cases, the existence of such a group assured the composer not only performances, but *better* performances than he could otherwise have hoped for. Composers profit from organizational ability, a knack for working in the world. This need not preclude a kinship with the outsider tradition of American composers, however, since the very act of creating one's own group places one outside the normal pattern of having to beg for performances.

Composing for one's own ensemble does seem to limit a composer in another way, by precluding large-scale music. Reich tried to escape that trap first by expanding his ensemble up to eighteen musicians and beyond, then by writing works for ensemble *and* orchestra, and finally turning to the symphony itself, when his growing stature enabled him to win commissions and assurances of adequate rehearsal time. Glass also writes now for the symphony, but before that he side-stepped the problem of enforced small scale by the same means with which rock groups have managed to fill indoor sports arenas with sound—amplification. If the growth of the symphony orchestra through the nineteenth century was partly a response to the democratization of music and the ever larger halls in which orchestras played, the advent of amplification was a further step in that direction—except that now the actual number of musicians could shrink, thus ideally combining the close, subtle interaction of chamber music with the volume of a full orchestra.

Amplification, generally augmented to a point where non-rock listeners become literally uncomfortable, is part of the connection between Glass and rock. Another is the very nature and configuration of his ensemble, or "band." Another is the palpable rhythmic kineticism of the music, even without a drummer. All that is missing are electric guitars, and younger composers like Glenn

Branca, Rhys Chatham and Paul Dresher have now turned to them. In 1982 there was an all-electric-guitar performance in SoHo of Riley's *In C*. Such affinities helped inspire the growth in New York of rock bands that were clearly influenced by this school of music—Talking Heads, above all. The rock appeal of his music won Glass club bookings that expanded his and the ensemble's earnings at a time when he was so busy composing he had no time to waste touring. And it attested still further to the variety of his audience, confirming that it was both permissible and enlightening to like more than one kind of music.

By every criterion except grudging mainstream respect, Glass is enjoying a success that few American composers have been able to equal. It may be an ephemeral success, as his detractors insist— the kind that will fade like the pop charts. But right now, Glass seems to be developing and diversifying his style and audience and supporting himself through commissions, grants, record sales and concert dates in a way rarely achieved in this dreary age of parsimonious foundations and stultifying academic appointments. Transitory or not, people *like* this music. For a serious composer in the late twentieth century, that is no mean achievement.

10

WOMEN COMPOSERS, PERFORMANCE ART & THE PERILS OF FASHION

LAURIE ANDERSON

By now the distinction between "uptown" and "downtown" new music probably means something even to those who live outside New York, as a distinction between academic sobriety and bohemian experimentation. In New York itself, "downtown" literally used to mean Greenwich Village. Now it refers more to SoHo or SoSoHo or Tribeca or whatever the acronyms of the moment are for still seedier, less developed neighborhoods between Houston Street and the southern tip of Manhattan. It was to these neighborhoods, most of them commercially zoned with large loft buildings that used to house light industry, that artists began moving when the Village became too expensive. The lofts were ideal for painters, and the rents were cheap. But as artists settled in, boutiques and other signs of trendiness soon followed, driving up the rents and driving out the artists.

For all the troubles Manhattan artists have with loft-converters and landlords, however, the downtown arts community still exists. It is a real community. People who live there feel a kinship with other downtown artists, even if they are working in different media. Artists will often work in more than one medium themselves. And artists in a given medium feel closer to fellow downtown artists of all kinds than they do to uptown artists in their own medium. Specifically, that means a downtown composer may feel more in common with neighboring dancers, painters and poets than with uptown composers—even if the composer was himself trained in an uptown bastion.

As in all "small towns," most everybody in SoHo knows everybody else. It is a scene full of ambitious, competitive people (for all the communitarian ethos), in the full glare of every kind of journalism from newspapers with a national impact to arts journals, national magazines and television. As a result, some artists suddenly become trendy and hot. They may sustain their recognition, or they may slip from view. At this writing, about the hottest, trendiest artist in SoHo is Laurie Anderson.

Anderson is a composer, but more visibly she is a "performance artist," which gives the first clue to her popularity. Performance art is the fashionable discipline these days, having succeeded painting, theater, dance and video, all of which enjoyed their place in the trend-setting sun over the past two decades. But there is more to her success than that; there are other performance artists, after all. Anderson owes her special recognition to her mixture of music and performance, and specifically to the way she embraced new-wave rock without becoming its slave. In all her guises she is a performer who seizes the attention and holds it. She has a delicious sense of humor, which is not all that common in either punk or the avant-garde. And she is a woman.

Anderson was born in 1947 into a large, well-to-do family and raised in Wayne, Illinois, west of Chicago. She took up the violin as a child and practiced it industriously until she was twenty-two years old. She has lived in New York since she came to Barnard College in 1966. At college she concentrated on art, with a B.A. in art history and an M.F.A. from Columbia in sculpture. She also studied privately with the artist Sol LeWitt, and for several years wrote art criticism for New York journals. Her performances began in the early seventies; she dates her first major piece in this genre, *As: If,* from 1974.

Her early pieces were short and clever, owing something to happenings and the post-Cageian avant-garde theater of composers like Ashley. She would play the violin, for instance, but in an unusual situation—like standing in a block of ice—that called fresh attention to this most familiar of actions. She wrote poetry, made conceptual installations in galleries, and recorded short songs and quirky instrumental pieces, all in preparation for her larger projects.

The most ambitious of these projects to date is called *United States I–IV*, an attempt to embrace and understand her native country, the inspiration for which came during her ever more frequent European performances. Earlier versions of separate sections were presented at the Kitchen and, as her popularity grew, a downtown converted movie theater. Her first LP, *Big Science*, consisted of "songs" from all four parts, and the entire extravaganza, spread over two evenings, received its world premiere in February 1983 at the Brooklyn Academy of Music.

All her work, including *United States*, is best described as solo opera—although in her larger-scale recent productions she has had accompanying musicians as well as assistants to help with the sound, lighting, tape recorders and slide and film projectors. Still, it is Anderson alone who is in the spotlight. The effect is like a highly attenuated art-rock concert, a stylized lecture or perhaps a poetry reading writ very large indeed, with every aspect of the poetic concept amplified and counterpointed by aural and visual imagery. The subject is herself on one level, but more generally, in the tradition of all autobiographical artists, her observations on whatever it is that is the subject of a given piece. In this sense, her work recalls Ashley's *Perfect Lives (Private Parts)*, but for reasons of both personality and style the effect is very different.

Anderson has said that the basis of her inspiration is words. In that way, too, she suggests Ashley and the text-sound movement of recent American poetry and composition. Anderson's words and her manner of delivering them, with exquisite timing, varied vocal inflections, and electronic and chemical alterations of her natural vocal timbre, can be both witty and insightful. A complete "song" from "Americans on the Move," Part One of *United States*, is as follows:

"WALK THE DOG," a song for voice, violin and electronics

I saw a lot of trees today. And they were all made of wood.
Well, they were wooden trees—and they were made entirely of wood.

Well, I came home today, and you were all on fire. Your shirt was on fire.
And your hair was on fire. And flames were licking all around your feet.
And I did not know what to do. And then, a thousand violins began to play.
And I really did not know what to do then.

   So I just decided to go out—
And walk the dog.

I went to the movies, and I saw a dog thirty feet high.
And this dog was made entirely of light. And he filled up the whole screen.
And his eyes were long hallways. He had those long, echoing, hallway eyes.

I turned on the radio and I heard a song by Dolly Parton. And she was singing:
Oh! I feel so bad. I feel so sad. I left my Mom and I left my Dad.
And I just want to go home now.
I just want to go back to my Tennessee mountain home now.
Well, you know she's not gonna go back home.
   And I know she's not gonna go back home.
   And she knows she's never gonna go back there.
And I just want to know who's gonna go and walk her dog. (Her dog.)

Well, I feel so bad. I feel so sad.
But not as bad as the night I wrote this song.

Close your eyes. OK. Now imagine you're at the most wonderful party. OK.
Delicious food. Uh-huh. Interesting people.
   Uh-mm. Terrific music. Mm-mmh.
NOW OPEN THEM!

Anderson's work is a compendium of pop culture and homey observations of day-to-day life, freed of high-culture pretensions and any overt attempt to express the ineffable. What lifts her texts beyond pop pastiche is her abrupt, glancing intimations of the erotic, the political and the cosmic. She presents a landscape of the ordinary made extraordinary through unexpected juxtaposition. Her work is seen through the eyes of a latter-day Candide, bemused and amused. Anderson's words are superior in wit and poetic resonance to most rock lyrics. But like them, they do not really find completeness apart from their musical accompaniment and performance. Bob Dylan's "poetry" has been derided, and perhaps rightly so, but he attains eloquence when he sings those same words to his own tunes.

In the context of downtown Manhattan avant-gardism, a better parallel to Anderson is Patti Smith, who started out as a similarly admired cult poet in the early seventies, began chanting and then singing her words to proto-minimalist rock, and then veered off in pursuit of mass rock stardom, which she almost attained—*did* attain, by every standard short of consistent commercial success.

Anderson, curiously enough, had a sudden and unexpected rock hit herself in 1981 with a tune called "O Superman (for Massenet)," backed by "Walk the Dog." It reached number two on the British rock singles charts, and encouraged a pop giant, Warner Bros., to support her in a nationwide American tour. But her single didn't have a similar success in the more conservative world of American pop radio and records. In any case, while Smith evolved ever more determinedly (and misguidedly) into the realm of commercially viable hard rock, Anderson's use of rock is so quirky that she could probably never hope to be more than a novelty item in that world. Then again, one thing pop is not is predictable.

She does make use of the spirit and instrumentation of new-wave rock, however, or at least of those art-rocking minimalists who have found their most powerful expression thus far in the music of Glenn Branca. But her own music, heard on her *Big Science* LP, sounds nothing like Branca's massive sonic assaults, while her theatricality transcends even Smith's compelling, bizarre public persona. Anderson's "singing" is not so much song as wildly varied and inflected narration. Her music is rockish, but also minimal and childlike in its precise spareness, electronic in its sound-colors and recorded effects, and "classical" in its sometimes frenetic, sometimes accomplished use of the violin (more accurately, electric violin). Her theatrics consist of an ingenious variety of visual devices and lighting effects, including hand shadows, party props and films, all conceived with a flair and executed with a precision that expose most performance art as well-meaning amateurism.

Performance art has a specific historical tradition, with antecedents in Dada, sixties happenings and rock. It can also be defined by its sources of patronage. Art galleries, at the same time that

127

they sponsored performances by such musical outsiders as Reich and Glass, offered a haven for performing poets, theatrically inclined dancers and artists who felt uncomfortable in new-dance or theater spaces—trapped by the expectations of those audiences and critics or unwilling to be judged in terms of long traditions with which they felt only a vague kinship.

Performance art flourished in New York in the late seventies, even though its direct precursors were not necessarily from New York. There were Gilbert and George and the Kipper Kids in London, Chris Burden in Los Angeles and many more. But the form found its most characteristic expression in New York, and there were similar experiments going on in theater and dance, as well—work by Robert Wilson and Meredith Monk, for instance, that was not usually called performance art but echoed or antici-pated many of the same concerns. All of this restless activity, one suspects, will be seen eventually as contributory to the renewal of musical theater, or opera, at a time when its traditional expression had been stultified both inspirationally and institutionally.

There were considerable differences between this new kind of "opera" and opera conventionally understood. Ashley's work indi-cates how music can play a lesser role in these collaborations, and how the very nature of collaboration can be more even-handed than it was in the days when composers dominated the proceed-ings. But the music itself, and the kind of performers it demands, have changed, too. In SoHo, the deemphasis of laboriously accrued performance technique has had several effects. One is that the less successful work of this sort falls victim to a clumsy naïveté of conception and, especially, execution. But there are disadvantages to virtuosity and advantages to a simpler technique, too—or, more precisely, to a technique evolved by an artist to suit his own needs.

An elaborate technical apparatus often sounds awkward in music that doesn't demand it. And the sheer possession of technique affects the willingness of a virtuoso to try something new. If a performer has stunted his youth struggling to master such a tech-nique, drawing almost all of his friends from a small circle of similarly minded performers, he may have neither the curiosity nor the inclination to explore beyond the conventional. Thus, the conservatories turn out armies of young performers dedicated to the past—or to "new" music that serves the assumptions of the past. Off on the margins, unrecognized by the establishmentarians, less technically practiced performers make music that speaks without the constraints of virtuosity—or is already developing its *own* virtuosity, better suited to its own expressive needs. Anderson, for one, regards her decision to stop regular practice of the violin as an act of courage. "Giving up practicing was one of the few things in my life that I am really proud of," she said. "I was becoming a technocrat, and I wanted to do other things, too."

A more rudimentary technique has other implications. It encourages artists to express themselves in related media, without excessive fear of humiliation because of technical shortcomings. An inclination to work in several artforms is hardly limited to SoHo artists, to be sure: one need only remember Schoenberg's paintings, which had a considerable technical finish. Yet in SoHo this sort of multi-art activity has become more and more common, and led to fascinating work.

Meredith Monk is perhaps the most complete example. She first established herself in the late sixties as a choreographer and dancer, although from the first her work partook of theater, happenings and performance art. It subsequently turned out that she had all along regarded herself as a composer, too. Now, not only do her solo and group compositions enliven her mixed-media events, but she has established a separate career as a vanguard composer, with several records and numerous performances to her credit. Her music consists of original and inventive extensions of a wide range of third-world vocal techniques, emitted over mostly lulling, simply triadic, repetitive instrumental accompaniment. On one level, this music, its harmonic basis especially, is minimal to the point of pretentious simple-mindedness. The trouble with such easy dismissals, however, is that this "simple-mindedness" can attain a rare evocativeness and expressiveness. Monk might not have been able to pursue her musical interests in a climate that did not tolerate the seemingly dilettantish.

Like Ashley and Monk, Anderson performs her own work, but in her case it is especially difficult to conceive how her music could function apart from her elfin presence. In the fall of 1981, an Anderson score commissioned by Dennis Russell Davies for the American Composers Orchestra was heard in New York. Orchestrated by an associate named Bill Obrecht and deprived of her poetry and personality, it sounded schematic, for all its passing charms—and, predictably, it outraged the conventionally minded. The piece, *It's Cold Outside,* was based on an earlier song, and it, in turn, included material later used in the song "Big Science" on the LP of the same name. The differences are instructive, suggesting that composers who evolve an original, idiosyncratic technique are ill advised to attempt the transferral of their ideas into an established medium without a sure grasp of that medium. Heard in an orchestral context, *It's Cold Outside* was simplistic. Relying on her standard electronic-rock forces and arranged and mixed with an unusual richness for the LP—the first time Anderson had specifically addressed herself to communicating as an artist through aural means alone—"Big Science" sounds wonderfully fresh and disorienting. And with her *Mister Heartbreak* LP of 1984, her exploration of studio technology and a dense sonic texture led to music of even greater innovative complexity.

By and large, however, Anderson can still expect to make her strongest impression in performance, combining the functions of composer and performer. In the eighteenth and nineteenth centuries, men like Mozart, Beethoven and Liszt were expected to present their own work, and be its best interpreter. Since then, in classical music, the two functions have separated. They were separate in popular music, too, when interpretive singers commonly crooned the tunes of others. But with jazz and rock, the two roles merged. Rock and folk-rock "singer-songwriters" now usually sing their own material exclusively, and listeners find it strange to hear their songs from anyone else. A few interpretive singers survive—Linda Ronstadt, for instance. But she is resisted by rock purists in part for her very "inauthenticity." The merger of composer and performer may mean a diminution of technical expertise. But the gains in sincerity òf personal expression, so prized in American culture since the sixties, are immeasurable.

Anderson's humor is unusual for a composer. In general, humor

translates only erratically into music. Apart from amusing subtleties for the connoisseur, musical humor is usually obvious parody
(Mozart's *A Musical Joke*) and heavy-handed overstatement (the
end of Beethoven's Eighth Symphony, with its protracted final
cadence), or more generalized bonhomie (Haydn) and all-purpose
perkiness (French neo-classicism). The humor of comic opera derives
largely from the words. The same might seem true of Anderson.
But the nature of her performance, her use of low-rent aural and
visual gags, is amusing, as well, and much of her instrumental
sound has a sweet, music-box quirkiness. Music still seems better
suited to the deeper emotions, however, and Anderson can make
haunting use of it for those purposes, too. But her wit clearly
entrances her audiences, and has helped secure her reputation.

So has the very fact that she is a woman, although that alone
explains little, since there are a lot of women composers these days,
especially downtown. For all the worthy historical reminders provided
by women's-music concerts, however, it remains true that until
quite recently, women simply had not made their mark as composers, even when they were welcomed as performers. Anderson herself,
with her characteristic blend of humor tempered by seriousness,
suggests one reason women were allowed to perform, and by implication why her own composition evolved out of "performance art":
"Women have rarely been composers," she said. "But we do have
one advantage. We're used to performing. I mean like we used to
tap dance for the boys—'Do you like it this way, boys? No? Is this
better?'"

The obvious underlying explanation for the low incidence of
women composers has been the general repression of female creativity
of all kinds. The romantic ideal, which still shapes our image of
the artist, is an exaggeratedly masculine one. It stresses aggression,
flamboyance, competitiveness, assertiveness. The conflicts within
present-day feminism about what a woman should be—equal to a
man, or equal but different—extend far beyond music. But it is
tempting to reflect that women are now entering all forms of
music, from experimental to mainstream avant-garde to jazz to
rock, just when the older ideal of tension and release building
to a climax and the aggressive imposition of the artist's will onto

the listener are becoming less fashionable. I earlier discussed this shift in terms of Orientalism. It may also have to do with a general feminization of our musical culture, a shift that encourages women to become composers and male composers to become androgynous.

As with any composer in this book, it is impossible to predict how far Anderson will develop or what her ultimate reputation will be. But the possibility of ephemerality seems particularly great with her, given her kinship with rock and the fickleness of the SoHo trendsetters. For all the advantages of a capital, its disadvantages are equally clear. The very volatility with which fashions change and cult darlings disappear can threaten an artist's income and self-esteem. The deleterious effects of the shallower kinds of media attention can damage even a traditionally "serious" artist, as seems to have happened with Leonard Bernstein. Deeper, more personal values, the kind best cultivated in geographic or spiritual isolation, can be mislaid in the pursuit of instantaneous success.

Anderson has shown a slightly disturbing tendency to play to her cult, to repeat and extend the coy humor that she knows can win a laugh. It is a tendency that has often been noticed in recent New York pop as well, with Patti Smith and the folk-singing Roche sisters. The very attainment of rapid success can be dizzying. One talented New York musical performance artist, Connie Beckley, a quiet and methodical worker, felt impelled to take a year's sabbatical just when she was winning international recognition. The onslaught of commissions and performance opportunities, she worried, threatened the integrity of her work.

It is ironic that contemporary composers even have to worry about such fears. In previous centuries, with a successful opera composer like Rossini or Verdi, it was assumed that artistic overextension was an inescapable consequence of success. Both men chose to retire in protest, the former early and permanently, the latter late and impermanently, but neither thought success improper in the first place. Anderson has such "troubles" now, and they may afflict her art. In the meantime, they stand as testimony to the renewed possibility of a new music that people actually clamor to hear.

11

*ELECTRONIC
& COMPUTER MUSIC
& THE HUMANIST REACTION*

DAVID BEHRMAN

Only a few years ago, electronic music seemed ready to sweep all
other music aside. Traditionalists worried nervously about music
composed by machines, and predicted a dehumanizing Armageddon. Today, outside a few specialist enclaves, one hears very little
about the subject. The odd loudspeaker still pops up at a contemporary-music concert, adding a bit of amplification, synthesized
sound or filtering to live instrumentalists. But otherwise, along with
their abandonment of serialism, composers seem to have forsaken
electronically generated or reproduced sound, as well.

In more subtle and pervasive ways, however, electronic music
continues all around us—in the amplification that accompanies so
many aspects of public life, in recordings and commercials, in rock
and jazz groups and even, after all, in new-music concerts. But the
field has changed. It is no longer necessarily an austere, abstract
medium; the bloop-and-bleep school of electronic composers turns
out to have been the serialists extending their idiom into electronics. And it is no longer practiced primarily in huge, forbidding
"centers" with expensive, ultra-complex equipment. Now, electronic music can be delicate and even sweet, performed live on
funky homemade equipment carried easily from place to place.
David Behrman, after a long career as a post-Cageian avant-gardist
and record producer, has become a leader of this school of newly
humanized electronic music.

"Electronic music" can in theory mean any kind of music that includes the electronic creation, preservation or amplification of sound. More realistically, the term should be reserved for the electronic generation of sound and the imitation of natural sounds or mechanically amplified musical instruments. The imitation can also be extended to include recorded material, altered or unaltered; collages of such materials are called *musique concrète*. Electronic music had its pre–World War II pioneers. But the genre really got its start with the perfecting of the tape recorder by the Germans during the war, which allowed composers to splice and rearrange sound. Soon thereafter, methods of generating and synthesizing sound became more sophisticated, and the advent of computer technology, with its heretofore undreamed-of ability to speed mental processes, was under way.

Thus, electronic music is really a phenomenon of the past thirty-five years. Its early practitioners, naturally enough, were linked stylistically with the prevalent musical fashions of the day. They came mostly from France, Germany and the United States, and they tended to huddle together in "centers" that allowed composers use of the then rare and expensive equipment needed to realize their ideas. Such centers sprang up in Paris, Cologne, Milan, New Jersey (the Bell Laboratories) and New York (the Columbia-Princeton Electronic Music Center).

The early centers offered access to large, expensive computers owned by universities or businesses. These computers' primary functions were not musical, however, and composers often had to work at odd hours and deal with a staff indifferent to their needs. Now, with the specialization of research and the shrinking of the size and cost of synthesizer and computer hardware, centers designed solely for electronic and computer music have become more common. The best known in this country is the computer-music research center at Stanford University. The Massachusetts Institute of Technology also has a computer-music center, and publishes a journal devoted to the subject. Stanford personnel helped develop similar centers in Paris—Pierre Boulez's Institut de Recherche et de Coordination Acoustique/Musique (IRCAM)—and at the Center for Music Experiment and Related Research of the University of

California at San Diego. Centers such as the one at Stanford are now run mostly by composers of a different sensibility than those who used to work at the Columbia-Princeton Center—Babbitt, Vladimir Ussachevsky, Mario Davidovsky. At Stanford, John Chowning, Loren Rush and others are closer in spirit to the acoustical mysticism of Alvin Lucier and Robert Ashley.

But the real revolution in electronic music extends beyond such centers, and has been made possible by the rapid development of technology. Formerly cumbersome behemoths, computers and synthesizers are now light, flexible and relatively inexpensive. This has come about through the progressive miniaturization of all electronic hardware over the past twenty years. Scientists and manufacturers did not miniaturize this equipment and make it widely available out of blind altruism. They did it in part because increased demand lowered unit costs, and in part because rock performers' and audiences' love affair with electronic sound, reinforced in the late seventies by the futuristic sound effects of computer games, broadened the market. Rock musicians and subsequently the public at large demanded equipment that was simple, portable and reasonably priced. Specialist manufacturers and even individual composers—like Behrman—were able to refine and compact this equipment still further by designing it for precise musical purposes. A synthesizer or computer that must accomplish varied tasks has to be far larger and more expensive than one limited to a single task. The result has been the spread of all kinds of electronic instruments, synthesizers and home computers. Philip Glass, for instance, based the tone color of his pre-*Satyagraha* ensemble music on the Farfisa and other humble electronic organs and pianos that also provided the insinuating little organ lines accenting so many rock singles of the sixties.

Vanguardists like Behrman, who are hardly rockers, took advantage of this revolution to liberate themselves from deadening institutional associations, and found in the process a whole younger audience that had bypassed lingering prejudices against electronic music. They also found venturesome rock musicians, weary of the stylistic limitations of conventional rock, who were ready to be influenced by *them*. Many of these composers made use of their new equipment and accessible idioms in live performance, rather than reclusively creating a tape in the studio. They mixed live performance with electronics, or used pure electronics altered in concert, or let the environment do the altering. Thus, one of the principal impediments of the old "electronic-music concert"—an audience sitting expectantly in a darkened concert hall, faced by two or more cold and impersonal loudspeakers—was overcome. In the old days, audiences didn't know when the music was beginning, when it was over and whether (or whom) to applaud. Now, the composer was onstage, alone or with assistants or live instrumentalists, and the concert proceeded like any other, except for the sounds that emerged.

This new mixture of live performance and live electronics was also seized upon by composer-performers already interested in improvisation—either improvisation within the tradition of classical avant-gardism, as with the group Musica Elettronica Viva, founded in Rome in 1966 by Rzewski and his allies, or the jazz avant-garde. Anthony Braxton, best known as a jazz musician, was involved with MEV for a while, and another MEV participant, Richard Teitelbaum, has had a long history of jazz performance along with his avant-garde concertizing. More recently, George Lewis, who first made a name for himself as an important young jazz avant-gardist, has combined his trombone improvisations with electronics and emerged in the "classical" realm as well—insofar as such distinctions have meaning at all any more. Lewis solidified his foothold in both camps by becoming music director of the Kitchen, the leading performance space for "downtown" music in New York, and programming "jazz" groups and even progressive rock along with the classical experimentalists.

Behrman's career exemplifies all these trends, except for any direct association with jazz. He was born in 1937 in Salzburg, where his parents—he was S. N. Behrman, the playwright; she was Jascha Heifetz's sister—were attending the summer festival. Raised in New York City, he studied composition privately with Wallingford Riegger and with Walter Piston at Harvard, and then returned to Columbia for a Master's. After collaborating with Henri Pousseur and Stockhausen in Europe, he was a member of the Sonic

Arts Union with Ashley, Lucier and Gordon Mumma. From 1970 to 1976 he worked with John Cage, David Tudor and Mumma at the Merce Cunningham Dance Company, and for a time he directed the Mills College Center for Contemporary Music along with Ashley. He lives now in New York.

Perhaps his most influential activity aside from his actual composing was his role as producer of a series of new-music records for Columbia Masterworks in the late sixties. This was during the enlightened era of Goddard Lieberson at Columbia, before the more aggressively pop-oriented Clive Davis took over. Behrman's recordings included a wide range of experimental music then ignored by the East Coast establishment. His best-known record was Riley's *In C,* which inspired a whole generation of minimalists and musical structuralists.

There has never been another series quite like Behrman's, and the reasons help explain a crucial problem faced by new-music composers of widely varying styles. Especially in this time of diminished musical literacy, exotic instrumentation and personal- ized notation, recordings have supplanted sheet music as the prin- cipal documentation of a composer's work. What made the Colum- bia series so influential was in part Behrman's taste and the vitality of the music he helped disseminate. But he didn't disseminate it alone; it took the distributing and promotional clout of a giant American record company to do that. Since then, those record companies were first seduced by greed and then paid the price for that greed in the partial collapse of their markets. Davis and others pursued ever greater mass pop success, cavalierly reducing the range and impact of their commitments to more marginal musics, among them jazz, the avant-garde, out-of-the-way pop and classi- cal music as a whole. When, in 1979, pop sales faltered—a decline attributed variously to a slumping economy, the end of the baby boom, the rise in record prices, the spread of home taping and the poor quality of too much of the pop music propagated by the record companies and top-forty radio—the companies retrenched, cutting back still further on their peripheral operations.

There were exceptions, above all the determined advocacy of mostly East Coast composers by Nonesuch Records (a component of Elektra-Asylum, which in turn is a division of Warner-Elektra-Atlantic, which is owned by Warner Communications). But for the most part, the major record companies have ignored anything out of the way. The result, as smaller companies filled the void, has been a fragmentation of the record market that parallels the fragmentation of the music audience. There are advantages to this fragmentation: a dizzying variety of music is available if you know where to look. But the disadvantage is that it is becoming increasingly difficult to *know* where to look. The proliferation of little labels, often privately produced by the composers themselves, has made distribution almost impossible. A record store can hold only so many records, and tends, like the major record companies, to favor the best-sellers. Thus, the neophyte new-music record consumer, unless he or she goes to the few shops that deal in such music, or to a specialty outlet like the New Music Distribution Service in New York, has no simple way of knowing what is available, let alone what is good. A customer is hardly helped by the monthly Schwann catalogue, which is supposed to list everything that is domestically available, but which has failed miserably to keep up with the realities of the American record market today. Schwann even lists "electronic music" separately and by label, rather than by composer like all other kinds of classical music. Schwann, too, has been taken over by a conglomerate—ABC Leisure Magazines—and seems to be suffering for it.

Records are more integral than ever to building an artistic reputation. Just as a young instrumentalist cannot hope for an international touring career without frequent recordings, so, too, a composer—and *especially* a composer of electronic music, so suited to the recording medium—cannot escape provinciality (even the provinciality of New York City) without disc exposure. Take Charles Dodge, a computer-music composer of considerable invention and imagination who doesn't happen to be a very successful hustler. As an unassuming professor of composition at Brooklyn College, in the absence of a concert circuit on which new electronic pieces can be regularly heard, he cannot hope for a national reputation unless he can record. During the years in which Teresa Sterne ran Nonesuch Records, Dodge was commissioned by the company to create an album-length work called *Earth's Magnetic Field* (1970), which attracted much favorable attention. But then his recordings receded to the tiny, erratically distributed labels frequented by most other composers. For years, he had a tape of a computer realization of a Beckett radio play, but couldn't interest any record company at all in it. Dodge may have been a great poet of the computer. But who was to know?

Behrman's mature style as a composer can be dated from 1966, when he designed his first electronic circuitry, and 1967, when his first piece composed for that circuitry, *Runthrough,* was performed by him and the Sonic Arts Union. *Runthrough* in its recorded incarnation is a busier, denser work than his more recent efforts. It sounds at first like some electronic washing machine churning through its cycles, and then settles down to purer electronic sounds. The actual score is improvisatory, designed for one or two players with one or two others handling the equipment; the players precipitate the sounds by activating a photo-cell with flashlights (that particular circuit was devised by Rzewski). The piece has several of the basic characteristics of Behrman's later work: homemade circuitry, using one thing to trigger something else, unskilled as well as skilled performers, simple results obtained by complex means, a freely evolving form.

Behrman is not a trained engineer. He learned what he needed to know mostly by reading and by corresponding with Mumma. The equipment he has designed has gone through several stages, but all of it conforms to a recognizable personal style and ideology. He is interested not in pure electronic sound but in its interaction with live performers, with the electronics responding to performers and modified in its design or on the spot by the composer.

His first equipment was "pitch-responsive," meaning that if the equipment perceived a certain pitch, it would respond with another pitch. Those responses were in just-intoned harmonies—pure intervals determined by the overtone series and free from distortion by the compromises inherent in the equal-tempered system that has defined Western harmony since the mid-eighteenth century. This lends all of Behrman's mature music a pure, crystalline quality. Paul DeMarinis, the California composer who contributes a fine Behrman chapter in Ashley's *Music with Roots in the Aether,* speculates that the very nature of these pitch-responsive devices will alter our notion of harmony's function. Conventional harmony and voice-leading were, he argues, the result of inherent acoustical laws compromised by equal temperament and the mechanics of conventional instruments. Electronic instruments are in theory freed from such compromises; they permit as pure a harmony as the human mind can imagine (although they introduce biases of their own). Thus, DeMarinis concludes, Behrman has been able "to use really rich harmonic material without having to deal with all the weight and forward direction usually associated with harmony. Without gravity."

Since those first pitch-responsive circuits, Behrman has extended his music's interactive capabilities, including one memorable collaboration in which sounds were prompted by clouds. Sometimes, as with his Cunningham works, the music responds to the movements of dancers. Sometimes he modifies speech. In 1982 he and DeMarinis offered a video and music installation called *Sound Fountain* at the Hudson River Museum north of New York City that combined sound with a direct invitation to an uninitiated audience to "play" the piece on specially designed instruments. But the main step forward has been the introduction of micro-computers, which enable the equipment to sense whole melodies, not just pitches, to respond with both pitches and changes in dynamics, and to modify its own responses in the course of a piece.

But what does all this technology *sound* like? First of all, a Behrman "piece" is something of a misnomer. Each new refinement of technology and software programming suggests new esthetic opportunities. His music consists of pieces that evolve over time, shifting imperceptibly into the next piece. "The form of the music," he once said, "is kind of a slow unfolding of the possibilities in the system."

His best and most characteristic recording offers two works that involve direct micro-computer and synthesizer responses to live instruments: woodwinds in *On the Other Ocean;* cello in *Figure in a Clearing.* Both are on a disc released by Lovely Music Ltd.— which is run by Robert Ashley's wife, Mimi Johnson, who also heads one of the most active artist-management firms specializing in vanguard performers. In each piece, the live performers contribute six pitches. The computer reacts to the order and timing of the notes and alters the synthesizer-generated harmonies accordingly, which in turn suggests new ideas to the improvising musicians. In *Figure in a Clearing*, there is a continuously accelerating or decelerating rhythm, "modelled after the velocity of a satellite in falling elliptical orbit about a planet," as well as one drone-producing sinewave generator. In both pieces, pure harmonies float weightless in mid-air, humanized by the "natural" sounds of the familiar instruments, which along with the synthesizer provide bucolic, pastoral melodies and intervals.

Behrman's work is meditative and personal. Although this music is in no way meant for a wide audience, and although Behrman himself is a shy, retiring man, it can please the uninitiated deeply. Behrman has recognized this curious relationship between an introverted music and an extroverted appeal. His work, he has said, "has a very private feeling for me, and yet I don't see why eighty-three million people couldn't enjoy that private feeling. Solitude could be a universal treasure in a crowded world."

The impact of Behrman's work is totally different from the hard-edged, cold, robot-like sounds most people associate with the term "electronic music." Yet the technology behind these seemingly simple sounds remains complex. Behrman's technology, in comparison with the more arcane reaches of computer-music research, is rudimentary. Yet a straightforward description of it can still lose the layman: "It uses half of a dual op-amp," says one such description in part. "The next stage is the compressor, which serves to neutralize amplitude variations, and cut down on loud transients. That uses the other half of the dual op-amp, plus a FET. Then there's a tunable resonant filter using three op-amp stages, and an envelope follower." And so forth. To what extent, one might wonder, does a listener have to be familiar with the intricacies of electronic technology in order to "understand" electronic music?

No more or less than the typical concertgoer need know the intricacies of harmonic analysis or the acoustical and mechanical workings of the piano. As a rule, composers have insisted that a dogged analysis of their compositional methods was not only unnecessary but a positive hindrance to its proper appreciation. Similarly, an understanding of the minutiae of electronic technology may be revelatory on some level for a sophisticated listener, but ultimately secondary to the musical message the composer is trying to convey. If an audience can find nothing in the music to enjoy, all the "understanding" in the world will not improve matters. An audience member who does enjoy a piece may be encouraged to ferret out its technical underpinnings—whether the piece be for electronic or mechanical instruments.

Naturally, in a new, rapidly evolving field like electronic music, the very presence of fancy new hardware can prove seductive to both composer and analyst. Electronics becomes a source of arcane terminology for critics to conjure up in lieu of a real explanation or evocation of the music. Composers can be sidetracked by the very novelty of confronting a new electronic technology. Just as some serialists lost sight of composition in their myopic fascination with technical "problems" to be "solved," some electronic composers become so obsessed with stunts that they stop making music.

The temptation to focus on a narrow set of solvable problems is great, in part because of the very openness of the electronic field. Among the alibis for electronic music's "failure" has been that composers are daunted by the very infinitude of possibilities. In theory, at least, electronic technology allows a composer to do anything at all. Music is usually made best within the context of a tradition—an understood set of guidelines, a past full of influences and models, and an open but comfortably circumscribed future. That is why a change within one style may be a genuine innovation, exciting to a composer and his listeners, even when something similar was done long ago in another style. In electronic music, next to nothing has been done, given the range of possibilities. In fear, composers fall back on the familiar or bury themselves in technological trivia.

Behrman has avoided that trap by developing a personal style that blends the familiar and the unexpected, and by evolving logically and steadily within terms he himself has defined. But the very familiarity of his melodic and harmonic materials, and the simplicity of his effects, might be challenged by brave-new-world electronic composers fixated on scientific complexity—Babbitt, for instance—who strive to create a musical idiom equally complex. Behrman's style is an unassuming one, consonant and even tuneful. He has the sort of personality one associates with the gentler hippies of the sixties, interested in the whole range of para-scientific phenomena—psychic healing, astral vibes and such like. It might seem easy to brand him a naïf who has lucked onto a technology he neither understands nor deserves.

The very notion of the electronic folk music made by Behrman, Lewis, Lucier, Brian Eno and many more looks paradoxical for just that reason. But this apparent paradox mistakes, I think, the functions of scientist and artist. An artist can be a scientist; many scientists are artists, avocationally or in their scientific work itself, the two functions being hardly antithetical. For a composer, this new electronic technology can be a tool in the same way that a violin serves a violinist. Just as audiences need understand little of the scientific and analytic principles behind ordinary music, a violinist can make deeply poetic art without being an expert either in the secrets of the Stradivari or in the finer points of the acoustics of a vibrating string.

Behrman is not at the creative forefront of the new computer technology. His work in instrument design is at a more practical, homey level—a part of the great American tradition of the garage tinkerer. He has his own vision of the relation between art and science that helps resolve the seeming tension between them. The very rise of uncertainty in contemporary science—mathematical problems impervious to resolution, irrationally "charmed" particles in physics—suggests that artistic intuition may be as valid an approach to reality as science at its most pragmatic. "It's possibly true that the arts are going to take over areas that used to be considered scientific," Behrman speculates. "As an electronic composer, I sometimes wonder whether the next step would be to detect psychic phenomena that have been beyond science."

Whether one likes the idea or not, electronic music is all around us—sometimes ironically so, as when a rock band intersperses its loud, dramatically amplified music with an "acoustic" set that consists of mechanically amplified guitars (i.e., their hollow resonating chambers) boomed electronically through the far reaches of an indoor sports arena. Electronic music in one sense is part of the everyday life of the most confirmed classical-music traditionalist; it was Babbitt who once pointed out that even a recording of a Tchaikovsky symphony is "electronic music." But there are those who will never be able to accept electronic music, no matter how interesting or accessible it is. Such people have grown up with the sound of acoustic music in their ears, and find anything electronically reproduced or amplified artificial. Virgil Thomson, so progressive and open-minded in other ways, calls any music coming from a loudspeaker "canned." For others, the exact reverse is true. Ashley says he has long preferred electronically amplified sound to mechanically amplified sound—in other words, to all the conventional instruments of classical music.

A compromise between those two extremes makes the most sense. Electronic music is just the latest step in the long and still evolving history of man's use of acoustical principles. Amplification can sound good or bad or just different, depending on the equipment and the openness of a given pair of ears. It is a sound in no way esthetically or morally inferior to any other, and for an imaginative composer today, it should constitute an almost irresistible field for exploration.

12

ENVIRONMENTAL COMPOSERS & AMBIENT MUSIC

MAX NEUHAUS

Most concerts take place in concert halls. Be they classical, jazz or pop, musicians assemble formally on a stage and are contemplated by row upon row of audience members, usually sitting in assigned seats. Even a club, with tables or just a dance floor, places the performers in a superior position that invites attention and admiration from afar. But music today also comes at us from a wide variety of other sources. Classical music filters in over the morning radio. Funk clatters raucously from portable "boxes" on the street. Muzak oozes out from elevators. And every once in a while, sometimes when one knows it's there and sometimes as a complete surprise, one encounters the work of an "environmental," "site" or "public" composer. Often as not, that composer is Max Neuhaus.

Such music is the aural equivalent of the work of visual artists like Robert Smithson or Christo. It is also directly connected with the conceptualists. What Neuhaus does is set up an electronic-music generating system in a public location and let the audience come upon it. Other composers take a more conservative approach, tape-recording environmental sounds and playing them back in a concert setting; the ex-post-facto "documentation" of a piece once actually installed in the environment can function that way, too. More boldly, the composer can rig the system so that it interacts with the environment or with passers-by. In all these cases the music, usually quiet and unobtrusive, can be beautiful in itself. It can enhance or contrast with the sound of the environment. And it can set a listener to thinking about the very nature of music, about the way in which a composer connects with a listener, about the role of shape and form in musical composition, and about the social and political implications of the ways we conventionally encounter music.

Classical-music lovers often impugn the credentials of experimentalists, implying that they are all mindless barbarians who do what they do because they are unequipped to do anything else. Neuhaus is invulnerable to such insinuation. Like so many supposedly wild-eyed experimentalists, he had a thorough and conventional training as a composer-performer. Born in Beaumont, Texas, in 1939, he took lessons in jazz drumming as a teenager with Gene Krupa and later attended the Manhattan School of Music in New York, where he received his Bachelor of Music degree in 1961 and his Master's in 1962. In the next few years, he established an international career as an avant-garde percussionist and percussion composer, touring with Boulez and Stockhausen and recording the music of Stockhausen, Cage, Earle Brown and Morton Feldman.

But in 1968 he gave all that up to compose electronic music. He spent a year in 1968–9 as an artist in residence at the Bell Telephone Laboratories in Murray Hill, New Jersey, which at that time was actively involved in cooperative experiments between artists and scientists. It was through that experience that he began to design his own circuitry, in the manner of David Behrman and so many of the younger composers of electronic music. And soon his works began to creep out of the concert hall.

In *Water Whistle*, for instance, which was presented in various swimming pools indoors and out between 1971 and 1974, Neuhaus pumped water steadily through a number of dime-store penny whistles. The whistles were at the ends of little hoses that branched off a central hose, and the whole complex was underwater. If water is pumped through a whistle underwater, the effect is the same as when air is blown through it above water. One hears a shifting, piping sound or, more precisely, a complex cluster of such sounds—except that if water is generating the sounds, they can only be heard underwater, with one's ears submerged. The piece as a whole, then, consisted of people in various states of undress—or leaning awkwardly from the side of the pool trying to dunk their heads for a moment—contemplating a gently dappled array of ringing tones. Most people could only do so for the length of a breath. Others managed to float on their backs with their ears submerged, or rigged up snorkel devices. Along with the sounds themselves, the experience inspired a good deal of innocent fun.

Radio Net, broadcast for two hours simultaneously over 190 participating National Public Radio stations in 1977, was an outgrowth of simpler phone-in pieces Neuhaus had created as early as 1966. Listeners could phone in from anywhere in the country to five regional centers and whistle a tune of their choice. The 190 stations were connected by telephone lines that fed into a central console in Washington, where Neuhaus—who happened to be sick unto death with the flu that day—mixed and modified them electronically. What one heard at home was a subdued whistling cacophony that any listener with sufficient imagination could feel part of.

In 1980 Neuhaus installed sixty-four little loudspeakers around the base of a gorgeous glass dome that sits above the central rotunda of the Como Park Conservatory arboretum in St. Paul, Minnesota. As visitors contemplate the flamboyant plants beneath the dome, the air is filled with relaxing, sustained electronic tones—which may help the plants grow, as well.

In his most dramatic confrontation with a noisy environment, Neuhaus won bureaucratic permission to install sound-generating equipment deep within an unused space covered by a grate in the middle of Times Square, just south of 46th Street in the narrow triangular island where Broadway and Seventh Avenue converge. There, in the midst of the twenty-four-hour-a-day din of street and crowd noise, subway rumble and big-city roar, emerges a rich organ chord, droning on indominitably in the face of it all. Many pedestrians don't even seem to notice the sounds, at least consciously; it's as if they simply assumed that something beautiful is just as likely or unlikely to assault them as something ugly, and all of it is best blotted out of their minds. Others stop for a moment, puzzled, and then hurry on. Still others linger, bemused. The piece is designed to remain there "forever"—or until construction of a hotel or the widening of Seventh Avenue destroys its resonating chamber; Neuhaus is already seeking permission to move his equipment to a site two blocks south.

Neuhaus may be the most noticeable and consistently effective environmental composer, but he is hardly alone. Several interesting variations on the idea have been put forward by others. Charlie Morrow is not concerned with electronics, but he has staged often humorous aural events involving live performers, including one especially memorable occasion on which he attempted, with what success we shall never know, to play music for fish in a bay off Queens.

Maryanne Amacher specializes in hours-long environmental documentation, taped or piped in live to a concert space from some distant location. Sometimes she will blend two different sites, but the editing is otherwise minimal. That might sound tedious, except that she has a sensitive ear for evocative sound, and her mournful tapes of pier noises and ships' horns from the Hudson River can be gently seductive.

There is a parallel, perhaps, between Amacher's tape recordings of distant sounds and a visual artist's photographic documentation of some far-away site event. Christo, for one, makes up much of his costs by peddling not only advance sketches and drawings of his projects, but also photographic and filmic documentation of "wrappings" that may have stayed wrapped for only a few hours. Usually, one can buy actual pieces of whatever material did the wrapping, as well. Indeed, so copious is this documentation, and so carefully prepared (some of it limited in numbers, in the manner of prints), that the documentation becomes the artwork, at least over time.

But the aural and visual documentation of a conceptual or site composition is problematic. "It's a very deliberate step of mine not to record the pieces," Neuhaus has remarked about his radio phone-in projects. "These pieces are not musical products; they're meant to be activities." The same holds true for his site compositions. "I try very hard not to have the installations even recorded, much less broadcast," he said. "They don't make sense to me outside of their context." Music is inherently less tangible than the visual arts. A piece of music cannot be purchased like a painting, and then be expected to appreciate in value. A recording is not quite like a print, either; it's too easily copied. And a notated score is only a guide to performance. Although there is a market for manuscripts by famous composers, a music-lover still loves sound, not written equivalents thereof. To "document" a Neuhaus piece visually would be pointless, since so much of it involves the actual confrontation with the sounds at a particular site. He has prepared such documentation, however, as at the 1981 *Soundworks* show of aural art at the Neuberger Museum on the campus of the State University of New York at Purchase. It all looked disappointingly second-hand.

Amacher might seem less rigid than Neuhaus about recorded documentation. But from another perspective, for her the actual site of the piece is where the audience gathers to hear sounds transmitted from the place her microphones are located. The formality of the occasion invites a different kind of concentration. So far, at least, she has not seen fit simply to release a recording of, say, her sounds from the Hudson River piers. Like Neuhaus, she is not so much concerned with the raw documentation of sound as in new concepts of confronting particular sounds with listeners in particular situations. A mere phonograph record would amount to the relinquishment of her control over the context in which her music is perceived.

Another interesting composer in this field is Liz Phillips, who devises pieces in which sound is actively modified by the environment or the audience. Phillips specializes in sensors that detect such variables as wind speed and direction, sunlight or the shadow or heat of a person's body, all of which then alter in various pre-programmed ways the electronic sounds that she has deployed. At its best, as in a delightful piece for the 1980 New Music America festival in Minneapolis, Phillips's work encourages a happily communal, festive response from passers-by.

Finally, there is the Englishman Brian Eno, most of whose environmental works have been installed here. Eno's "ambient" music, as he calls it, exists both on records—he is a well-known rock musician, used to making money from record sales—and in the sites for which it is intended. His *Music for Airports*, for instance, can be purchased in record stores and played anywhere. It and others of his "ambient" pieces have also been installed for limited periods in the La Guardia Marine Air Terminal in New York and the Minneapolis–St. Paul airport, and at the University of California at Berkeley Art Museum. The Minnesota and California installations were part of New Music America festivals, which have become the principal annual showcase for environmental music.

All of these composers pose fundamental questions about the musical experience. It has been commonly assumed, for example, that music must have a beginning, middle and end; that it is an art that exists over time; that rhythm is essential; and that a composer's task is to arrange sound as a juxtaposition of tension and climax. Neuhaus thinks he has turned all this on its head. "Traditionally," he wrote in a privately printed manifesto, "composers have located the elements of a composition in time. One idea which I am interested in is locating them, instead, in space, and letting the listener place them in his own time." Although Neuhaus grants that good music can still be made in a concert hall, he himself is determined to expand the art beyond those walls. "One obvious way to realize that idea is to transport the music of the concert to the public space," he says, "and in some cases this works very well. Far too often, though, the results of removing this kind of music from the esthetic and acoustic context for which it was conceived are serious compromises in the sound of the repertoire performed. Rather than trying to fit these forms into situations where they have basic conflicts, it seems a more positive direction to look at the unique acoustic and use characteristics of these spaces, use them and make new kinds of music that work there."

All of this presupposes a populist ideology, based on an impatience with the elitism that characterizes most American composers. "I'm not interested in making music exclusively for musicians or musically initiated audiences," he continues. "I am interested in making music for people." "We have been in an area of over-intellectualization for a long period, to the point of absurdity," he said some years later. "I demand from a listener no previous knowledge of my work or of any other work of any composer, but simply to listen, and I also take on the burden of providing a situation where it is most likely that he would listen."

When this is accomplished, however, it poses new demands on the listener—demands similar to those implied in Cage's *4'33"* of silence. Ideally, all listeners are at all times actively engaged in a dialogue with all that they perceive, busily balancing the responses of their own ears, intellect and emotions. Practically, for a listener comfortably settled into a particular style of the past (Beethoven, Dixieland jazz, fifties rock & roll), many of those more alert, sensitized responses become blunted by habit. Encountering unusual music in unusual circumstances can resensitize a person, encouraging a new awareness of the continuously shifting sounds all around, which is what Cage had in mind. Hearing Neuhaus's *Times Square* is an especially powerful way of confronting ambient noise, and of engaging in the meditative exercise of trying to perceive the totality of sound at any given moment as form. To experience any of these ongoing environmental pieces is like passing by a painting on a museum wall. You are invited to contemplate it for as long or as little as you like; it is the moment-by-moment sensation of the piece—plus whatever complexities are in the sound or its generation or presentation, as well as whatever degree of sophistication and knowledge you bring to the experience—that determines the length and depth of your interest. And an awareness of these different factors can double back and deepen your awareness of, say, Vivaldi.

As Neuhaus's comments about the music of the concert hall transported elsewhere indicate, we already encounter music outside the spaces for which it was conceived—not only at amplified live performances such as a lawn seat at Tanglewood or the Hollywood Bowl, but with recordings. One reads frequent complaints about masterpieces demeaned by the inappropriate contexts in which they are now encountered—Beethoven's Ninth Symphony as background music for shaving. Music can indeed be defined by its context. Some people are automatically inclined to take music more seriously if they hear it in Carnegie Hall than on the radio; hence the eagerness with which the promoters of various déclassé musical forms rush out records with titles like *Country Comes to Carnegie Hall.* Beethoven's Ninth may be trivialized if encountered too often and too casually. But perhaps a different, less insistent, more insinuating and continuous music is very much suited for such circumstances.

That is exactly what the inventors of Muzak had in mind, and Neuhaus has been eager to denounce the intrusion of auditory treacle and to erect an esthetic that differentiates his own work from Muzak. One awkward question for site composers, at least at sites where a reasonable number of people are likely to hear their work, is this very problem of intrusion. It is a peculiarity of the human physiognomy that it is easier to avert one's eyes than one's ears. Thus, site composers have had a difficult time convincing bureaucrats that their works would be welcome. An example was Neuhaus's long-sought-after project to install sound in the echoing underground passageways that connect the subway with the various buildings of Lincoln Center. Still, there seems little ultimate differ- ence between that and a giant, building-high metal sculpture in a public square that thrills some and offends others. "Silencing our environment is the acoustic equivalent of painting it black," Neuhaus grumbles in his manifesto. Most environmental music is fairly quiet and fairly pleasing, anyway, although that may be to overcome potential objections as much as anything else. For all we know, Neuhaus may be secretly itching to install some mega-volumed, grotesquely dissonant aural monstrosity in the Cloisters.

The very tenacity with which environmental artists like Neuhaus and Christo pursue their projects in the face of governmental indif- ference and community hostility becomes a part of the overall process of their art—a way of dramatizing the eternal relationship between artist and society. It took Neuhaus four years to win approval for his Times Square installation, and he is now working on the seemingly quixotic project of trying to reshape artistically the contours of all of New York City's mobile sirens. Since 1977 he has been dreaming of an international phone-in project, the first stage of which is now scheduled for realization in Holland in 1985. Christo's battles become part of the massive documentation that follows any of his projects, thus giving substance to what in reality is a day-to-day struggle of attrition against red tape. Sometimes, however, especially with a more modest, short-term project, things aren't nearly so dramatic: funding is obtained with a sponsor in mind, and the piece is installed with a minimum of fuss. With or without political struggle, environmental art is inherently political in the larger sense of reflecting and illuminating the changing relationships among music, composers, patrons and audiences. Electronics has liberated musicians from the confines of acoustical space, and made it less necessary for anyone who wants to hear a piece of music to pay for a ticket or a record. For better or worse, music is in the air these days. Composers like Neuhaus are doing their best to make that music and our perception of it a more artistic, less unthinking experience.

13

MUSIQUE CONCRÈTE & COMPOSITION BEYOND MUSIC

WALTER MURCH

Some of the subjects of this book may seem far afield from the traditional conception of a composer. Some of them "compose" things that look more like poetry or theater than music. But what are we to make of Walter Murch, who is a sound editor, film editor, scriptwriter and director of Hollywood movies, and who doesn't even think of himself as a composer? Why, one might ask, is he included here at all?

The abrupt answer is: Because I have designated him a composer. If that seems an arbitrary, eccentric or arrogant extension of the critical imperative, remember that one consequence of experimental and electronic music has been a new attention to the creative role of the listener. If, as a professional listener, I choose to extend my creativity still further and call somebody a composer who really isn't one, that is my prerogative.

But a more cogent case can be made for Murch's inclusion. Although he may not consider himself a composer, or at least primarily a composer, he still works in a specific, established idiom of electronic music—that of *musique concrète,* which was pioneered in France after World War II and which directly influenced Murch when he was growing up. *Musique concrète* means an electronic music consisting of a collage of real, or "concrete," sounds: in other words, of sounds recorded and then manipulated and juxtaposed in various ways. The alternative is synthesized sound, created electronically from scratch. Murch's work in this field, even though it is for film soundtracks rather than meant as a statement by itself, deserves consideration by people interested in all forms of artfully organized sound. His career suggests that the decline in appeal of twentieth-century classical music, combined with the rise of alternate technologies and art forms obtusely ignored by traditional composers, have lured away talent that might in previous centuries have been applied to composition.

Murch was born in New York in 1943, the son of Walter Murch, the "romantic realist" painter of everyday, often mechanical objects. The younger Murch never formally studied a musical instrument (except for three months with the flute at the age of nineteen). But when he was eleven, he discovered the tape recorder, at just about the time, in the early fifties, when tape recorders were becoming generally available. The discovery changed his life. Unlike the typical "sound nut" or high-fidelity cultist, Murch was not so much interested in the circuitry and workings of this new machine as in its artistic potential. It is a bias he retains today; surrounded by the most sophisticated sound-mixing equipment, he evinces a laconic diffidence: "I'm lucky if I can keep my head above water," he says. "I can describe the results that I would like, and I have an intuitive feel for when something's gone wrong, but that's about the extent of it." All through his teens, Murch played with his tape recorders, capturing sounds from friends and the radio, splicing busily and otherwise experimenting in *musique concrète*. He knew the term, recalling, "I was very interested in the early fifties in Pierre Henri and those guys in France. I had copies of their records and I was consciously working in that style." For Murch, the exciting thing was the way *musique concrète* maintained a contact with real life but transformed it, too.

By his late teens, Murch had developed other interests. Unable to imagine how he could make his hobby into a living, he went to Johns Hopkins University and on to graduate work at the University of Southern California film school, that cradle of so many of America's brighter young movie-makers. His interest in film developed gradually, and he concedes that one reason he went to graduate school was to avoid the draft. At USC, he formed a close friendship with another student, George Lucas. "Lucas and I had a kind of Huck Finn–Tom Sawyer blood bond while we were up for a Warner Bros. scholarship at USC, and it came down to between me and him," Murch recalls. "We were waiting outside for the final interview and we said, 'Well, one of us is going to get it, but whoever gets it, if he gets a chance to help the other guy, he'll do it.' He got it."

And he helped the other guy. In 1968 Murch got a telephone call from Lucas, asking if he wanted to come to San Francisco and work on the editing of a film by Francis Ford Coppola called *The Rain People*. Murch did, and at the same time found himself involved in Lucas's first feature. While still at USC, Lucas had made a short entitled *THX 1138 4EB* that had attracted considerable attention. Now a protégé of Coppola, he was ready to transform it into a feature film, to be produced by Coppola's then new American Zoetrope. Murch was enlisted not only as sound recorder, mixer and editor, but as co-scriptwriter as well. The film came out in 1971, and since then he has functioned as sound or film editor (the titles vary, but his function remains fairly constant) on such films as both *Godfathers*, the original *American Graffiti*, *The Conversation*, *Julia* and *Apocalypse Now*, for which he won an Oscar. He also worked on the screenplay for *The Black Stallion* and, as of late 1983, was working hard to close deals to direct his first two films—*Return to Oz*, which he has co-written, and then an entirely original Egyptian horror film entitled *Intrusive Burials*.

But it is *THX 1138*, as the feature version was called, on which I wish to concentrate here. The reason is its very nature—a futuristic allegory grounded in realistic detail, with very little dialogue or conventional background music and hence a soundtrack made up almost entirely of "sound effects." Murch's subsequent work in sound has been equally inventive and precise, and some of his particular effects—the whirring helicopters in *Apocalpyse Now*, for instance—are as striking as anything he's done. But *THX 1138* was Lucas at his most experimental (so far—he says now that when he returns to directing, it will be in experimental work for a limited market). Its unusual nature allowed Murch his fullest freedom as a creator of "sound montage," as one of his credits read. Unfortunately, no soundtrack album of *THX* was ever released: the film, a victim of battles between the distributing studio and the young, still powerless Lucas, did not do well at the box office, and in any case Murch's contribution was rather too venturesome for a commercially oriented soundtrack release. But the film is still worth seeing at its occasional revivals. And, for all its visual dazzlement, it is well worth encountering with one's eyes closed.

Murch's soundtrack is a floating cloud of realistic and electronically altered or generated effects. The characters in the film are narcotized robots who move dreamily through a dehumanized world of electronic gadgetry, disembodied voices and computer-controlled appliances. The sonic ambience is subtly grating, distorted, metallic, on edge. Nothing is ever quite clear for any length of time, with a distracting electronic babble that mirrors the psychological displacement of the characters. As the film builds to its climax, the soundtrack is gradually filled with intimations of urgency, crackling short-wave cross-talk, soothing voices of robot authority figures, screaming tires and the roars of jet cars. The sound score both echoes and evokes the visual images, often suggesting things that we do not actually see and leaving it to the viewer to imagine effects Murch does not bother to supply. They are rarely missed, so potent is the power of audio-visual suggestion; when they are, the loss contributes to the sense of disorientation. The result is fully the equal of any similar collage score by a practicing electronic-music composer, with additional coherence provided by the imagery. It is a piece of electronic music-theater by Lucas and Murch together. It is, in short, opera, the soundtrack is music and Murch is a composer.

Film has long lured composers. In the "silent" era, they provided generalized mood music that could be performed by anything from a full symphony orchestra to a desperately improvising organist or pianist. Similar idioms continued into the early sound films, now accompanied by referential sound effects that reminded an audience that it was in fact seeing *and hearing* a sound film: doors slamming, car tires squealing.

By the late thirties, the role of the Hollywood composer was well established. The film business had already attracted some leading younger composers—Erich Wolfgang Korngold had been a boy wonder of European opera before he settled in Hollywood. Most of the Hollywood composers wrote in a style modernistic enough for fashion but familiar enough not to alienate audiences— high late-romantic bombast and sentimentality, in short. With the rise of Nazism, more prominent composers gravitated to Los Angeles. The sun and the already active immigrant community were lures, of course. But the composers also hoped for work in film; and it can be argued that the immigrant community, which at its height made Los Angeles the capital of the exiled Central European cultural community, grew up around the composers. As it happened, however, the better the composer, the less likely his chances with the studio bosses; for varied reasons, neither Stravinsky nor Schoenberg ever scored a Hollywood film.

In recent years, the purveyors of late-romantic kitsch have staged a comeback, and been renewed by such younger, eclectically facile craftsmen as John Williams and Jerry Goldsmith, who have benefited from the nostalgia that is part of the shared sensibility of Lucas, Coppola and Steven Spielberg. Indeed, their love for symphonic scores, and their ever greater ability to commission them, may partially explain why Murch's purest soundscore came early in his career. Other film composers have timidly ventured into modernist idioms, such as Leonard Rosenman and Alex North (who often collaborates with the classical iconoclast Henry Brant). Important "serious" composers continue to achieve effective results in the medium, as John Corigliano proved with his luridly dramatic music for Ken Russell's *Altered States*. And there has been an increasing use of pop composers and groups, too, with the initial planning for some films based on the expectation of a multi-million-selling soundtrack album.

While the role of composers within Hollywood films has stead-ily evolved, there has also been a less tangible shifting of creative energies between film and music, and among the various kinds of music. The San Francisco film scene that engendered the feature version of *THX 1138* was born at the USC film school. There is never a reason why a particular constellation of talents suddenly assembles: it could be something in the air, or some turning point of a given industry or art form, or just blind luck. In this case, directors as disparate as Lucas, Murch, Hal Barwood, Matthew Robbins, John Milius and Caleb Deschanel were all at USC in the mid-sixties, and they all have made their mark on Hollywood, mostly from four hundred miles to the north. The very intensity of this group makes one wonder if certain art forms have their "day," attracting creative talent that might otherwise have gone elsewhere. It has been suggested that many fine European film directors would once have gone into the theater, opera or even composition. Murch, for one, certainly demonstrated a musical ability, broadly defined, with his teenage tape-recording. But an old-fashioned music-education system failed to recognize his talents; music teachers were perhaps understandably unaccustomed to looking at record-ists as a source of musical talent. And although he was raised in an artistic milieu, Murch by his own admission didn't really know what he wanted to do, and was no more than normally interested in movies as a boy. Perhaps he felt drawn to film eventually because it was a way of expressing visual concerns without directly compet-ing with his father. But that is armchair psychoanalysis. Murch drifted into a medium that was vital at the moment, and wound up contributing to it rather than to some other. Like music.

The same phenomenon can be observed among composers and performers who might once have gravitated naturally to classical music, but who now turn instead to jazz or pop. Linda Ronstadt, for instance, proved in *The Pirates of Penzance* that, with training, she could have become an opera singer. Her high-school chorus teacher, following the time-honored tradition in which promising young singers are discovered, had her singing opera arias as a teenager. But she chose rock & roll instead, where she saw excite-ment and creative vitality—and glamour and money, as well, to be sure. As with Murch, the methods by which musical interest and performing talent are gauged seem so erratic and stultified today that many slip through the net. That they have found other outlets for their musical interests may reinvigorate music as a whole.

The transferral of creative energy in film away from Los Ange-les allowed young San Francisco filmmakers to establish their crea-tive freedom from both studios and unions and still stay close enough to the movie industry to make their mark on it. What that freedom meant for Murch was everything. In Los Angeles, he would have had to battle endless union restrictions and to concentrate in one specialized aspect of sound or film editing. In San Francisco, he not only could but had to do it all. "All" included recording his own catalogue of sounds for any contingency, since San Francisco lacked the libraries of sound effects that are commonplace in Hollywood. That ensured a freshness the standard effects could not provide. On *THX 1138*, for instance, he worked without an assistant and spent a year merely collecting the material he would subsequently use in the three weeks of actual mixing. The sound editing, in turn, took place simultaneously with Lucas's editing of the film, thus ensuring an unusual synchronism of effect. Murch has been free in other ways, as well. Instead of rushing from picture to picture, with limited personal responsibility for anything he worked on, he has done barely one film a year, but has been paid well enough to lead a comfortable life. In addition, he has worked almost exclusively with Coppola and Lucas, thus ensuring a supportive personal relationship with his artistic peers, rather than a constantly shifting employee status under a sequence of bosses.

It was during his planning and execution of the *THX* soundtrack that Murch evolved his theory of film sound. His 1970 production notes isolated three basic soundtrack elements: what he called "working effects," in which "the visual is absolutely dominant, the sound merely follows it like a puppet"; "evocative effects," with a "symbiotic synergistic relationship of sound to picture; one reinforces the other"; and "musical effects," in which "the sound is absolutely dominant; the visual is the slave." But he also suggests that "an evocative effect can very easily be a musical effect, in fact it is a very arbitrary separation." And that "*all* sound is evocative." At still another point, he reminds himself to "think of *musique concrète*: do not be limited by what you see on the screen; it would be much better if nothing were related than if everything were."

For Murch, we have transcended the "post-silent" era, in which audiences needed to be reassured that they were seeing a sound picture by a sound effect for every visual cue. Just as Cage and the experimentalists trust the listener's creativity, so Murch counts on listeners to fill in aural information with a minimum of prodding. He recalls a scene in his first film, Coppola's *The Rain People*. The screen depicted a busy gas station next to a freeway. The full onslaught of possible sounds—traffic rushing by, idling cars, people's voices, mechanical labor—seemed far too much. The solution was silence broken by a single wrench dropped in the distance on concrete. "There was something about the evocativeness of that sound that made you fill in the rest from your own experience," Murch says. As he put it in his *THX* production notes, "Sounds can be eliminated under the right circumstances because the audience will actually hear the sound even if it is not there. Less is more." Or, as he said in explaining a technically unrealistic machine-gun effect in *Apocalypse Now*: "Ultimately, who is to say what is the sound? The sound is what's in your mind, not what is on one piece of magnetic tape."

Murch is opposed not only to the use of stock sounds from libraries but to any kind of processed or all-purpose sound. Some stock sounds have taken on a life of their own, however, and people now expect them and perceive them as real even though they are nothing of the sort. Examples include the crunching impact of a film fist hitting a film jaw, or a booming gunshot. Neither sounds anywhere near so palpable in real life, but by now film audiences will accept nothing less. So Murch will sometimes use them, too, as part of the larger process of heightening an otherwise drab reality. The final criterion is emotional effectiveness, not crude verisimilitude. But often excitement is best achieved by reinforcing a sound's very realism. "I'm extremely interested in the emotion of sound, as conveyed through the space it operates in," he has said. He likes to "take a sound and dredge it into the reality it is supposed to be part of."

I earlier called *THX* an opera, and that designation was not entirely tongue in cheek. *THX* is the most complete realization in all of Murch's films of his inclination to replace the old, discrete categories of dialogue, sound effects and music by an organic collage that takes elements of all three and weaves them into a contrapuntal texture with the film images themselves. That, in turn, is evidence of the concern among the young San Francisco filmmakers for all aspects of a film's sound, whether it be a tub-thumping John Williams score or a futuristic little click. This new sensitivity to sound encouraged a serious upgrading of theater sound systems in the late seventies, with the beginnings, now, of a similar improvement in the long-primitive sound of television—and hence the restoration of balance between the aural and the visual in media long dominated by the visual. Murch's knitting together of the various elements of film sound and imagery amounts to the largely unselfconscious creation of a new form of musical theater, another way of using music and sound to support drama—and hence a modernday reinterpretation of the same ideal of Greek tragedy that inspired the Florentine Camerata to "invent" opera, and Wagner to create his music dramas. But beyond all theorizing about the function of sound, the sensuous impact of Murch's collages can be, as he puts it, *fun*.

Murch is not alone; all modern film composers and soundeffects specialists have to confront these issues. Rock performers are already dealing with them from their more strictly musical perspective, in their increasing use of video to create visual realizations of their music. A purer parallel to Murch's work is the radio documentaries of Glenn Gould, the late Canadian pianist. Starting in 1967 with a program entitled *The Idea of North*, Gould developed what he called "contrapuntal radio," in which several simultaneous monologues are woven together, the whole constructed with explicit debts to traditional musical models.

Without necessarily intending to, Murch, Gould and others working in this field have extended our notion of music. They have extended the ideal of the composer, as well, or, perhaps more accurately, they have resurrected an older ideal of the composer as craftsman, as opposed to romantic Promethean. A man like Murch, for all his disclaimers of technical knowledge, clearly loves the painstaking, day-in-and-day-out work of bending over a mixing console in a dark studio, getting things precisely *right*. "One thing that interested me about film," he once recalled, "was that it was a craft—it had its own appeal the way that carpentry or making shoes has an appeal. You're working with tools; it has its own power." Add to that its status as a glamorous and creatively exciting field that can offer lucrative and enlightened patronage to someone interested in working with sound, and you have the birth of a new kind of composer.

For all his self-image as a humble craftsman, however, Murch is also a composer who wants to reach an audience, to move it emotionally. One reason he chose film instead of the isolation of academic electronic music is that film offered him the chance to do what he wanted, yet have an impact on people's lives. "Underlying all I have been doing, all I am saying, is my belief that the real power of film lies in its ability to alter our subconscious awareness in the same manner as dreams," he wrote in 1974. "The fabric of a film is composed of many threads. At one time one thread is more evident, at another, another. Perhaps that's what makes sound useful in speaking directly to the subconscious. Deep films have a power over our lives similar to deep dreams—a power that is mysterious in its sources, in the paths through which it moves." Wagner could not have said it better.

14

THE ART ENSEMBLE OF CHICAGO

A discussion of jazz might be expected to begin with an attempt, however feeble, to define it. All definitions are tricky, but that of jazz is controversially so. There are jazz polemicists who refuse to accept the term at all. Others accept it, but only for a specific and brief historical period. Some think it inseparable from race; others vehemently deny that connection. Simply put, jazz is a musical movement that originated around the turn of the century among black musicians in the American South, gravitated north to Chicago, and then spread out into the world. It is marked, usually, by a lively attention to rhythm and by extensive improvisation. Its practitioners are aware of their own tradition: jazz plays its own club and concert circuit, has its own record labels or subdivisions, and its own scholarly and critical apparatus. But if you try further to pin down what it *is*, it disappears like a mist.

Although many whites are jazz musicians, the overall place of jazz within American culture parallels that of blacks within our predominantly white culture. The attitudes of that white culture, and of its European progenitors, have evolved over the years, but it is safe to say that, beyond lip service, the average white intellectual still does not recognize jazz as anything like the cultural equal of his own greatest art music. Classical musicians have approached jazz with a curious mixture of admiration, patronization, indifference and scorn. From the naïve jazz borrowings and flavorings of such composers as Debussy, Stravinsky and Krenek to Gunther Schuller's "third stream" music, composers attempted to adapt selected stylistic attributes of jazz to their own fixed practices, just as composers before Bartók had borrowed folk tunes. In nearly all cases, the borrowed music remained foreign and exotic. Whatever the virtues of jazz-influenced classical pieces, they had little to do with the spirit and essence of jazz itself. While jazz may have been quaint or modish or exciting for American intellectuals, it wasn't—and isn't—considered really *serious*.

And yet there are those who have argued that jazz (and, some-times, popular music) has replaced classical music as the serious musical expression of our time, or that it constitutes America's *only* serious artistic contribution to world music. Henry Pleasants, the distinguished American critic of both past classical music and pre-rock pop and jazz, contends in *The Agony of Modern Music* and subsequent books that avant-garde composers' excessive complex-ity and dissonance and their resultant loss of audience have condemned them to irrelevance, and that the true music of our time, that which expresses its spirit and sensibility, is popular. (For Pleasants, free and dissonant jazz falls into the same trap that ensnared classical avant-gardism; when he says "jazz," he means the kind before bebop, the kind lots of people actually liked.)

But Pleasants remains the gadfly, so much so that recently he has begun to despair; instead of a pioneer, he worries, he has been nothing but an eccentric outsider. For most American intellectuals (not to speak of British intellectuals, since Pleasants lives in London), jazz remains alien. Even if they profess respect, it seems such a vast, distant world that they don't make the attempt to come to terms with it. They seem to have three principal reservations. First, that jazz is simplistic in relation to the more refined products of Western art music. Second, that improvisation is an inherently primitive kind of composition. And third, the implicit racist under-current to the first two complaints, that jazz is black and therefore inferior.

Certainly Western art music has had a longer sustained devel-opment than jazz, and has found more varied ways to build large-scale structures. But we have already seen that complexity cannot be equated with quality. In any case, on its own terms, music of the jazz tradition has attained enormous complexity, if that is a criterion for anything in itself, particularly in the realm of rhythm. Even the seemingly complex cross-rhythms of some twentieth-century scores pale beside the rhythmic polyphony of African drumming, and that complex vivacity has been absorbed into much of jazz and Latin music.

A more serious concern is the very reliance of jazz upon improvisation. From the beginnings of jazz, set material, whether notated or not, alternated with improvisation, and the balance between the two has varied from decade to decade. Today, it is common in new jazz to see musicians come out and set up their music stands, even if there remain crucial elements of improvisation in their work. But the Western art musician's disdain for *any* improvisation is expressed succinctly by Elliott Carter, who remarked that "a musical score is written to keep the performer from playing what he already knows and leads him to explore other new ideas and techniques."

Improvisation has been called "instant composition" by, among others, George Lewis, the young new-jazz and avant-garde trombonist, composer and electronic musician. The difference between such instant composition and composition of a more considered kind depends on the degree of thought and planning. What composers like Carter worry about is that the supposed "freedom" of improvisation can become an avenue for the reassertion of hackneyed instinct. Yet it's nowhere near so simple as that. In fact, all music blends composition and improvisation, and as recently as a century ago there was considerably more improvisation in Western art music than there is now. The filling out of a bass line into improvised accompanying harmonies and ornamental flourishes in baroque music, or the piano improvisations of the romantics, or the freedom with which great singers before the early twentieth century approached the written score—all attested to the extent to which Western audiences once valued spontaneous creation. It can even be argued that the steady stifling of that practice has contributed to the decline of Western art music's accessibility and appeal.

American intellectuals have kept their distance from jazz for a third, more dangerous reason: racism. Leaving aside for the moment the extent of the "blackness" of jazz, it is still *perceived* as a product of the underclass. As such, it serves as a symbol for so many American intellectuals' sad alienation from their own country—from its diversity, democracy and chaotic energy. The sight of black people under any but the most sanitized circumstances inspires fear among whites in this country. And the sound of black music, be it pounding funk-pop or the driving energy of jazz, evokes, if not fear, then a disquietude that precludes intimacy. (There is also reverse racism: whites attracted to blacks and their culture for the same reasons that scare the white majority. The result is the white hipster, more soulful than a soul brother—Norman Mailer's "white Negro.")

Although it was originated by blacks, jazz became known to whites through white bands, a situation that lasted at least until the Second World War. In the twenties and thirties, such musicians as Paul Whiteman and Glenn Miller, both of whom are considered lightweights today, were far better known, in concerts and on nationwide radio, than comparable or superior blacks. Black polemicists argue with some fierceness that jazz is an *inherently* black cultural expression, and that whites who attempt it are invariably inferior. This seems extreme. It ignores the many fine if less than strikingly original white jazz musicians. It also ignores, more significantly, white musicians who made important creative contributions to both black jazz and, especially, pop. Sometimes this was simply a matter of talent. At other times, it seemed that, inadvertently, through the imposition of attributes perceived by blacks as proof of the whites' inferiority—stiffness, rigidity, obviousness—they managed to transform the tradition into something different. If such new music appealed more to whites than what the black "originals" had done, that wasn't merely because the whites looked whiter or got more airplay or promotion. In some cases it was because their music conformed more closely to what whites wanted to hear. The black polemicists also ignore the continual interchange between black and white music in this country. American black music is not all direct from Africa; it has absorbed elements of Scottish-Irish folk songs, white pop and classical music. And to think of jazz and pop as exclusively, characteristically black is to abandon black classical musicians to a curious limbo. They aren't all Uncle Toms, any more than Yo-Yo Ma has betrayed *his* race by playing the cello.

As early as the twenties, jazz was the rage not only in New York but in Europe, as well. It was adopted by classical composers as a fashionable new flavoring and by younger Europeans who formed their own jazz bands. Since the Second World War, the growth of European jazz has been so rapid as to call into question the assumption that jazz is an inherently American music. Jazz by this time is no more exclusively American than it is exclusively black. A particularly interesting development of European jazz has been the constellation of musicians—many of them Americans, but many others Europeans—that has gathered under the aegis of the German ECM record label. There is even an "ECM style," cool, controlled and elegant.

The history of jazz since the late thirties, from bebop and the tougher "hard bop" to the cool-jazz reaction to the impassioned outbursts of "free" jazz and beyond, can be seen in three ways. It was purely esthetic, a series of artistic developments evolving logically from the preceding phases. Or it was a sequence of dominant individuals who bent the music to their personal idiosyncrasies. Or, finally, it was a series of successive attempts by black innovators to define a territory that was theirs, beyond that of their eager white imitators.

These successive stylistic steps, whatever their cause, alienated jazz from its mainstream audience in precisely the same manner that classical composers had drifted from the classical mainstream earlier in the century. Particularly difficult for the conservatives to accept was "free" jazz, with its frenzied, heavily dissonant improvisations that lacked any easily perceptible form. In popular favor, jazz was replaced by pop-jazz fusions, pop, rock and country. Although there remained a good many vital musicians working in the older idioms of both jazz and classical music, mainstream jazz and classical audiences drifted more and more into nostalgia, the museum-like recreation of dead work. This was slightly more difficult in the case of jazz, given the close identification of composers and performers, and the continued presence of the original versions on records. But as the century wore on, many important jazz festivals became arenas for increasingly aged performers, answering nostalgic needs. There were even jazz repertory ensembles, playing arrangements from the past.

While "jazz" was slipping in terms of public perception into the past, younger jazz musicians found themselves forced into new modes of survival. While there had always been some distinction between jazz and popular music, jazz up until the fifties had been, in a real, financially remunerative sense, popular. But thereafter it was no longer possible for many progressive jazz musicians to make the music they wanted to make and still to hope realistically that lucrative club dates and record contracts would be their reward. Not that that had always been possible for some of the true innovators before them. But at least there was a functional club circuit. In the sixties, that circuit was drying up. As a reaction, musicians devised alternatives. Black jazz players especially banded together to form cooperatives. The cooperative provided rehearsal space that might double as a concert hall. Management ideas or volunteers were shared. Sometimes private record labels were formed. Above all, the cooperative ideal extended the longtime communal interaction of the jazz band itself into the realm of practical life.

Perhaps the best known of such cooperatives is the Association for the Advancement of Creative Musicians. The AACM was founded in 1965 by Muhal Richard Abrams, a pianist, and three other musicians in Chicago—a symbolic location, given that city's role in the dissemination of early jazz to the world. The AACM serves a political purpose as well as a musical and economic one. It takes young black musicians discouraged by the hostility or indifference of the white world and imbues them with new purpose. One example was the young George Lewis, who felt ignored and frustrated about his music and his black identity at Yale, and who was put on the path toward his mature style during a stint in Chicago. AACM musicians were inherently political, even if they didn't always write music for the barricades. They epitomized the movement among blacks to recapture and explore their own history, cultural and otherwise. That meant specifically a return to Africa for inspiration in music, dress, religion and life. It meant an extension of the cooperative principle beyond music to include society on all levels. It meant a more or less insistent concentration on blackness as a thing in itself. It also meant some remarkable music. "The spirit of the AACM permeates just about everything I stand for," says Lester Bowie of the Art Ensemble of Chicago.

Out of the AACM came a variety of artists and performing groups—Abrams, Anthony Braxton, Leroy Jenkins, Leo Smith, Air, the Creative Construction Company and, above all, the Art Ensemble. The ensemble coalesced out of the AACM Chicago scene in the mid-sixties, spent two years abroad, and has had the same personnel since 1970. Each member plays more than one instrument, and two have elaborated their names to attest to their African roots. Here is the band, with all the instruments played on its most recent album as of this writing, *Urban Bushmen:* Lester Bowie, trumpet, bass drum, long horn, vocals; Joseph Jarman, sopranino, soprano, alto, tenor, baritone and bass saxophones, vocals, bass clarinet, B-flat clarinet, bassoon, piccolo, flute, alto flute, conch shell, vibraharp, celeste, gongs, congas, tom-toms, whistles, bells, siren, bass pan drums; Roscoe Mitchell, soprano, alto, tenor, baritone and bass saxophones, piccolo, flute, bongos, conga, B-flat clarinet, bamboo flute, gongs, glockenspiel, whistles, bells, pan drums, vocals; Malachi Favors Maghostut, bass, percussion, melodica, bass pan drums, vocals; Dougoufama Famoudou Don Moye, trap drums, bendir, bike horns, whistles, congas, djimbe, djundjun, donno, bongos, timpani, chekere, conch shell, long horn, elephant horn, gongs, cymbals, chimes, wood blocks, belafon, cans, bass pan drums, vocals. This list not only suggests the members' fascination with musical cultures all over the globe, but also is a literal measure of the ensemble's growth during the past fifteen years. Of late, the group has called its travels "two-ton tours," and the designation is probably apt as an attestation to the sheer weight of instruments and equipment.

The group's artistic growth has been more complicated. Art Ensemble recordings fall into two types: studio sessions and live performances. The difference is mostly one of microphone placement and the presence or absence of the stimulation or distraction an audience can provide; laborious multi-tracking and re-recording would not suit the Art Ensemble's improvisatory esthetic. To judge from its earlier discs, Art Ensemble performances of the late sixties and early seventies were improvisationally bolder if less compositionally venturesome than they are today. The group demonstrated an especially free-wheeling readiness to attempt *anything*: swing, bebop, hard bop, cool jazz, free jazz, blues, soul, gospel, extended theatricals, African ritual evocations, you name it. That range has been sustained throughout the group's career—indeed, the sheer breadth of styles at the Art Ensemble's command, and its musicological thoroughness and care, make this a kind of traveling compendium of black musical history, with any implied didacticism transformed effortlessly into art. Jazz may indeed be regressing into moribundity in its more geriatric festivals and its college repertory ensembles. But, at the same time, it is attaining the status of a truly classic art—the status its proponents have claimed it enjoyed all along. One good measure of that status is this new, unselfconsciously deployed command of jazz history and styles evinced by the most vital musicians of the younger generation. The members of the Art Ensemble can evoke all kinds of jazz—or "black classical music," as some prefer to call it—at will, just as the Guarneri String Quartet's repertory spans the centuries of Western art music.

What has changed about the Art Ensemble since 1970, some feel, has been the spontaneity of the improvisation and the balance between improvisation and at least partial composition. All improvising groups have their ups and downs. When the Art Ensemble seems flat, its music can fall into familiar, predictable patterns. The critic Robert Palmer has written that "their improvisational gambits began to harden into routines—the mysterious-bells-and-gongs routine, the honking-saxophone-free-for-all routine, the jazz-quintet-as-percussion-orchestra routine." Yet, as Palmer concedes, such clichés can still be enlivened by the heat of a great performance. And lately there has been an apparent tendency to rely just a bit more than before on composition, allowing for sharply differentiated sections and a greater complexity and unanimity within some portions of the evening. Like nearly all jazz, each "piece" of an Art Ensemble performance is usually credited to an individual member, although some sections receive group credit. The actual extent of composition, beyond the "tune" and, perhaps, the basic arrangement, varies from case to case, and every piece is subject to group input as well as modification in the course of performance. In recent years, however, it has seemed as if the individual responsible for a given number has invested a greater degree of compositional planning before the improvisation begins. Before, despite all the styles essayed, the typical individual section was a solo, the others chipping in improvised accompaniment. Now the most common impression is of a vanguard big band.

An Art Ensemble concert is like nothing else in music. At its most conventional, the group breaks down into a front line of Bowie, Jarman and Mitchell, but the list of equipment indicates the frequency with which players shift from instrument to instrument, confounding traditional jazz configurations. Sometimes everyone takes up a member of the same family—all percussion, for instance, or all winds, or even all vocals—and creates a homogeneous texture. At other times, they turn to instruments with which they are not commonly associated, and bring to them an outlook unbounded by conventional technique. Sometimes the music is structured by a regular rhythm, often a rhythmic riff from a recognizable jazz style. At others, pulse dissolves into a coloristic flux. The moods can range from swing to bebop to "free" jazz to eerily ritualistic impressionism to jaunty recollections of every corner of jazz and third-world musical history. Nothing seems overextended or perfunctory: the group possesses that sense of intuitive rightness of form and texture that distinguishes all fine music. The concerts even expand beyond music altogether into theater—not just flamboyant displays of personality, but make-up, costumes and planned routines ranging from the comic to the shamanistic. These theatrics serve to unify the Art Ensemble's diverse musical inspirations in the same way that classical avant-gardists, from Schoenberg to David Del Tredici, Laurie Anderson and Walter Murch, have turned to theater for a focus that music itself, at a particular stage of its stylistic evolution, may have lacked.

Most of this book deals with individual composers. This and the final chapter, however, concern groups that create their own music—creative collaboratives. I have already discussed the expanded kinds of collaboration in new music-theater pieces. Groups carry such collaboration one step further, by institutionalizing it.

Improvisatory collectives were much in vogue in the sixties, and were hardly confined to jazz or even music—the Grand Union was a particularly notable example in the field of experimental dance. Yet most groups do not extend the collective ideal to its extreme. In jazz and rock bands, improvisatory or otherwise, creativity is usually not shared on an equal basis; some members are songwriters and some, just performers. Not all groups are harmonious within themselves, either. Sometimes acrimony spurs creativity, as seems to have been the case with the Who. But at their best, bands serve, in Greil Marcus's wonderful phrase, as "images of community." They mirror the communal aspirations of their audiences even as they embody a new kind of collaborative art.

The Art Ensemble's members have active solo careers, which give them the chance either to explore private compositional concerns or to collaborate with other members of the same new-jazz scene out of which the ensemble itself arose. Some years—1981, for instance—the ensemble's members spend more time apart than together. But they remain intensely proud of their communal character. "There's always somebody who knows something about everything," says Bowie. "Our group is like that. We have five different people with five different lives and sets of experiences which are brought in to make one music. This isn't a band where the leader dictates the way everything should be done. Everybody writes, brings in material and does extra studies."

Collaborative composition is not necessarily superior to individual creation, as proven by Maoist composition by committee. The practice flies in the face of the romantic Western image of the artist, and if a group's chemistry is insufficiently potent, members can feel ignored or inhibited. With the Art Ensemble, some critics felt that the solo albums released by members in the late seventies and early eighties contained more thoughtful, venturesome material than their Art Ensemble discs of the same period; Mitchell in particular was faulted for withholding his best inspirations for his personal use.

But on the whole, as with the best rock bands, it seems that the tensions and complementary attributes still inspire a creativity that would be impossible for the members on their own; Mitchell's solo albums may contain more extreme, vanguard statements than he generally achieves with the Art Ensemble, but the Art Ensemble in turn harnesses those inspirations in the service of more communicative and, perhaps, resonant art. The best recent example of this synergistic phenomenon is the Beatles, none of whom equaled on his own what the group had been able to achieve—even when, in its last years, every "Beatles" song was in fact composed by an individual. There was still something about the group identity that enhanced both the creation and the reception of its songs.

The Art Ensemble thinks of itself in esthetic terms; hence its title, which is not just a way of making a political statement about black creativity, although it is that, too (the group has subtitled its recent tours "Great Black Music, Ancient to the Future"). The name is also a spur to rethink the place of art in society, white and black. In the dominant white culture, art is supposedly universal, floating free above ordinary life, and ordinary life includes politics. The members of the Art Ensemble want to return art to a more integral relationship with the community's day-to-day activities.

"In ancient days, the music gave you something to help you with your life, whether you had to write poetry or load a truck," says Bowie. "But today people come to the music expecting less real benefit from it, and consequently, they are less inspired."

"Different kinds of music evolved for different situations," Moye continues, "and the function of the evolved musician of ancient times was to create music that would help make work easier, along with music for different festivities. It wasn't art for art's sake. Music had a definite function in people's lives."

Those functions aren't all prosaic. The Art Ensemble's obsession with ritual and magic incantations is part of a broader return to African spiritual values on the part of some black intellectuals. Africa serves their music the way the Orient inspires experimental musicians, but with an even greater sense of personal, ancestral kinship. In both cases, music is reinvigorated with totemic intensity. But the Art Ensemble is hardly all grim primitivism. What is most enlivening about its performances—and no audio disc has been able to capture the impact of those performances, for the very reason that so much of the experience transcends sound alone—is the way music and mood can shift so suddenly from gravity to levity and back again. It is the emotional range of the Art Ensemble that seems especially heartening, its ability to embrace the most serious and the most frivolous of human feelings. Life does that, and art should, too.

15

MYSTICAL ROMANTICISM, POPULARITY & THE VARIED FORMS OF FUSION

KEITH JARRETT

The Art Ensemble of Chicago can be light-hearted and fun. Keith Jarrett is usually serious, not to say humorless, not to say self-important. He is different from the Art Ensemble in so many ways that he can well serve to suggest the range of styles that now exist under that vague rubric, "jazz."

Jarrett is probably the most popular jazz musician playing today, as measured in concert attendance and record sales and not counting such rock- and pop-jazz cross-overs as George Benson or Chuck Mangione (who was in the first band Jarrett ever played with, one of Art Blakey's ever shifting assortments of young musicians in the early sixties). His very popularity sets him apart from most jazz musicians; jazz now counts for less than five percent of the total annual record sales in this country, an even smaller percentage than classical music.

Yet if he is too popular in the eyes of some jazz purists, that is not really why they discount his work as not being jazz at all. The real reason is his pervasive classical training, which colors all his work and which has led him, in recent years, to a style that is as much classical as jazz. Yet his music still appears on jazz labels and appeals primarily to a jazz audience, even as Jarrett himself appears with ever greater frequency as an orchestral soloist and has his works played by classical ensembles. Jarrett thus stands as one of the more complex instances of fusion in music today. And at the same time, the fluidity with which he passes from jazz to classical to popular attention might seem to reinforce his own determined feeling that such categorizations do more harm than good.

In its simplest outline, Jarrett's career so far has moved from classical to jazz to classical again, although he remains pigeonholed in the public mind as a "jazz musician." He was born in Allentown, Pennsylvania, in 1945, of Scottish-Irish and Hungarian descent. His racial background is mentioned only because so many people assume that he is black. That assumption is a comment on racial stereotypes in jazz—and, perhaps, despite his own apparent annoyance at the confusion, on his own willingness to exploit such stereotypes, since he wore his hair for years in what looked like an Afro.

Born with perfect pitch, he was a classic child prodigy who began piano lessons at the age of three. His childhood recitals consisted of not only classical scores but also little pieces and improvisations of his own. In his early teens, he toured with Fred Waring and his Pennsylvanians, and at fifteen he undertook formal study of composition, with a piano recital a year later devoted entirely to his own work. He then proceeded to the Berklee School of Music in Boston as a scholarship student, and was subsequently offered another scholarship to study with Nadia Boulanger in Paris.

But by then he had broken off this seemingly smooth evolution into yet another promising young American classical composer. Instead of Paris, he moved to New York and, after a few months of semi-starvation, he caught on with the jazz musicians there, having been noticed at a Monday-night open audition at the Village Vanguard. After playing briefly with Blakey and Rahsaan Roland Kirk, he joined the Charles Lloyd Quartet, with which he toured internationally and became more widely known in the jazz world. He started his own first group, a trio, while he was still with Lloyd, and his first real recognition came from European critics and audiences. When Lloyd disbanded his quartet in 1969, Jarrett formally organized his trio, now with Charlie Haden, bass, and Paul Motian, drums, and in 1972 they added Dewey Redman, a saxophonist; Redman and Haden were former Ornette Coleman sidemen. Between tours with his own group, Jarrett played with one of Miles Davis's more innovative bands, but since 1971 he has been completely on his own. That has meant four different kinds of music-making: small jazz groups, solo piano improvisations, interpretations of classical scores by others and his own orchestral compositions, usually with himself as piano soloist.

Jarrett's small-ensemble work takes up only a small portion of his time these days, although it dominated his career in the early seventies, and he does continue to work with a quartet that includes the Scandinavians Jan Garbarek, Palle Danielsson and Jon Christensen. All groups that improvise from agreed-upon chord changes, or switch between pre-composed material and improvisation, involve some sort of interchange among equals—although in a trio, when the bass and drums assume the role of "rhythm section," the soloist takes the predominant part. With his quartet, however, Jarrett achieved a greater parity than some similar groups have managed: Cecil Taylor, for instance, often seems to tower over his bandmembers. Jarrett, in contrast, shared much of the melodic material with Redman, while Motian and Haden elevated their functions far beyond a merely supportive role.

This music had and has its charms, but it is not the music that has won Jarrett his greatest renown. The style of these ensemble performances demonstrated considerable variety, and not just between the more vigorous, driving work of the American quartet and the cooler approach of the Europeans. The full quartet was often not enlisted, for instance, leading to all manner of duets and trios in unlikely combinations (there are also duet records with musicians not in either of the quartets), and Jarrett's ensemble compositions readily transcended the improvisatory routines common to the quartet configuration. But in one crucial sense, this ensemble music was traditional. At the time when other former Miles Davis pianists—Chick Corea, Herbie Hancock, Josef Zawinul—had forsaken the "acoustic" piano for electronic keyboards and jazz-rock groups, Jarrett remained faithful to the concert grand. For a while, that looked like commercial suicide. It didn't turn out that way, and now Jarrett seems like something of a prophet of the renewed jazz commitment to acoustic sonorities.

It was in 1972, with his first solo piano record and first disc for ECM, *Facing You,* that Jarrett's major reputation and popularity began. His solo albums continued with *Solo Concerts, Köln Concert, Staircase,* the ten-disc *Sun Bear Concerts, The Moth and the Flame* and *Concerts.* They have included pipe-organ improvisations, with such coloristically lavish effects as register stops set at the halfway point to achieve unexpected shadings and microtonal pitches. In fact, these ominously thick-textured organ mood pieces, in their similarity to the sixties *Klangfarbenschule,* are the closest Jarrett comes to any recognizable form of contemporary classical music.

But it is Jarrett's piano recitals that present the purest picture of his artistry. He sits at the keyboard, silently, until inspiration strikes. Then the music pours forth, accompanied by the most body English and extraneous humming and singing since the halcyon days of Glenn Gould. Jarrett's acknowledgment of the audience—unless he is disturbed by undue noise or a flash camera, when he will break off to denounce the offender—is curt and abstracted, as if he resented merely human disruption of his trance.

His music, however, provides what his person withholds. It is a floating collage of bits and pieces of pianistic styles from all of jazz and classical music history, executed with a virtuosity that commands respect among classical musicians (although some have complained of his tendency to let his left hand subside into vestigial chordal accompaniment of the extravagant lyrical filigree of his right). Free-form collages, like the more generally eclectic idioms favored by so many classical composers today, can easily lose focus, but Jarrett's music sounds ordered by a highly persuasive formal intuition. For all the variety of styles invoked, his work in this genre is always recognizably his, and the pieces rise and fall with a purpose that carries the listener along, willingly. The harmonic idiom is tonal and conservative, shot through with motoric passages, hammering repetition, churchish chordal passages and swelling climaxes, redeemed from bland familiarity by the stylistic range and the passion of the playing. The effect is of a shifting prism of idioms, few of them less than fifty years old and hence a kind of dream museum of the interchanges between jazz, blues, gospel, old-time pop, hymns and classical music that marked the early days of jazz itself. No wonder Jarrett, normally so wary of admitting to any sort of influence, has confessed an intense admiration for Charles Ives (among jazz pianists, he has spoken with special warmth of Bud Powell). Even though he rarely makes use of specific quotation, Jarrett's procedure, apart from his "spontaneous composition," is similar to the eclectic collages that have been employed with increasing frequency by classical avant-gardists. It also recalls the "return to romanticism" of such composers as Rochberg, Del Tredici and Rzewski, although in his motives and the actual sound of his music Jarrett differs as much from those composers as they differ from one another.

In recent years, he has begun to appear as a piano soloist in the works of others—notably in concertos by Colin McPhee, Peggy Glanville-Hicks, Alan Hovhaness and Bartók and solo pieces by G. I. Gurdjieff—and he has won warm praise from classical critics for his efforts. His own classical composition predates such appearances by several years. His first album in this vein was a two-disc set of string and brass music, *In the Light,* the composition of which had been made possible by a Guggenheim fellowship. His classical efforts have now expanded to include *Ritual,* a piano score recorded by Dennis Russell Davies, symphonic pieces and what amounts to a full-scale piano concerto, *The Celestial Hawk.* This last was originally meant to be performed with the Boston Symphony, but was dropped after a single rehearsal, without explanation. It was subsequently given its first performance by the Syracuse Symphony conducted by Christopher Keene with Jarrett as soloist, and was recorded at the time of its Carnegie Hall premiere.

Jarrett's classical compositions are considerably less effective than his improvisations, solo or group; they sound like student essays in styles already mastered long since by other composers—sometimes quite pleasant, but derivative and naïve in a way his other music is not. There are earnestly neo-baroque and neo-classical pieces for brass or strings with flute, guitar and piano solo parts, for instance, mostly reminiscent of Hindemith. Or there are bland mood-pieces with sustained strings and saxophone solos. Sometimes, as in *The Celestial Hawk,* there are attractive coloristic effects that dovetail into the quasi-improvisatory solo part, and those sections suggest that Jarrett might one day speak more forcefully with his own voice. But he has not done so yet, and the reasons lie in his background and attitude.

All composers are forced to some extent to concede that they don't know where their ideas come from. Even with computer scientists struggling to build models of the conceptual process, we still must fall back on the idea of "inspiration" to explain that leap from contemplation to the actual moment of creation. Most composers struggle to subject such inspiration to rational control. They harness it in forms, they conceive of work as problems to be solved, they slog through the long valleys between inspirational peaks with steady piecework.

Jarrett will have none of this. When he approaches the piano, he tries to make his mind as blank as possible, in order to clear himself to be a channel for inspiration from the beyond. Just how he thinks of "the beyond" he guards as his jealous secret. But he is known to have pursued study of such mystics as Gurdjieff and pop philosophers as Kahlil Gibran, and his album of music Gurdjieff composed in collaboration with his Russian composer-follower Thomas de Hartmann attests to those inclinations.

He discusses the music that results from his inspirational raptures as if it were something entirely separate from himself: "I'm not in a position to describe in words where it comes from," he once said. "I've been letting it happen all by itself so much that I'm looking at it as something completely independent of me, which it really is. I'm just transmitting it. The one thing that has governed what I've done, throughout my musical career, has been not to identify with something I did. The minute I would identify with what I'm playing, I wouldn't hear the next thing, and that's particularly true of solo playing. You just cannot go and improvise music if you're hearing what you do and considering it to be yours. The music is so much stronger than the person who's playing it that you have to be very, very careful. It can destroy you or it can enrich you, and if it enriches you and you get stronger, it gets that much stronger. So you're never in a secure position, you're never at a point where you have it all sewed up. You have to choose to be secure and like stone, or insecure but able to flow."

Sometimes, he has even talked about his playing as if it transcended music altogether, and about how perilously open he feels in the midst of it: "What I do isn't about music. It's about an experience beyond sound." And he worries that as the frail reed of the music, he may be destroyed: "Death hovers around quite a bit at a solo concert—the possibility that I might not live through a concert because of how vulnerable I am to anything that happens. It's like my ego isn't strong enough to protect me at those moments. Sometimes I feel as if I'm putting my finger on an electric line and leaving it there."

Such mystical imagery is impervious to rational challenge. Jarrett has often been perceived as an egomaniac, but an equally likely interpretation is that he is a genuinely romantic artist misplaced in a cynically unromantic time—defensive, temperamental, uncomfortable with the way he expresses himself in words and convinced of his higher destiny.

The common complaint against improvisation—a complaint made by Ornette Coleman as well as Elliott Carter—is that its supposed freedom is really an excuse for all sorts of undigested fragments of the subconscious to float unedited to the surface. For a conventional composer, the way around that problem is to let inspiration come (the "improvisatory" part of composition) and then to rework the material to invest it with form and craft. Jarrett has faith in the uncontaminated purity of his original inspiration. Hence, his way to ever purer work is to leave himself ever more open to inspiration. And although sequential listening to several of his solo piano improvisations reveals all sorts of recurrent mannerisms that he hasn't yet purged, those improvisations as a whole remain mightily impressive.

But in his orchestral writing, his limitations show through more clearly, and suggest the general difficulty that composers who are secure in one style may have in stepping too blithely into another. Jarrett seems unwilling to work to correct his deficiencies. His formal education apparently stopped short of a thorough study of twentieth-century composition and orchestration, and so his scores sound not only received but dated. There are many jazz performers today whose work parallels vanguard twentieth-century composers, with a dissonance and complexity of language that shows them to be part of their time. One thinks of Cecil Taylor's brilliantly virtuosic, dense piano textures. Or Anthony Braxton's sometimes self-consciously rationalistic scores. Or Leroy Jenkins's more eclectic but passionately hard-edged, tightly focused pieces. Or George Lewis's extensions of a gentler, softer "downtown" idiom. Jarrett has stopped short of all of this. Just as his small-ensemble and solo work is open to the charge of conservatism, his classical scores remain determinedly neo-classical and consonant. Gary Giddins, the jazz critic, has complained about Jarrett's "unrelenting lyricism." "Is one experiencing genuine depth of feeling or the trappings of feeling?" Giddins asks. "How tough is the center, and how resonant the ideas that spring from it?"

There is an irony in Jarrett's seeming inability to transcend his influences. As a young piano student, he spent a good deal of time with Bartók's music, and the modalities and timbres of Bartók's folk-inflected style color much of Jarrett's music today. Yet Bartók stands as the premier example of a composer who subsumed his influences into a strong personal style. What distinguished his treatment of Hungarian folk melodies was not his ethnomusicological researches, admirable though they were. Bartók's mature idiom grew from his ability to absorb those influences and recreate them as his own. Past composers had sweetened and adapted folk music into the prevailing classical styles of their day; Bartók let it inspire him to speak with his own voice. If Jarrett could turn inward, blending his conscious mind with his mystical subconscious, and *work* to make a similarly personal synthesis of a still wider range of music, he might achieve something really remarkable.

As it is, he stands as a curiously nostalgic, updated extension of Gunther Schuller's "third stream" music. Jarrett has fused classical music with jazz more naturally than Schuller usually managed, and in an accessible idiom that has won him a genuine audience. But he has still not found a way to develop and extend his idiom through traditional compositional means, and his concentration on the beyond and his defensive isolation have cut him off from the musical currents of his time, be they classical, jazz or popular.

That isolation may qualify him as another of those loners who have given shape to American music. But it has not made him very popular among his peers. There is a clear backlash against his widespread success of the early-mid seventies, when he seemingly won every jazz and pop poll and was just making his first bid for classical recognition. Now Giddins is not alone in his doubts, and there is also a feeling that Jarrett has snobbishly abandoned jazz for the classics. There are racial jealousies, and envy of his record sales—in a time when leading jazz artists are forced to issue their music on private or specialty labels, Jarrett has several major record contracts, and his *Köln Concert* has sold over three-quarters of a million two-disc sets. Such jealousy is part of the larger paranoia that jazz as well as classical musicians feel about the pop-celebrity phenomenon and associated image-building techniques—as if the only difference in popular appeal between Cecil Taylor and George Benson were the latter's larger promotional budget. As it happens, Jarrett has avoided the big-time show-biz syndrome of managers and press agents, and he tries to avoid interviews. Yet his very reticence has fueled his image, and people resent that image.

More charitably, one should remember that Jarrett is a romantic in his soul as well as his music. For some people, that's just fine—they like his music and find his reclusiveness intriguing. Others worry that he has limited himself by not coming to terms with his time. But who knows, with this most strictly private of persons, what he actually listens to and what he allows himself to be influenced by? For all his pretensions and faucheries, both musical and personal, it would be premature to discount him. Anyone who can make music as wonderful as the best of his solo improvisations deserves more than one chance to grow and be heard.

16

FREE JAZZ, BODY MUSIC
& SYMPHONIC DREAMS

ORNETTE COLEMAN

In his own sometimes beautiful, sometimes limited way, Keith
Jarrett represents a true fusion of jazz and classical music. In his
own totally eccentric and original way, Ornette Coleman has achieved
a similar fusion. But Coleman has also attempted to blend his jazz
with nearly every music there is, except that he wouldn't call it a
blending because he only grudgingly recognizes categories in the
first place. And for all his fame and for all the influence he has
exercised, Coleman is a classic example of the sort of loner I have
honored throughout this book—an outsider whose sense of alienation has only been exacerbated by race, and who has never accepted
anything unthinkingly throughout his life.

Born in Fort Worth, Texas, in 1930, Coleman is almost entirely
self-taught, apart from a passing influence from a cousin who was
a music-teacher and a saxophonist. He worked by himself with
harmony and other technical matters, all part of his goal to play,
"once the mechanics have been absorbed, as free and natural a
music as is possible."

Coleman started out as an alto saxophonist, switched for a
while to tenor since it was a more popular instrument at the time,
and eventually reverted to alto as his main instrument, although he
has experimented with other reed instruments and takes up the
violin and trumpet in his concerts, as well. In his teens he played

with bebop, rhythm-and-blues and rural dance bands in Texas and elsewhere in the South. Some critics feel that his jazz style was shaped by that experience, and that it foreshadowed his return to jazz-funk. But even then he had trouble adapting to the tastes of others. "I was in a dance band one time," he recently recalled, "playing some standard theme like 'Stardust,' and it was my turn to solo on the chord changes of the tune. In that situation, it's like having to know the results of all the changes before you even play them, compacting them in your mind. So I did that, and once I had it all compacted in my head I just literally *removed* it all and just *played*." Time after time, for some reason, he got fired. Once, a group of disgruntled blues buffs beat him up.

For a long while, his luck was no better in Los Angeles, where he first wound up in 1952. After suffering rejection and humiliation by white musicians and black musicians both, and working as an elevator operator at Bullock's department store, Coleman finally began to catch on with the Southern California jazz circuit—but only after a two-year return to Fort Worth followed by a two-and-one-half-year second sojourn in Los Angeles. By 1958 he was on his way at last, making his first records and winning the recognition he has retained until now. His first major California band included Don Cherry and Billy Higgins, who had worked with La Monte Young, the pioneering minimalist, in his early period as a jazz experimenter.

Coleman's troubles—and his originality—lay in his unwillingness to conform to jazz formulas: the common understanding in a band of the "chord changes," or harmonies, of a given tune, and then a set pattern of choruses and solo improvisations on those changes. Coleman would "compact" or ignore the bar lines or play some polytonal variation on the theme—all in response to his own inner voices. For those unaccustomed to such carryings on, he sounded out of tune or willfully incompetent. To more sympathetic ears, his music seemed suffused with the plaintiveness of the human voice, as if Coleman had somehow managed to transform his instrument from a piece of metal tubing with keys and a mouthpiece into a direct expression of emotion. With his early albums, he began to win important admirers, not least Gunther Schuller, who helped provide him access to New York. Coleman's opening engagement at the Five Spot in New York in 1959 is widely taken as one important symbol for the advent of avant-garde jazz.

The music that defined this new avant-gardism was made with a quartet consisting of Coleman, Cherry on trumpet, Charlie Haden or Scott LaFaro on bass and Ed Blackwell or Higgins on drums, plus a few other loyalists. (In 1978 Cherry, Haden and Blackwell formed a band devoted to Coleman's music and musical principles called Old and New Dreams, with Dewey Redman, another Coleman and Keith Jarrett sideman, taking the saxophone part.) Coleman's albums from this period carried such prophetic titles as *The Shape of Jazz to Come, Change of the Century* and *Free Jazz.* The music was actually more varied than "free jazz" stereotypes suggest, but it all attested to Coleman's blues roots and his seemingly casual redefinition of modulation. Jazz, like classical music, had grown ever more complex, and musicians as disparate as John Coltrane, Sonny Rollins and Charles Mingus had tried to come to terms with that complexity. Coleman's apparent side-stepping of the problem proved enormously, sometimes deleteriously, influential. Polytonality, dissonance and apparent anarchy reigned in his improvisations—and gave rise to a host of truly anarchic lesser imitators.

It might seem tempting to view Coleman's development as a jazz equivalent to both Cage's revolution and the reaction against it. In other words, to see "free jazz" as a barn-burning destruction of the mannerisms and clichés into which too much jazz had fallen, followed by a series of new formal structures liberated from older jazz's deadening traditions. But there are troubles with this scenario. One is the affecting homages to older jazz in Coleman's playing. And Schuller, for one, perceived a form beneath the apparent anarchy: "His musical inspiration operates in a world uncluttered by conventional bar lines, conventional chord changes, and conventional ways of blowing or fingering a saxophone. Such practical 'limitations' did not even have to be overcome in his music; they somehow never existed for him. Despite this—or more accurately, *because* of this—his playing has a deep inner logic. Not an obvious surface logic, it is based on subtleties of reaction, subtleties of timing and color that are, I think, quite new to jazz—at least they have never appeared in so pure and direct a form." Coleman, in any case, never approved of the term "free," with its connotations of anarchic license. Like so many fine American eccentrics, he had a *system*.

That system, which he calls "harmolodic theory" and about which he has been preparing a still unpublished theoretical treatise for years, seems singularly opaque, especially in his own descriptions of it. It has something to do with a free interchange of clef signs by members of an ensemble, resulting in a kind of random, parallel polytonality in the choruses; something with a new equation of melody, harmony and movement; something with an assertion of compositional ideas over the limitations of instrument design, inherited artistic methodology and rote improvisation; and something with a blend of tempered and non-tempered scales, and hence of Western and third-world instruments and musical esthetics. Perhaps Coleman's theory will support a more lucid explanation than that, although I have never encountered one, by him or anyone else. Whatever its objective merits may be, however, it clearly serves a subjective purpose for Coleman, providing an underlying pattern for his surface restlessness. In so doing it conforms to the role idiosyncratic theory has always played for vanguard composers. I have already suggested that role in such composers as Wagner, Schoenberg and Babbitt. Their theories serves as much to clarify instinctually arrived-at practices as to lay guidelines for other composers. In Coleman's case, "harmolodic theory" would seem to correspond to that collection of particularly American crackpot theorizing of which Harry Partch's forty-three–note scale is but another recent example. Partch believed deeply in his ideas, and his explanations make sense; there are those who take his theory very seriously. To less finely tuned ears, however, and given the inevitable imperfections of his own instrument-construction, it all sounds slightly ill-tuned—as does much of Coleman, which is why he had trouble keeping gigs before people started to take *him* seriously.

The "free jazz" of the mid-late fifties was widely influential, but it took place well over two decades ago, and Coleman has been incessantly active since—often in public, with concerts and record-ings, and just as often in private, during long periods of withdrawal from public life. These sabbaticals may have served to give him the freedom from public expectation that he needed to innovate, or to master new instruments, or to allow his audience to catch up by listening to more accessible imitators in his absence. The sabbati-cals also reflect a continuing sense of frustration with the music business. In any event, they echo similar patterns of withdrawal practiced by jazz musicians of comparable stature—Sonny Rollins and Miles Davis, to name two.

Coleman's most notable stylistic excursions since "free jazz" have been large-scale symphonic music and danceable funk-jazz. His best-known symphonic piece is called *Skies of America*, which appeared on the Columbia label in 1972. The score had originally been intended as a third-stream composition in the most obvious sense—for his jazz group and a symphony orchestra. But for various reasons having to do with British labor and visa regulations—the piece was recorded with the London Symphony Orchestra—what we have on disc is Coleman's saxophone alone, plus orchestra. Subsequent performances at the 1972 Newport Jazz Festival and in Paris restored the quartet, and the "complete" score was finally performed in his home town of Fort Worth in 1983.

Coleman has always made use of recurrent personal themes—short, choppy tunes that recall the blues or nursery rhymes and that pop up over and over again on his records. Here, he has explained, those themes represent the world's various musical cultures, all part of the ecumenicalism alluded to in the title. Although the record is banded into different "cuts," this is actually no more a collection of individual numbers than is an Art Ensemble of Chicago performance. The effect is sectional but unified. Coleman uses the orchestra according to his best "harmolodic" principles, with driv-ing polytonal passages—sometimes on their own and sometimes supporting his own soaring solos—alternating with slower, grander statements that recall the chordal calm of the American folk symphonists. There are, certainly, moments of naïveté and clum-siness in the conception, arrangement and execution of this fresco. But the overall impact is Ivesian in scope and in spirit, too. Very few first efforts are so powerful as this. It seems a great pity that, for all sorts of reasons, some of them self-inflicted, he has been unable so far to pursue his orchestral dreams.

Coleman has offered many explanations for the title *Skies of America*. One was that he had been inspired by the sky above Montana during a stay with the Crow Indians on a reservation there. On another occasion, Coleman had this to say: "I grew up in Texas, in the South, where there was lots of discrimination, lots of problems for minorities. Sometimes the sun is shining and beautiful on one side of the street, and across the street, just maybe three feet apart, there'd be big balls of hail and thunderstorms, and that reminded me of something that happened with people. In America, you see them all enjoying themselves and next moment they're all fighting. They're the same way as the elements. When I titled that piece, it was to let me see if I could describe the beauty, and not have it be racial or any territory. In other words, the sky has no territory; only the land has a territory. I was trying to describe something that has no territory."

Coleman's attempts to abolish territorial imperatives extended to the very question of what kind of music this was. Although it was produced by a staff classical producer, Paul Myers, it was released by Columbia's jazz division. Worse, the company insisted on banding the record into a sequence of "songs" that could be comprehended by the jazz-pop public and abstracted for radio play. "I just wrote it and put it out just as a person that'd write a piece of music and put it out," Coleman recalled. "Someone at Columbia told me if I titled all the pieces I'd get more airplay, but basically they were trying to keep it from having the image of a symphony. I realize now it was another social-racial problem. People say, 'Well, you're a jazz player.' I've always thought of myself as a composer who also performs music. I'm classified as a jazz saxophonist. It eliminates people from trying to find out if I've done anything else. I still don't know how it works, and maybe that's because of being an outsider."

Skies of America was Coleman's last recording until a disc called *Dancing in Your Head* appeared in 1977. *Dancing in Your Head* is both a documentation and an elaboration of a trip Coleman took to Morocco in 1973 that had been organized by the critic and clarinetist Robert Palmer. It includes an actual field recording of a jam between Coleman and the tribal musicians of Jajouka. Brian Jones, the Rolling Stone, also made a record of these musicians' incessant, timbrally piercing dance music. Most of Coleman's record, however, is his own music inspired by that experience. The music partakes of Moroccan music but also of rock and disco, or so it seems—as well as themes from *Skies of America*. It sticks in the mind in a riveting way, but it breaks through the more comfortable limitations of pop with its insistent abrasiveness.

The band on *Dancing in Your Head* was called Prime Time, with which Coleman has performed since 1977—but only in public, really, since 1981. Its most characteristic document on records as of this writing is called *Of Human Feelings*. Released in 1982, the disc was recorded in 1979, and circulated as an underground cassette and test pressing (under the title *Fashion Faces*) for three years. But that merely meant that by the time it was released, a larger public, primed by previously released records by such Coleman disciples as James Blood Ulmer and Ronald Shannon Jackson, was ready for it. Prime Time plays a funk-oriented fusion music, thus re-establishing Coleman as the progenitor (with an assist from Miles Davis's electronic fusion music) of the funk-jazz and punk-jazz of the downtown Manhattan art-rock-jazz scene. The musicians alternate lead and rhythm parts, sometimes all in different keys but with an unrelievedly driving, dancing energy.

It might seem a long way from *Skies of America*'s "symphony" to *Of Human Feelings*' tribal stomp. Actually, the road may be a detour, but it is fairly straight. Coleman has composed for other "classical" forces, including string quartets. When *Skies of America* was released, he had ideas for further symphonic projects, especially one called *The Oldest Language*. This was (and still is) a two- to three-hour piece for a 125-member ensemble that includes two musicians from every U.S. state and one each from twenty-two different world cultures; the number twenty-two is a bit of numerological mysticism from the Crow Indians. But he couldn't get Columbia or any far-sighted manager to take the financial risk.

"After I recorded *Skies of America,* I wanted to continue in that direction," he said later. "But if you're a musician in America, you have to find a person who can take what you do and make it part of the mass system. And, because everything is in categories, you have all these people who buy only classical music or Broadway music and never go out and get any other kind of record. I've tried to express sound in all the forms it is expressed in, but I'm called a jazz musician, and, to make a long story short, I've never found that person who could give me the kind of help I needed."

Coleman's decision to return to an overtly dance-oriented music reflects his lifelong commitment to "body music," with his interest since childhood in blues and country dance music and his absorption in third-world musical traditions. Both "ear music" and "eye music" are perceived in the head, which leaves much of ourselves unaccounted for. There is a school of thought—or feeling—which holds that Western art music went wrong when it denied its indebtedness to dance. If harmony, as Ernest Ansermet and Leonard Bernstein have argued, conforms to universal acoustical laws, so does rhythm correspond to the cycles of the body, the intake of the breath and the beating of the heart. When music ignores that primal connection, it betrays its essence. In re-emphasizing body rhythms, Coleman was thwarting not just the mandarins of modernist art music, but jazz elitists as well. To a traditionalist, jazz may not mean a thing if it ain't got that swing. But swinging is one thing, vulgar popular dancing quite another, and rapprochements with genuine popular dance music strike most jazz purists as crude and crass. For Coleman, ever suspicious of categories in the first place, any musical idiom can be played well or poorly. Prime Time's dance music is, by almost any elitist standard except the most stuffy, artful enough to engage the head even as it galvanizes the body.

But there were other, more practical reasons for Coleman to create his own idiosyncratic dance music. He was still seeking to penetrate the "mass system," and this seemed one way to popular success. And with the momentary frustration of his orchestral ambitions, he realized—a realization that also affected Philip Glass—that amplification could compensate for a lack of access to large-scale ensembles. "I've always wanted to work with an orchestral set-up," he said, "but I could never afford a full orchestra. I noticed that the groups that always had a fuller sound were rock groups, with amplified guitars and all. So I figured I could use that instrumentation to achieve the sound I want, that fuller sound, and expand my writing at the same time. I'm not writing strictly for electric instruments or anything, though, I'm just taking advantage of what that sound could mean to me in the context of the music I'm composing at this time."

Coleman's need to express himself with larger, more varied ensembles is natural enough; indeed, enforced small scale has been one of the more severe limitations of much classical new music in recent years. But his decision to opt for amplification—beyond the timid reinforcement of acoustical instruments that nearly all jazz performers use for balance or to fill a hall—speaks to a different issue. That is the seemingly steady augmentation of volume that audiences demand or promoters impose in concerts of jazz and popular music. In rock, amplification is so constantly loud that a number of well-known musicians (most notably Pete Townshend of the Who), plus uncounted "roadies" and backstage personnel, are partially deaf. Amplification has even infected the theater, where both musicals and spoken dramas are now routinely miked. All this has to do with the public's need for ever greater impact. Since dissonance and radical formal innovations are risky, the best way to answer this need is to increase the volume. Ever louder music also has something to do with the sheer volume of city life today, and with the ease with which radios and high-fidelity equipment can be turned up to unnatural levels. Concert amplification enables audiences to experience mega-volumes of wattage denied them by their own limited budgets and sharp-eared neighbors.

In moving into funk-jazz, Coleman might have seemed to be venturing upon already well-trodden turf. In fact, he was coming at the problem from a somewhat different perspective than the purveyors of rock-jazz fusion music in the late sixties and early seventies. Jazz has always had an uneasy relation to pop—"uneasy" mostly, perhaps, in the minds of jazz aficionados who try to make rigid distinctions between the two. It seemed clear enough that jazz made use of popular tunes of the day as a basis for improvisation. But whereas pop was simple and song-oriented, based on the lowest level of commercial calculation, in jazz individual artistry and virtuosity took precedence.

Jazz began to shift away from easy accessibility with the advent of bebop in the forties. But up until the sixties, it was still possible for a recognized jazz musician to make a decent living from his art. He could play major concerts, he could put out records on major labels, he could hope for extensive airplay that would help sell records. The "British invasion" in rock after 1964 signified the final and decisive shift of the public and the music business to mass-audience electric pop and rock. By the late sixties, jazz's percentage of the market had begun to shrink toward that of classical—both pushed into their insular little corners, some people felt, by greedy record executives concerned only with maximizing short-term profits.

One result was a raft of rock-jazz fusion attempts starting in the late sixties. Charitably considered, jazz musicians perceived an energy and a direct vitality in the best rock and saw a way to make a new, different, clean-lined, fresher music than they had within the confines of jazz. Uncharitably, they sold out, as fast and ignominiously as they could, by abandoning artistic conscience, distorting the pure acoustic sound of their instruments in favor of electronic alternatives or cultivating a glutinous, amplified texture that buried the individuality of whatever acoustic instruments remained.

Both sides can find examples to prove their points. Coleman played a part in the evolution of a genuinely innovative jazz-rock fusion, but Miles Davis, with his *Bitches Brew* album of 1969, was the true pioneer. Soon thereafter, it seemed, every promising young jazz musician, and some not so young, had "gone electric," just as the folkies of the mid-sixties had followed Bob Dylan and embraced the proud assertiveness of rock & roll. Yes, there were overt popsters from a jazz background, like Chuck Mangione. But there were also John McLaughlin with his Mahavishnu Orchestra, Hancock and Corea, and Josef Zawinul and Wayne Shorter in Weather Report. At its best, this music achieved a telling synthesis of the driving energy and formal clarity of rock with the complexity of jazz. But even as it won sales from the mass audience, jazz record sales retreated overall, with the mainstream jazz audience clinging ever more desperately to the past. In so doing, it provided an exact parallel to the audience for classical music, which likewise had increasing difficulty accepting the new. Both audiences may have had their reasons; their nostalgic historicism wasn't necessarily "wrong." But the turn to the past made new artists in both fields feel increasingly cut off from their public. For the best jazz-rock fusionists, this sense of alienation could be mitigated for a while by healthy record sales. But by the late seventies, the market for innovative jazz-rock fusion had shrunk, and the situation was complicated by the sudden decline of pop record sales overall. A number of such musicians have now returned, chastened, to the jazz fold, like Corea, or issue distinct pop-jazz and pure-jazz recordings, like Hancock.

The true avant-gardists, electric or otherwise, were forced into the social role of "artist" whether they wanted it or not, finding themselves eventually in precisely the same position as their classical avant-garde confreres. The "loft jazz" movement in New York in the seventies was the result, and was periodically invigorated by refugees from less hospitable cities that had generated significant local movements but found it difficult to sustain them—Chicago, St. Louis, Los Angeles. The scene grew for the same reasons that experimental artists of all sorts moved to lower Manhattan—cheap space and the sense of possibility an artistic community can provide.

For a while, the jazz vanguardists held themselves apart from the white bohemians. But soon shared involvement in improvisation and new sonic possibilities brought them into an alliance of convenience, along with a lively common curiosity about their different traditions. They worked with the same instrumentation in the same forms, and they exchanged players frequently. By the late seventies, loft jazz became less visible—in part because the loft-jazz movement had spawned a number of younger musicians who were then given access to jazz clubs that had previously shunned them, but also because some elements of the new jazz had been absorbed into and had significantly altered the overall experimental scene. These new-jazz musicians could claim artistic status on sociological as well as esthetic grounds. They found performance opportunities not just with the jazz clubs that had once rejected them, and with new ones that sprang up in response to their activity, but in avant-garde "artistic" performance spaces such as museums, galleries, concert halls and even rock clubs. They applied for and won the same grants as their classical brethren, and they toured to the same places in Europe. It was, in short, a shared scene, under the same, undifferentiated "sky." Just as the classical avant-gardists had their own management organizations and record distributors, so, too, did the jazz people—such as Outward Visions, Inc., which represented several key members of the jazz vanguard by the early eighties, and the New Music Distribution Service, which was founded by Carla Bley and Michael Mantler and which served as a leading record-distributor for jazz and classical independent labels alike.

These small labels—Philip Glass's Chatham Square was an early prototype—differed from "vanity" labels and presses only in that the artists behind them were significant, the kind major labels used to release before they became fixated on the mass market. These new small labels concentrated on the music of their founders and their close associates, and often failed to sustain themselves beyond one or two releases. In the jazz world, a leading example, with a nicely symbolic name, was Artists House, the initial leading artist of which was Ornette Coleman.

The difference between the funk-jazz of the late seventies and the commercial rock-jazz of the late sixties was that the former attempted to blend the improvisatory freedom and innovations of jazz with the most vital black pop of the seventies, while the latter tended to be a more calculated borrowing from the white pop of the sixties, and quickly degenerated in the seventies as white rock softened out into the middle of the road. Like so much jazz itself, funk was inspired by Africa and a renewed interest in the basic forms of black music. George Clinton, with his funk band Parliament-Funkadelic, Larry Graham and a variety of disco producers and composers evolved a bass-heavy, minimally insistent communal dance music. They in turn had been inspired by Sly Stone and by James Brown and the soul musicians of the sixties, who had been the models for some of the harder white rockers; these things can become dizzily incestuous. But the new funk-disco (the two forms were polemical opponents for a while, but their similarities outweighed their differences) was not so dependent on song form or lyrics; it even owed debts to such pioneering jazz-rock fusionists as Davis and Jimi Hendrix. Funk could thus merge easily with both the jazz experimenters and with such subsequent novelty pop forms as the quick, rhythmic chanting of "rapping." It was with such downtown funk-jazz musicians of greater or lesser artistic pretensions as Ulmer, Jackson, James Chance and Material that Coleman renewed his claim to leadership. His first New York concert in three years at the Public Theater fell on the first day of the 1981 Kool/Newport/New York Jazz Festival—a characteristic way of attracting mainstream attention while maintaining a defiant independence.

Where Coleman will go from here remains a mystery, probably even to himself. Ever the earnest naïf, he hired the man who boasts he brought the Beatles to America, Sid Bernstein, to be his manager. Whether Bernstein could have gotten him access to the "mass system"—or could have overcome Coleman's own apprehensions about that system—seems doubtful, and soon enough the two fell into legal wrangling. Coleman once attended a question-and-answer session with Elliott Carter, and was struck by the similarities of their positions: "When he described what his music was going through, it reminded me that he had the same problem, as far as how many people have heard, or are into, his music." But so far, at least, Elliott Carter has not hired Sid Bernstein to be his manager.

Perhaps Coleman can achieve that magical blend of artistic originality, mass audience, adulation and integrity that seemed so possible in the sixties. One has to applaud him for refusing to accept the stereotype of the white artist, coddled by grants and the academy into illusory success, but trapped by that same coddling. Just as likely, Coleman's latest foray at the windmills of popular approbation will end with another round of embitterment and private exploration. Which may, in turn, lead to further stylistic adventure and another, as yet unforeseen kind of fusion. That's the way it is with American outsiders. They may not be happy with their lot, but sometimes their very alienation preserves the intensity of their innovations.

17

LATIN MUSIC, FOLK MUSIC & THE ARTIST AS CRAFTSMAN

EDDIE PALMIERI

Ornette Coleman is a name that people who know nothing about jazz might have heard. Beyond his own territory, very few people have heard of Eddie Palmieri. What he does bears strong resemblances to "Latin jazz"—that fusion of the American jazz tradition with the rhythms and instrumental colors of Latin music. Latin jazz has been a recognized subgenre since Dizzy Gillespie pioneered it in a serious way in the late forties. More recently, mainly through the efforts of Carlos Santana and his eponymous bands, there has been a recognized subgenre of Latin rock, as well. Palmieri's music might be said to combine rock insistence with rhythm-and-blues and soul fervor. Yet what he does is neither jazz nor rock nor soul. As composer, arranger and performer, Palmieri is perhaps the most respected exponent of Latin dance music in the United States. But he is no staid traditionalist; his excellence derives in large measure from his very refusal to confine himself to traditional Latin forms. He is always pushing to expand and transcend those forms. His efforts have won him a faithful following in the country's growing Latin community. But he has been unable to reach an audience beyond that community, and thus stands as another instance of an American artist trapped by circumstance—in his case, a restive kind of success within a subculture that has not yet blended smoothly into American culture as a whole.

According to the 1980 census, there were nearly fifteen million people of Hispanic descent in this country. Although Latins are regarded as one undifferentiated mass by the white, English-speaking majority—assumed to be Puerto Rican in the East, Cuban in Florida and Mexican in the Southwest and West—they are in fact highly diversified as to their national origins. In a sense, English-speaking blacks constitute the largest minority in the United States. But blacks have been here for a long time, speak the language and have so continuously and forcefully influenced American popular music that it is sometimes difficult to think of black music as separate from the white mainstream—although in many respects, of course, it most certainly is.

There can be no such confusion about Latin music. Artistically and sociologically, it is a ghetto. Latin music plays its own concert circuit, with its own record labels, radio stations and (usually Spanish-language) fan magazines. Some artists appeal to narrow national audiences; the most successful overcome parochial loyalties and reach out to Latins as a whole. A successful performer can make money on the Latin circuit. But such success is purchased at the price of a steady pattern of exploitation and corruption that is less obvious now in the upper reaches of the mainstream pop-music business. And whatever success a Latin performer does achieve is soured by an awareness of the much greater success available on just the other side of the street, and by the strictures that tradition and subcultural rigidity place on a creative composer.

Eddie Palmieri knows those strictures all too well. Born in New York's Spanish Harlem in 1936 of Puerto Rican descent, he was raised in the South Bronx. His family was musical, with his mother insisting on piano lessons; Eddie's older brother Charlie is now a noted Latin pianist and bandleader, too. Rejected by the High School of Music and Art, Eddie started a dance band with schoolmates at Monroe High School in the Bronx. For a while, he switched from piano to the timbales, a Latin drum set, and his experience playing percussion has reinforced the strongly rhythmic impetus in his piano playing and band arrangements. By his early twenties, Palmieri was a member of some of the most popular Latin bands of the day, culminating, from 1958 to 1961, with Tito Rodriguez's big band.

This was a crucial period for American Latin music. The field was dominated by Cubans, whose own musical tradition was rich in both undiluted African rhythms and elegant dance forms. Today's modern American Latin music, known as "salsa" (usually translated as "hot sauce"), is practiced primarily by Puerto Ricans, who make up the largest Latin community in the Northeast. But it is based firmly on Cuban traditions. When I accompanied a group of American rock, jazz and Latin musicians to a Cuban music festival in 1979, the Cuban audiences gave the Puerto Ricans, Panamanians and Dominicans who made up the American Latin contingent a decidedly cool welcome, and with good reason: their own groups, from the traditional Orquesta Aragón to the jazz-rocking Irakere, outclassed the salsa musicians on every count. To be fair, the Cubans hear Latin music all the time, and at this festival, the first of its kind under Fidel Castro's regime, they wanted more rock and jazz, which for them were the novelties. On the other hand, Palmieri was not among the American group; these were musicians affiliated with the Fania All Stars. One suspects the Cubans would have thought more kindly of him.

When Castro came to power in 1959, it wasn't only the import traffic in Cuban cigars and rum that suffered. The steady flow of musicians and musical ideas from Havana was cut off, too, and it took a long time for American Latins to build up a working heritage of their own. Palmieri, who formed his first professional band in 1961, was very much part of that construction project. His group, or *conjunto*, played the dance music Latins wanted to hear. But he added to it an unprecedented front line of trombones that extended the traditional Cuban trumpet flourishes with trombone effects reminiscent of such jazz musicians as J. J. Johnson and Kai Winding.

Palmieri's role in this *conjunto*, as in all his subsequent music, has been fourfold. He is the composer of some but not all of the pieces, he is the bandleader, and he is the pianist, which in his bands is a prominent role, with frequent solos and a texture designed to make one almost continually aware of the instrument. His fourth role is that of arranger, which is more important than it might

sound, and which overlaps his compositional role in ways sometimes hard to sort out.

Arrangers in jazz, in large-ensemble popular music, on Broadway or in films can have widely varying functions. Often they are
pure craftsmen, executing the ideas of others as faithfully but face-
lessly as possible (in fact, Palmieri sometimes has such assistants
working on the details of the arrangements under his guidance).
But often, again, the arranger becomes the key creative force in the
collaboration, rather in the manner an active producer in television
can determine the artistic content of a documentary or commercial
more than the writer, cameraman, actors or even the director. An
arranger of this sort takes the "composition," which may be nothing
more than a tune with implied harmonies, and determines the
entire shape and sound of the piece. In small-ensemble jazz, the
same thing happens, except that the elaborations are developed
improvisationally, often as a round of solos among the band members.
In big-band-jazz and Latin orchestras, the arranger partially usurps
the role of the improvising performers. Sometimes he merely provides
a plush backdrop against which soloists still improvise. But sometimes he actually *composes* a score based on thematic material supplied
by the titular composer. Gil Evans at his most creative is an example from jazz of such a composer-arranger. The distinctiveness of
Palmieri's best records and performances derives in part from the
excellence of his players (above all, himself on piano), but in larger
part still from his mastery of this dual creative role.

Latin music is primarily a dance style, and as such should not
be automatically slighted by highbrows, any more than Ornette
Coleman's funk-jazz. Abstraction has its place. But to brush kinet-
ically reiterative music aside—especially music with such a strong
and clever rhythmic counterpoint surrounding the basic impulse—
seems extreme, not to say philistine. In any case, Palmieri's earliest
idiom was not just dance music, it was an artifact of a specific
cultural enclave. Such self-contained musical circuits, functioning
free from high art or mainstream commercial attention, exist all
over America, threatened by the mainstream but somehow manag-
ing to survive. Country music was like that for a long time, bitterly

resisting the innovations first of Nashville itself, with its strings and spangles, and later of the Texas "outlaws," with their hippie-rocking ways. Today, purer and less commercial forms of country music—country-flavored "folk music," bluegrass, "old-timey music" and the like—carry on at specialized festivals and on their own concert and college circuits, with their own record labels, fan magazines and radio broadcasts. Stars of other isolated genres include Jimmy Sturr, with his mightily popular polka band, and Flaco Jimenez and his lilting "Tex-Mex" accordion playing. Some of these musicians have attracted poetic and academic documentarians, from the anthropological wanderings of the Lomax family to the loving films of Les Blank.

To what extent are such musicians "artists," in the sense I have been using the term throughout this book? They are not really constrained by the heightened commercial pressures of the mass music market; they might idly dream of conquering that market, yet for most of them, their dreams are just that. But they are constrained by an even more stultifying force, and that is the expectations of their intensely conservative audiences. In America, "folk" music is inherently conservative—artistically conservative, not politically conservative, although it is that, too, often as not, despite Woody Guthrie and Bob Dylan. There are reasons for such conservatism. If an immigrant community looks back to an "old country," it has a natural tendency to preserve the idioms and styles that were popular at the time of the emigration. Thus, when black musicians try to reclaim their "African roots," they turn to tribal rhythms rather than to the modern extensions of such rhythms practiced by contemporary African pop stars like Fela. Similarly, the German polka bands of south Texas or the Polish and Lithuanian bands of Chicago harken back to a time in which the polka was popular in the old country; they are not trying to keep up with what they would regard as the adulterated folk-pop traditions of present-day Germany, Poland or Lithuania. It is not music that is being served here, but nostalgia—idealized memories of a subcultural Garden of Eden. This conservatism is heightened if the emigrants fled for political reasons. It is further strengthened if they do not easily adapt to the dominant American culture, but continue to speak their native language and to sustain a self-contained cultural identity.

Even when stylistic evolution does take place—the fusion of Mexican dance music and German polkas in the Tex-Mex *Norteño* music of the Rio Grande valley, for instance—new subgenres evolve slowly. This traditionalism has partly to do with the need for escapist entertainment. It also persists because the romantic notion of "artist" is only rudimentarily developed within many of these cultures. As in "serious" European music until the past couple of centuries, musicians are considered craftsmen who are expected to execute the dominant style as well as they can. In classical music, it was only at the outset of the romantic era that artists routinely felt free to experiment far in advance of their audience's tastes, as in Beethoven's late string quartets. There had, of course, been isolated eccentrics (Gesualdo) and determined reformers (Gluck) before them. But as a rule, up until the early nineteenth century, an artist did not conceive of his task in terms of radical stylistic innovation. It would be rash, given the problematic relationship between composers and audiences today, to presume that the evolution away from this esthetic of servitude represented an unqualified advance.

Mozart, for all his troubles with his patrons, could at least hope that in Vienna or Prague his ideas might be prized. The subcultural "folk" musician has less hope of this kind, unless he can transform the entire value structure of his tradition or escape it altogether. Bill Monroe did that with his "invention" of bluegrass music around 1940. But ordinarily, if a maverick like Coleman or Palmieri comes along, he must either adapt or persevere blindly until he succeeds in imposing his ideas. Coleman managed such a revolution, but only because "jazz" was rapidly developing an "artistic" tradition of its own, and only after years of isolation that may have crippled his sensibility to the point of idiosyncrasy. Palmieri has succeeded off and on, too, as in his La Perfecta *conjunto* and its trombone front line. But he has not been able to sustain that success.

One might think that innovation within a folk tradition would be prized and publicized by a progressive intelligentsia. But in folk music, the intelligentsia is often more purist than the audience.

Country audiences will accept distortions of their traditions in the direction of middlebrow pop, if not tough rock. But country purists remain fierce defenders of the pre-Nashville status quo. Thus, innovation is possible within such a style only if the composer can balance personal inspiration with a sure sense of what his public will accept. One example of this dilemma is John Fahey, who took an encyclopedia of folk and country-blues guitar styles and wove those styles into an hypnotic personal expression based on repetition and extended solos. Fahey found a new audience with West Coast hippies. Hedy West, one of the best "purist" folk singers in the country, met a different fate. She is prized among nostalgists for old-time folk songs both here and in Europe and is also a trained classical composer. But she sees no connection between her "serious" composition and her folk singing, even when she allows herself to make up new songs. Instead of evolving a new form of American art music based on folk models, she feels torn between the cultivated and the vernacular, unable to settle on a "serious" compositional style.

As I have argued, though, anyone can be called an artist who strives for artistic self-expression by individualizing a given style. On that criterion, Eddie Palmieri is very much an artist; certainly he has struggled enough. Palmieri managed to sustain his La Perfecta trombone *conjunto* from 1961 to 1968, when the band broke up and Palmieri broke down: "I was wallowing in self-pity," he said later. The reasons for this professional and personal collapse were several. Palmieri has never been a clever businessman. At that time, he was feeling the strain of trying to contain his ideas within a dance-band format. He was even branded as "pink" by right-wing Latins for his insistent retention of Cuban stylistic traits. And the rock onslaught had crashed straight into salsa just as it had into jazz. Rock and its first gigantic festivals, highlighted by the success of Carlos Santana, proved such a potent lure to audiences and young musicians alike that the very existence of salsa seemed threatened. By the next year, however, Palmieri had begun to reconstruct his career and extend his musicianship, and in the mid-seventies, both he and salsa regained a reasonably vital health. Palmieri's mature music is still too little prized, even among aficionados of jazz-rock and dance-rock. To the basic salsa conventions—played with a rare, ebullient spirit that secured the loyalty of traditional salsa audiences—he added chromatic, improvisatorily bold piano solos (McCoy Tyner was probably the closest parallel) and passages indebted to classical and experimental music.

In the late sixties and early seventies, he made two records that attested to his social concern and his desire to broaden the stylistic and popular base of Latin music. Palmieri is a voracious reader and self-improver. One of the reasons his performing and recording career has been erratic is that he is forever taking time off to study sociology or music theory or, simply, to practice the piano. *Justicia*, from 1969, was an explicit cry for social justice, and musically an homage to such socially concerned composers as Richard Rodgers and his *Slaughter on Tenth Avenue* ballet and Leonard Bernstein and *West Side Story*; the song "Somewhere" from that musical, sung in English, appears twice on side two, as a recurrent theme. In between comes instrumentally conceived, jazz- and soul-influenced Latin music, culminating in an eleven-minute instrumental on side two marked by venturesome, virtuosic solos. Four years later, he attempted something even bolder, a fusion of soul music and salsa entitled *Harlem River Drive*. Here, the effort was undercut by some not always very interesting English lyrics and some not always very persuasive soul music; the mixture sounds heavy and crude, the Latin ebullience weighed down by second-hand soul riffs. But the experiment is redeemed by the last number, "The Seeds of Life." Here some fine soul musicians, including the guitarist Cornell Dupree and the drummer Bernard Purdie, achieve a true blend of salsa excitement and soul passion, the music driving forward with a thick, electric authority, rumbling and bass-heavy, yet enlivened by Latin percussion. The album was uneven, but brave at its best. Yet sales were disappointing; the record was either ahead of its time or too optimistic in its faith in the willingness of Latin and black pop audiences to explore beyond the familiar.

Palmieri's best-known record is *The Sun of Latin Music* from 1975. Here overt stylistic cross-breedings were set aside in favor of a straightforward Latin record—for Coco, a straightforward Latin record label. But by this time, Palmieri was less capable than ever of making a formula salsa disc. The arrangements are shot through with elegant, unexpected touches—a sweet, flowing string passage in the first piece, for instance, or the uneasy, proclamatory piano solo with electronic and percussion effects at the beginning of side two. Without parading its fusion credentials, the record emerges as a satisfying blend of Cuban dance rhythms, South American percussion and timbral color, jazz complexity and soul fervor. The album won him recognition as the premier salsa musician. Three years later, he reached the apex of his recorded career to date. The record, *Lucumi Macumba Voodoo,* was ambitious in two ways. Artistically, this was a panorama, inspired by South American religion and rhythms, of the varied influences that shaped contemporary Latin music. The lyrics, as on *Justicia,* were in both Spanish and English. Although the record is permeated with jumping Latin dance rhythms, the arrangements are more varied than ever, lapping beyond the prescribed categories of salsa. Yet this is no arcane "personal statement," either; it retains its popular roots, and hence its potential appeal to a popular audience.

Unfortunately, the record failed in its second ambition, to bring salsa and Palmieri to an audience outside the Latin community. By this time, Palmieri had moved up to a major, mainstream pop record label, Epic, which is part of CBS. But his new disc failed to achieve the cross-over success he and Epic hoped for. Its failure was abetted by two factors, one out of his control and one, theoretically, within it. By the mid-seventies, there was eager talk among salsa's New York partisans that salsa would be the "next big thing," the next cross-over phenomenon to rival the earlier successes of black and country music. The Latin industry succeeded in getting the Grammy Awards to establish a Latin category, and Palmieri won the first two years. But just as rock had blunted salsa's development in the late sixties, disco deflected its growth in the late seventies. There was an irony to that, since disco, with its pounding, primal beat, had been widely hailed as a recrudescence, after a half-decade of bland white pop, of black and Latin influence—mixed, to be sure, with a newly assertive gay sensibility and the more progressive elements of "Europop." But the disco formula, during its commercial ascendence in the late seventies, proved stultifying to all but a few composers whose needs it happened to suit. Palmieri was far too subtle, diverse and complex to fit inside the disco strait jacket, and the mainstream audience and even the rock intelligentsia lost sight of him again.

Part of his problem was his own ambivalence about venturing beyond his ethnic nest in the first place. At one point, in his insistent assurances to his salsa fans that he was not betraying the Latin tradition, he claimed that he would speak only Spanish at his concerts. He also denied that he ever listened to classical music and even that what he played could be called "jazz." All of these protestations were sad and absurd, the fears of a man who knows he wants to liberate himself but who worries that he will lose his artistic center if he does.

As of 1983, the Latin-salsa scene has partially recovered from the disco onslaught, and Palmieri is still a star within that scene. Aficionados sometimes complain that he appears too often with pick-up groups, unwilling as he is to assume financial responsibility for a full-time band and to tour indefatigably to sustain such a band. But his album from late 1981, *Eddie Palmieri*, while back on a Latin label, Barbaro, and abjuring his more extreme cross-over ambitions, was still a classy, deft and imaginative record. And he has begun to venture out to new-wave rock clubs with a Latin band and into jazz clubs with a quintet. For all his personal unpredictability, Palmieri has a reputation within the Latin world so supreme by now that he can have his pick of the best musicians almost any time he wants them. And given a reasonable period of rehearsal, the conventions of salsa are so commonly understood, and the nature of his innovations so well known now as well, that even a pick-up group can play his music with excitement and feeling. Furthermore, the very looseness and changeability of the ensembles may provide a freshness that might otherwise be lacking, at least in live performance.

Still, Eddie Palmieri's case is a sad one. Some composers are willing to abandon their roots. They either accept a mainstream style, be it pop-rock or, as with a black "serious" composer like Olly Wilson, academic modernism. Or they wander off into uncharted eccentricity. If they stay with the music with which they were born, however, they will be condemned to obey a narrow master. Palmieri may serve the Latin community expertly; Mozart himself served his patrons with some wonderful music. Being a popular, expert musical craftsman is not a dishonorable way to live one's life, if that is what Palmieri wants. But he has given evidence of wanting more. Ultimately, Mozart broke free; Palmieri's time for doing that may be growing short.

18

URBAN POPULAR SONG,
THE BROADWAY MUSICAL,
THE CABARET REVIVAL & THE
BIRTH PANGS OF AMERICAN OPERA

STEPHEN SONDHEIM

Just as there is a deep division between classical and popular music in this country, there is also a division between popular music before and after the mid-fifties—before and after rock. Rock fans often reveal a lamentable ignorance about the traditions of the American popular song before the electric guitar. But in precisely the same way—prejudice that can be measured generationally—the older aficionados of pre-rock pop too frequently condemn rock as a plot against musical truth and beauty. There are marked differences between the two styles, insofar as something so diverse as the whole tradition of American popular music can be simply divided in two. But there are similarities, as well, and both sides are foolish to ignore them.

White American popular song before rock was based in spirit on folk models but in form on European art music. Simpler folk songs and their manifestations as country music and "race music" had some of their roots in the church, to be sure, and there were exceptions to the prevalent urbanity and gentility, most notably the ragtime craze of the first decade of this century. But by and large, even those popular composers who took note of native traditions were careful to domesticate them into the accepted ballad forms of the day, as Stephen Foster did with Negro spirituals. The process was precisely the same as that employed by "serious" composers, such as Dvořák with his evocations of Czech folk melodies—or of spirituals.

In a time before records and the radio, songs were composed for the educated amateur or for theatrical revues, including the minstrel shows. Songs for the home tended to be sentimental, as did so much of the parlor music of the time; indeed, the ballad "After the Ball," with its massive sheet-music sales in 1892, is sometimes cited as the first real hit single in American history. Show tunes and dance-band marches and polkas could be livelier, and Broadway songs enjoyed the added advantage of the publicity attendant upon the show itself.

The American musical comedy—and hence the American popular song and, eventually, the Hollywood musical—that emerged at the turn of this century owed much to Central European operetta and to its English variant epitomized by Gilbert and Sullivan. This was, in essence, opera, but stripped of its high-art pretensions and defined by a tuneful humor and sweet sentimentality that placed it at least ostensibly in the realm of entertainment. The form's high point came between the wars, when such composers as Jerome Kern, Irving Berlin, George Gershwin and Richard Rodgers achieved a blend of melody, wit and sensual sophistication that ensures the continued popularity of their work to this day. Formally, however, the musical comedy rarely transcended the revues that inspired it. The plots were formulaic, vehicles for the great singing and acting stars of the time, and the lyrics dealt in simple situations with simple, declarative tunes to match.

Well before World War II, however, there had been attempts to create a true American opera based on the Broadway musical. "Opera" in this sense did not mean something snobbish and highbrow. It meant an attempt by composers to express themselves as directly and originally as they could within this vital form of indigenous American musical theater. There was a clear precedent for making opera out of popular musical theater: Mozart himself had done something similar with the German vaudeville *Singspiel* in *The Abduction from the Seraglio* and *The Magic Flute*. American composers were further encouraged by the energy and seemingly inexorable internal evolution of the musical, combined with the sterility of "serious" American opera—a sterility that had at least as many sociological explanations as strictly musical ones. Three composers should be mentioned here: Gershwin, with his *Porgy and Bess,* which has been acclaimed as the greatest American opera; Kurt Weill, a European expatriate who adopted the form of the musical and composed some superior examples before writing, in *Street Scene,* another "great American opera"; and, finally, Leonard Bernstein, who composed a fine musical with *West Side Story* and something more ambitious with *Candide,* and who has not yet given up his goal to provide us an American opera that is both popular and respected. All three men refused to rest content with the simpler forms they were expected to fill. And Weill and Bernstein were explicit in their intention to make the leap from musicals to opera.

American opera up until the 1930's was a primitive thing. If American intellectuals were crippled by an undue deference to Europe, American high society was positively transfixed by its European betters. The American preference for European musicians continues to this day, as a quick count of American-born music directors of leading American symphony orchestras will reveal. In Europe, opera was originally a princely entertainment made graciously available to the lower classes—apart from a few exceptions in Britain and Germany, in which the popular dispensation came from a civic-minded upper bourgeoisie. When opera was nationalized in Central Europe after World War I, the precedent for a democratic opera, already established, was institutionalized by the new republican states. Government subsidies kept ticket prices within reach of the average person, and an innovative tradition prevented the repertory from becoming fixed on a few warhorses. American opera was the province of nouveaux riches who aspired to European class and glamour: before the advent of film and recording stars, an opera singer was as exotic a creature as the arts could provide. For a while, American opera houses emulated Europe in competing for new operas. But when new music began to sound unpleasant, the need for novelties was easily assuaged by exciting new singers and flashy new productions.

In all of this, the American composer was a decided afterthought. The annals of the Metropolitan Opera—which for a long time was America's only opera house offering even close to a full season—do reveal the periodic American-opera premiere. Such works as Deems Taylor's *The King's Henchman* or Louis Gruenberg's *The Emperor Jones* were earnest, unoriginal settings of librettos with American themes, forgotten as soon as they were premiered. Later, there was a whole school of folk opera, epitomized by Douglas Moore and Jack Beeson. Too often these works sound dated and selfconscious, and the cynical anachronisms of Gian Carlo Menotti and Thomas Pasatieri sound even worse. There were a few exceptions to this gloomy picture, but nearly all of them—including *Porgy and Bess*—grew out of alternate means of patronage than the conventional opera company. Most striking were Virgil Thomson's two operas to texts by Gertrude Stein. *Four Saints in Three Acts* enjoyed an enormous chic success in 1934, the American equivalent of Berlin's *Threepenny Opera*. But neither it nor the even finer *The Mother of Us All* of 1947 has yet been performed at the Metropolitan.

The avant-garde music-theater events of the past two decades are even further removed from the conventional operagoer's taste, which by now seems fully satisfied by singing and the more primitive forms of melodramatic acting. Yet works like Glass's *Satyagraha* have emerged from that tradition and will eventually enter the operatic repertory, and more and more seemingly marginal experimental composers are showing signs of turning to the operatic stage—and are being encouraged to do so by such far-sighted operatic music directors as Dennis Russell Davies (who, symptomatically, is based in Stuttgart, not America).

Gershwin's *Porgy* dates from 1935, Weill's *Street Scene* from 1947 and Bernstein's *Candide* from 1956. We have not been deluged with serious musicals since, or with vital new American operas by composers who emerged from that tradition. In fact, the musical itself is in trouble, with revivals (*The Pirates of Penzance,* no less) ruling Broadway along with recyclings like *42nd Street.* Broadway has profound esthetic and sociological problems of its own. If the audience for American opera is conservative, so is that for the musical comedy—a middle-class public in search of escapist entertainment. The financing of any Broadway show, and especially a musical, has grown so perilous as to discourage artistic innovation. And Broadway's rules, or habits, hardly help, demanding as they do eight shows a week and thus dissuading gifted singers from voice-threatening strain.

It is this context in which the success of Stephen Sondheim must be considered. Sondheim was born in 1930 into a well-to-do New York family. A precocious child, he showed youthful musical talent and studied piano for a couple of years. But when he was ten, his parents divorced and Sondheim spent time at a military academy—which he enjoyed—before moving with his mother to a farm in Pennsylvania. Their next-door neighbor was an old family friend who became a second father to Sondheim—Oscar Hammerstein II, the lyricist who collaborated first with Vincent Youmans, Rudolf Friml, Jerome Kern and Sigmund Romberg and later with Richard Rodgers. Sondheim credits Hammerstein not only with inspiring his first efforts as a lyricist and composer, but with the firm and detailed criticism that enabled him to perfect his craft. At Williams College, Sondheim first thought of majoring in mathematics, but eventually gravitated to the music department, where he received a firm technical basis. He was so successful that he won a two-year scholarship upon graduation for further study at Princeton with Milton Babbitt.

Even in the early fifties, Babbitt was a radical avant-gardist, and had completed the early formulations of his total-serialist theory. But he was also a lover of musicials and had spent time writing them and popular songs in that idiom. Sondheim's apprenticeship with Babbitt suggests that he had a talent for "serious" music, and that his preference for the musical was his way of side-stepping the dilemmas posed by musical modernism. "Steve was terribly bright, ambitious, and could have been good as any sort of composer," Babbitt later recalled. "But there was no question that Broadway was where he wanted to be."

Although he had been trained as a composer, it was as a lyricist that Sondheim was first type-cast in New York. He had a part-time scriptwriting job on the *Topper* television show and left that to write songs for an aborted musical revue. His first Broadway credit was as lyricist for Bernstein's *West Side Story*, and after that he provided the words for *Gypsy*. His first success as both lyricist and composer came with *A Funny Thing Happened on the Way to the Forum* in 1962. That was followed by the short-lived (nine performances but prized by its cult) *Anyone Can Whistle* of 1964 and a return to the role of lyricist for Rodgers's *Do I Hear a Waltz?* in 1965.

Sondheim's verbal felicity has remained with him throughout his career. He has that gift for clever rhymes that has distinguished lyricists since W. S. Gilbert ("beauty celestial the best you'll / agree" from *Follies*, for instance). Better still, he has the ability to link musical construction with verbal cadence, to let the rhythm of the words shape the structure of a phrase. To take yet another of many possible examples, the song "Broadway Baby," again from *Follies*, includes a stanza that begins "At / my tiny flat . . ." This is an unexpected rhyme, to start with. And it helps define the melodic structure of the song itself.

That sense of melody, shape and overall formal design only really came into its own after 1970, with *Company* (*Forum*, for all its cleverness and charm, was not much more than a revue). *Company* was Sondheim's first real collaboration with Harold Prince, the producer-director, and it marked the beginning of a creative relationship that has defined his career since. Prince had co-produced *West Side Story* and produced *Forum*, but from *Company* on he and Sondheim worked together as closely as lyricists and composers had traditionally done on Broadway. Indeed, their complementary attributes—Prince the knowing showman, Sondheim the introverted, selfconscious artist—make for a synergy that recalls the working dynamics between Richard Strauss and Hugo von Hofmannsthal. "The reason I like to work with Hal Prince is that we have the same point of view, but we're abrasive," Sondheim once said. "We see the large and small parts exactly the same, but it's the middle ground where we disagree violently, and it causes a lot of good work to be done. I love to write in dark colors about gut feelings. Hal has a sense of audience that I often lack."

Company formed a trilogy with *Follies* (1971) and *A Little Night*

Music (1973), mirroring and exalting a certain early-seventies sensibility. The basic Broadway audience was and is a conservative one. But New York has a brittle, more sophisticated side, too, shared by the people who create and perform the productions. The Prince-Sondheim shows, with their alternating, overlapping irony and sentimentality, effected a marriage between what has been called the suburban "bridge-and-tunnel crowd" and the witty, nostalgic, sometimes homosexual element of contemporary New York. The lyrics and the dramatic situations were close enough to most people's lives to seem comforting. But they were also peppered with a sophistication and even a kinkiness that could titillate. These shows were celebrations of marriage and love, yet their seeming normalcy was undercut and contrasted with wit and camp (especially in *Follies*, with its parade of veteran female performers). The Sondheim-Prince shows avoided cliché, as so many Broadway productions these days fail to do. They evoked nostalgia without being fettered by the past. And they each had their conceptually bold sides, as well. *Company*, a celebration of marriage, was riven with acerbic asides about modern mores. *Follies*, a tale of two marriages set at a reunion of Ziegfeld-type showgirls, offered a feast for Broadway nostalgists in a clever, contemporarily complex package. And *A Little Night Music*, which took a Mozart title for an adaptation of Ingmar Bergman's Mozartean film comedy, *Smiles of a Summer Night*, was a waltz-musical that conveyed much of what Ravel attempted in *La Valse*, without the Old World ennui.

Sondheim's melodies are shaped differently from those of Broadway's past in part because his way of working is different. What makes his best songs so fine is their synchronism of words and music, the music supporting the text and the text defining the music, with both the sense and the sound of the words playing their parts. "Send in the Clowns" from *A Little Night Music* is Sondheim's best-known song. It lacks his characteristic wit and naughty patter, but otherwise it can stand as representative of his method. The song emerges from the four-note phrase announced at the very beginning by the clarinet. That fragment is repeated and varied (the title phrase itself is one of those variants) in a broken, musing fashion; the entire song is built up of these four-note fragments and their extensions. That hesitation reflects perfectly the dramatic state of the protagonist. The lyrics are full of a sweet suggestiveness, intimations of acrobats soaring and falling as a metaphor for love, and the allusion to clowns evokes both lovers and love itself. This is not a tune in the more traditional sense—several successive melodic ideas, neat and hummable. But it may be more true to the needs of the drama, and a more deftly artful piece of musical composition, than some of those older tunes, as well.

Sondheim's sensitivity to the marriage of words and music, and his ability to reflect the realities of his own time, can also be heard in his wittier, wickeder songs. "Poor Baby" from *Company,* for instance, is a study in cattiness, a sequence of women casting doubt on a male friend's current companion—a litany of bitchiness that builds into a complex ensemble texture. Sondheim's songs often build that way, from simple (or not so simple) melody and accompaniment to complicated set pieces. His musical idiom, especially in this trilogy from the early seventies, is happily historical, invoking styles and procedures from every corner of the American popular song repertory. And not just popular song, but opera, too. In that context, his most ingenious musical structures may not seem all that innovative; since Mozart's time, opera has offered ensembles of a richer complexity. But the proper standard of comparison is not opera but Broadway. And in any case, Sondheim invests his seeming conservatism with musical touches of his own, and enlivens his music with the contemporary spirit of his lyrics. Besides, in a time in which composers like George Rochberg are elevating the past into an esthetic for the present, Sondheim's eclecticism seems positively fashionable.

Company and *A Little Night Music* were hits; *Follies,* although it ran for a year, lost its entire investment. *Pacific Overtures* of 1976 and *Sweeney Todd* of 1979 were conceptually bolder but only marginally successful at the box office, while *Merrily We Roll Along,* full of fine, cleverly interlocking songs but crippled by its awkward book, closed precipitously. *Pacific Overtures* is about yet another kind of marriage—an audacious attempt to recount the story of

Japan's Westernization through a mixture of Western musical comedy and Kabuki drama. The resultant fresco was hard for audiences to identify with—all that foreignness in the musical and dramatic idioms, the lack of a single romantic hero or heroine, the distance from contemporary life. Yet some of the music was quite remarkable in its marriage of Japanese and Western sounds and effects. And the lyrics were as charming as ever ("If the tea the Shogun drank will / Serve to keep the Shogun tranquil").

Sweeney Todd, the tale of the "demon barber of Fleet Street" who allies himself with a maker of meat pies as a way of disposing of his victims, is the most operatically ambitious Sondheim-Prince collaboration yet. So grandiose are its ambitions, in fact, that controversy has arisen as to whether it actually is an opera. Beverly Sills plans to stage it at the New York City Opera—in the regular season, not in her summer operetta season. It belongs in the regular season; it is certainly as "serious" as, say, *Cavalleria Rusticana.* *Sweeney Todd*'s operatic aspirations lurk everywhere in the score. The story itself is a wonderful one, mixing Dickensian atmosphere, Grand Guignol humor, lyricism and terror in a way that seems perfectly suited to its creators' sensibilities. The two principal figures are superb dramatic creations, and superb vehicles for stars as persuasive as Len Cariou and Angela Lansbury. They can, as with most of Sondheim's leads, be portrayed by either singing actors or acting singers. But some of the vocal writing for the other roles is operatically overt, as in the high trill for the soprano ingenue. And the score's formal construction is Sondheim's most organically far-reaching to date. The idioms range from baroque-style evocations of the street cries of London to Weill and Stravinsky, full of dissonance and bitonality. With its mosaic construction, rapidly shifting moods, recurrent leitmotifs and complex ensembles, *Sweeney Todd* belongs on the operatic stage far more deservedly than most of the new operas that jostle for position there.

Sondheim has not attained his status as America's finest living composer of musicals without doubts being voiced. Classical critics fault him for not doing his own orchestrations. Others complain of his supposed inability—a reflection of his own guarded personality, Leonard Bernstein has suggested—to express simple, direct, intense emotion, and of his tuneless tunes. They have accused him and Prince of mixing up genres that should be kept separate, and of being more devoted to campy exploitation than genuine emotion.

Broadway composers have traditionally farmed out their orchestrations; even Bernstein has done it. Sondheim attributes his delegation of the task to a "lack of time and skill." It seems indeed unfortunate when a composer abdicates that part of his work, however: orchestration is not just fancy dress but part of a composer's very expression, and not to bother with it is to depersonalize that expression. But such a division of responsibilities may be just another example of the new kinds of collaboration practiced not only by Sondheim and Prince but by Robert Ashley and Laurie Anderson, as well—a different assignment of the creative tasks, and one not to be scorned if it happens to work. Sondheim's regular orchestrator is Jonathan Tunick, who has collaborated with him since *Company*. Tunick is clearly attuned to Sondheim's method and style, and by this point must be credited along with him for the originality that results. "Steve is very exact in his intentions," Tunick has said. "He doesn't concern himself with instrumentation at all, but he gives me a very thorough piano score that contains every detail of harmony and rhythm, as well as melody."

Orchestration is a superficial matter next to the innate distaste some critics feel for Sondheim and the entire world they believe him to epitomize. Arlene Croce, reviewing the *Follies* cast album—which, incidentally, curtails some songs and eliminates others to compress the show onto a single disc—suggested that the rhyme of "celestial" and "best / you'll" implies the old women are "bestial," and called "the dowdy spectacle of their exhibition not only ironic and sad but actively disgusting." Even Sondheim's champions must admit to a disturbing undercurrent in his work, without necessarily sharing Croce's lurid vehemence. There is a sometimes cynically vulgar, manipulative side to Broadway, and it has infected the conception and execution of Sondheim's work—mostly, one suspects, through what he likes to think of as "Hal's sense of audience."

Many of the more moderate complaints against Sondheim seem to be about "flaws" perceived by his admirers as virtues. As a man of today, Sondheim refuses to accept the pat, sweet directness that once defined our national character, at least as that character was projected in musicals and musical films. Although he echoes elegant interwar artifice, he is inevitably different from the great masters of the American popular song—more fragmented emotionally and musically, drier, more ironic, more ambivalent. And he would only deny himself were he to attempt to be anything different than he is. Sondheim was once quoted as saying, "At least half my songs deal with ambivalence, feeling two things at once. I like neurotic people. I like troubled people. Not that I don't like squared-away people, but I *prefer* neurotic people." On the other hand, his songs are not all *that* tuneless. And what they lack in directness, they gain in subtlety and complexity. If his work approaches opera, that hardly means other composers cannot write old-fashioned, simple-minded musicals. Indeed they do, season after season. Sondheim's major contribution may even be a conservative one, sustaining the conventions and the intellectual respectability of the traditional Broadway musical. Perhaps the creative moment for formulaic simplicity has passed, at least if it is to be achieved with genius.

Or perhaps not. The obvious source for the renewal of the traditional musical lies in rock. The two worlds, once so seemingly antithetical, have already begun to merge. Performers like Linda Ronstadt and Rex Smith have made acclaimed Broadway debuts, and composers like James Taylor, Paul Simon and Melanie have shown interest in the form. Rock is distinguished from the curdled manifestations of latter-day Tin Pan Alley and Broadway by its directness of expression. That openness recalls the earlier days of Broadway itself, so it is at least possible that, should rock composers be lured to Broadway, they could revitalize American musical theater. But rebirth is hardly guaranteed. The relative freedom that rock composers enjoy in the studio cannot be matched on the stage, given Broadway's collaborative esthetic and perilous financial insecurity. And the most likely candidates for such a cross-over—singer-songwriters such as Simon, Taylor and Randy Newman—are hardly simple and straightforward, themselves.

Sondheim stands for a different sensibility, which was responsible for the revival of cabaret life in New York in the early seventies. The composers and performers who led this revival were part of the same spirit that infused Broadway and blended so compatibly with suburban conservatism. Like Sondheim, they sought a more overtly dramatic expression through music. Their concerns were partly nostalgic, to bring back singers and styles that had been obliterated by rock. The cabaret revival was fueled by the growth and increasing self-assertion of New York's homosexual subculture, and it paralleled the commercial decline of Broadway. With the revitalization of theater attendance in the late seventies, and with the rise of disco, New York's cabarets lost some of their frenetic trendiness. The energies that came together in the cabaret revival have by now dispersed. Barry Manilow energized and vulgarized middle-of-the-road pop. Bette Midler is trying to establish a place for herself in films. Some performers have ventured into disco and dance-rock, and others are still to be seen in actual cabarets.

Sondheim, whose "Send in the Clowns" has probably been massacred in more different ways in more different cabarets than any other single song, was never a direct part of this movement; he merely shared its sensibility. Neurotic as ever, he is a slow worker who must always struggle to justify his place in the still undeniably commercial world of the Broadway theater. In a way, one wishes he had allowed the abstractly artistic aspect of Babbitt's influence to push him toward opera from the outset. But not really. What lends Sondheim's work its fascination is its very tension between art and entertainment, a tension mirrored in his creative relation-ship with Prince. He may be torn, and his conflicts may inhibit his art. But the very essence of his art *is* conflict, so that to wish away the tension would be to wish away the art.

19

ROCK, POPULISM & TRANSCENDENTAL PRIMITIVISM

NEIL YOUNG

Neil Young is a rock star. As such, he might seem the antithesis of artistry to those who regard rock as musical barbarism. But not all rock is barbaric, and some is barbaric in the best sense—more direct, more passionate, more aggressive in the expression of human feeling than too much contemporary music allows itself to be.

But Young is in some respects an atypical rock star. In 1972 he had his biggest hit album, *Harvest*—number one on the charts, every rocker's dream. But for a whole range of reasons, he opted out—not out of rock itself, but out of the compromises and disorientation that massive success too often entails. As he once put it in a program note about the biggest single on *Harvest*, "Heart of Gold," "This song put me in the middle of the road. Travelling there soon became a bore so I headed for the ditch. A rougher ride but I saw more interesting people there." That statement doesn't just characterize Young's relationship to mainstream popular music and to the music business in this country. It also suggests the relationship—once instinctive, now deliberate and hence "artistic"—of rock & roll to pop music, and of the best popular music to establishment culture. It may be rougher, it may be cruder, but for many, it's closer to real life.

Young is noteworthy for several reasons: the quality of his songs, the idiosyncratic charisma of his performing style, his elevation of rough simplicity into art. But another distinction is his sheer, determined longevity in a field that prizes the transient fashions of youth. Neil Young got started a little later than the oldest still-functioning rock stars, men like Bob Dylan, Paul McCartney and Mick Jagger. But he has sustained a first-class body of work longer than any of them, and except for Pete Townshend of the Who, no one has more trenchantly addressed the issues of rock's essence and survival.

As such, he stands as a refutation of the present-day conservative reaction against rock and the populist esthetics on which it is based. The 1960's saw a good deal of leftist, communal, idealistic rhetoric spilled about, much of it inspiring but much of it overblown and exaggerated. In the seventies, the forces of the right regrouped, and by late in the decade, with the baby boom over, campus protests a dim memory and many of the most vital voices of the sixties forced into marginality, the Tory counter-revolution seemed almost complete. Rock was kids' stuff, we read. Or it had sold out. Or it was never much to begin with, a cynical plot by the music business all along. Young proves not that "rock is art"— although I think he *is* an artist, and an important one—but that it is at least possible to express oneself artistically and be an unashamed rock & roller all at once.

Rock arose in the mid-fifties out of a marriage of black rhythm and blues—a hotter, urban variant of basic blues forms—and white up-tempo country music. As it developed, it quickly incorporated other strains of popular and folk musics: the older Tin Pan Alley, with its cheeriness and sentimentality, and an encyclopedia of black rural and urban styles. From the start, people perceived rock as sexual and rebellious, and both damned and welcomed it as such. In the sixties, such rebelliousness came to color the whole spectrum of social and political concerns that defined the decade. Yet for every protest marcher, there were a hundred young people who didn't march, and who still valued this music for its capacity to entertain or express personal feeling. The Byrds, often as not in their bland "cover versions" of Bob Dylan songs, sold many more records than Dylan, but it is he who is remembered as the American musical voice of the sixties. In the seventies, this rebelliousness was co-opted by the very cultural system it had challenged. By the late sixties, the corporate record business discovered rock with a vengeance, and in the seventies, music grew into an industry to rival the movies. As rock stars became millionaires, they found it difficult to sustain the innovation that had seemed routine with the Beatles or Dylan, or to espouse personal or political change. That was partly because the mood of the country had shifted. But it also reflected the stars' absorption into the system.

It is in this context that Young's career must be measured. He was born in Toronto in 1945, the son of a still notable Canadian journalist who was divorced from Young's mother in 1958. Young and his mother moved to Winnipeg, where during his teens Young was a member of rock bands and later, back in Toronto, a solo folk singer and again a rocker. When he was twenty-one, Young gravitated to Los Angeles, and has lived there or on a ranch south of San Francisco ever since.

Young's first band in Los Angeles was a pioneering country-rock group called Buffalo Springfield—pioneering because at that time country music was regarded as the province of red-neck right-wingers, and hence antithetical to rock. Later, after his solo career was already under way, Young joined up with Stephen Stills, who had been in Buffalo Springfield, David Crosby of the Byrds and Graham Nash of the Hollies to form Crosby, Stills, Nash and Young, a massively popular folk-rock band that specialized in complex vocal arrangements with innovative harmonies and song structures. But, always the congenital outsider, Young quit that band—several times—and spent the seventies on his own, in sometime partnership with a rough-and-ready rock band called Crazy Horse; in reunions with some or all of Crosby, Stills and Nash; or in other, more ephemeral musical alliances.

The real dividing line in his career came in 1972, after the success of *Harvest*, his fourth solo album. That album offered much that still defines his work: romantic longing, mystical transcendence, Western imagery, folk and cowboy musical idioms and the solidity and drive of rock & roll. But it sweetened his sensibility with an unusually overt fixation on romantic love, and with string arrangements that softened the music and recalled the ballads of Crosby, Stills, Nash and Young; two songs even offered the London

Symphony Orchestra as back-up. Young decided to "head for the ditch" for several reasons. He had long oscillated between lyricism and aggression, and clearly saw the need to swing sharply away from the extreme lyricism of *Harvest*. He felt dehumanized by success, which demanded tours to indoor sports arenas with minimal audience contact, and constrained by the expectations of his fans. He was horrified by the drug deaths of two friends. And he had his own health problems—epilepsy, a slipped disc and excessive drinking brought on by all his other troubles.

Rock was born in clubs, small halls and recording studios, but by the seventies the biggest stars were commonly playing in arenas that seated twenty thousand or at festivals that attracted audiences into the hundreds of thousands. Although amplified music is meant to allow a minimum number of instrumentalists to create a maximum impact, music at this scale is inevitably distorted—especially if the songs being played were intimately conceived. Gestures must be broadened to the point of coarseness, and the arenas, designed for sports, usually muddy the sound. Almost invariably, bands that tour regularly to such facilities must fall back on the simplest of music combined with the flashiest of stage shows. Sometimes such restrictions encourage imaginative solutions to the problem of mass theatrical art—solutions unequaled since Max Reinhardt's popular spectacles. David Bowie's 1976 tour, for instance, offered a Brechtian bare stage pummeled by intense white light. And Pink Floyd's tours mix massive props with film and live action. But for most bands in such halls, the possibilities seem limited, and Young felt that pressure.

Further pressure comes from fans' expectations following a hit album. In theory, a "star" has a greater latitude than an unsuccessful performer. In practice, tour audiences demand the familiar—either actual songs or, more insidiously, new songs in the same style. If the artist is insecure, and most are, he is encouraged to repeat himself even when his instincts might tell him to push forward.

Drugs and rock are synonymous in people's minds, and the connection is real. Not only have many rock stars flaunted their drug usage, but some have died from it. Rock lyrics glorify the drug experience, and many teenagers make rock concerts occasions for drinking and drugs. Young himself has apparently never been much interested in hard drugs. But the guitarist of Crazy Horse overdosed and died from heroin just before Young's big post-*Harvest* tour, and did so the night after Young had fired him because of his inability to play his parts. Shortly thereafter, a "roadie"—someone who performs such tasks as moving equipment and tuning guitars during a rock tour—with whom Young had been close died from the same drug. All this forced Young into reclusion. And when his self-indulgent first film, *Journey Through the Past,* was critically dismissed, he was widely discounted as another sixties burn-out.

Yet the early seventies was not the end of Young's mature career, but the beginning. He reached within himself for a series of deeply personal, tortured, musically sparse and grating records that culminated in *Tonight's the Night,* a harrowing portrayal of heroin and the damage it can do. In 1976 he re-emerged into the wider public arena with *Zuma,* an album full of renewed vision. By the late seventies, he had recaptured his audience and solidified his critical reputation with the impressive retrospective *Decade* and an album called *Rust Never Sleeps,* which deals with rock's aging, the relationship between folk music and rock and the new punk-rock upheaval that was challenging rockers of Young's generation. Then in 1982 and 1983, he came forth with the strange, endearing, indomitably eccentric *Trans,* which wedded folk-rock to synthesizers, computers and electronic filtering in a lively if volatile marriage, and a quirky rockabilly revival album, *Everybody's Rockin'.* By this time he had surpassed his idol, Dylan, in sustained creativity (and perhaps sustained eccentricity, as well), although Young himself prefers to avoid the comparison.

For a while, as a way of recontacting his audience and making meaningful music, he experimented with anonymous performances in small clubs. But there is an unfortunate elitist implication to such slumming: it denies most of the fans who genuinely want to see an artist the chance to do so. By the late seventies, Young had devised a conceptually clever stage show that made sense in arenas. And he had turned rock's primitive simplicity into the conscious basis of his musical style.

Simplicity defines Young's music, clarifying his position as a precursor of the new-wave simplicity that transformed rock & roll in the late seventies. Paradoxically, his earnest musical innocence is only highlighted by the flashy surface complexity of an album like *Trans*. Young's simplicity gives even some rockers pause—the kind of studio professional who favors dulcet vocalism and technically dazzling instrumental virtuosity. Young has a perilously insecure, quavery, nasal little tenor and a guitar style based on a few functional chords and licks. But his vocal and instrumental expressivity casts new doubt on the links between quality and complexity. Art can be called the formalization of vision through craft, but the craft must transmit the vision. Too often, the vision is obscured instead. Perhaps, both experimental composers and neo-primitive rockers believe, we need a lesser craft through which some sort of vision may shine unimpeded. Wilfrid Mellers, in his ornately over-analytical yet right-minded book on the Beatles, argues that popular music serves a function by reminding Western man of music's essence. Yet if Western art music has become overrefined, pop music, too, has a tendency to "evolve" into fancy fuss. Young is determined to haul rock back to its basics, to rekindle its power to communicate within self-imposed limits. "It is practically the only question of the age," Jean Renoir once said, "this question of primitivism and how it can be sustained in the face of sophistication." Without belaboring the comparison, Young might be said to have something of Renoir's childlike humanism.

The root of his style is "folk music," but that term needs explanation. Folk music used to mean any music of the folk. By the early sixties, however, the term had taken on a second meaning: music composed in a folk style by urban singer-songwriters—Dylan, preeminently. By the mid-sixties, Dylan had expanded into rock, which horrified folk "purists" but seemed logical enough, both musically and conceptually: rock was, after all, by this time the true music of the folk, and hence a "folk musician" avoided it at the peril of antiquarian esotericism.

Every "folk" has its traditional music; the folk meant in American "folk music" is mostly of Scottish-Irish descent, musically speaking—such song structures, poetic imagery and modal scales have affected nearly all traditional American music, black spirituals and blues very much included. Scottish-Irish-American songs are strophic, outwardly simple but prone to haunting twists and turns within their austere outer conventions, and a sometimes apocalyptic imagery, as befits the stern mysticism of the religion these peoples brought with them from the old country. In America, "country music" is also very much a form of folk music, especially before it got slicked up by Nashville and Hollywood; Dolly Parton is, or was, as poetic a composer within the country-folk idiom as this country has known, until she decided to sacrifice her art for stardom.

In one sense, rock is merely folk music writ large; certainly that seems the case with Young. But the enlargement transforms its subject. What can sound intimately intense as folk music, confiding and personal, becomes grand and proclamatory when it is inflated by the gigantic amplifiers and speakers that make up a rock band's touring sound system. In his live sets and on his records, Young alternates between "acoustic" music, which is folk or country music unadorned, and rock. *Rust Never Sleeps* dramatizes the connections between the two by ending with a grinding hard-rock version of a song about rock & roll offered in folk guise at the beginning. The first is sweet and quietly anguished, the second defiant.

That album posed the problem of retaining a simple, unselfconscious style when selfconsciousness had intruded into the creative process. It is a problem that has afflicted all music: indeed, one can trace the isolation of composer from audience over the past century to the spread of historical selfconsciousness on both sides—composers measuring themselves against the past, audiences retreating into the past. The very existence of something called "rock criticism" encapsulates the dilemma: members of the intelligentsia obsessed with an art form that epitomizes, often as not, anti-intellectualism. Clearly, it can be profitable to think deeply about even the most non-intellectual art, and clearly not all rock is non- or anti-intellectual. But the possibilities for falling into pretension or ludicrousness or irrelevance remain great. Smart rock performers have to walk the same wire, and Young has managed to do so with delicate skill.

He succeeds in part because of his own musical expressivity. His tenor may be shaky, but it is also vulnerable and emotive, and he maintains his subtle, frail vulnerability in even the most violent rock songs, thanks to amplification. His singing also refutes those who prize one conventionalized vocal or instrumental technique above all others. Sometimes the attainment of a standardized technique precludes other kinds of artistry, or blinds one to other techniques (as with opera-lovers who hear nothing in East Indian singing). Young's voice suits a time in which directness of personal expression—"sincerity"—is prized far more than in opera or the suaver days of inter-war American pop. Similarly, his guitar style, with its long, minimally repetitive lines and low, throaty pitch-ranges, answers a deeper need than many a high, flashy, note-ridden guitar solo. Young's solos—in a song called "Like a Hurricane," for instance—attain a quite wonderful arching reach. Instead of busy, brilliant roulades of notes, they sound like some keening singer, climaxing once again when all passion seems surely spent.

Like any great composer, Young varies and extends an idiom that is a common language for him and his audience. It might be foolish to measure his music against the complexities of an Elliott Carter. But it would be equally silly to expect from Carter the emotional directness of Young. While he works in traditional folk and folk-rock styles, Young enlivens those styles with all manner of delightful, off-balance twists. A deft, telling little song like "Love Is a Rose" ("Love is a rose but you'd better not pick it / It only grows when it's on the vine / A hand full of thorns and you'll know you've missed it / You lose your love when you say the word, 'mine' ") jogs along sweetly, but escapes the musically obvious with its curious repetition of the tonic note and its odd little tag-refrain. Young's longer ballads avoid sameness not just through the quality of their lyrics, but by the sheer epic weight of their strophic reiterations. As with minimalism, not all repetition makes artistic sense. But the *right* repetition, artfully accomplished, can become a statement in itself.

The balance between words and music varies in all work that combines the two, rock included. In rock that equilibrium has been tilted by most rock critics' backgrounds. Rock has been a liberating force in American culture precisely because it does not demand musical literacy. Rock musicians are usually self-taught, and can bypass the need to read notation because the tape recorder has recreated an oral culture. Rock critics, too, come most often from a literary background rather than a musical one, and hence feel uncomfortable with musical description and analysis. They are happier with words, and hence too much rock criticism concentrates unduly on the lyrics. Young's lyrics invite such concentration; in fact, one admiring California poet, Tom Clark, arranged lines from Young songs and published them in a mimeographed edition. Yet, like all song texts, they remain inseparable from their music and performance, especially since Young has always said that he composes words and music simultaneously.

Young's poetic imagery places him securely within the romantic camp. He is the eternal seeker—after love and the elusive perfect woman, after childlike innocence, after mystical ideals. Love is the pabulum of pop. What distinguishes Young's treatment is the vividness of his metaphors and descriptions, the range of his canvas. In a song called "Cortez the Killer" on the *Zuma* album, he paints a misty-eyed vision of Aztec society on the verge of annihilation by the conquistadors:

He came dancing across the water
With his galleons and guns
Looking for the new world
And that palace in the sun.

On the shore lay Montezuma
With his cocoa leaves and pearls
In his halls he often wandered
With the secrets of the worlds.

Then, after a few more such verses, with no transition, Young is lamenting a lost love who has stepped inexplicably into this dream-Arcadia:

And I know she's living there
And she loves me to this day
I still can't remember when
Or how I lost my way.

With one stroke, Young has linked and enriched two disparate emotional worlds, offering images of non-Western man as a feminine victim of European rapine, and of the mythic dimensions of obsessional love. Conversely but similarly, in a song called "Star of Bethlehem," after some gentle, mournful musings he suddenly enlarges the scope to invoke Christian redemption: "Maybe a Star of Bethlehem wasn't a star at all."

Young is a Canadian, and has sometimes described himself as a "world citizen," but his songs celebrate America. He has lived here since the mid-sixties and counts now as a true immigrant—indeed, he may soon become a U.S. citizen. Like Robbie Robertson and the other songwriters of the Band, a nearly all-Canadian group, and even like the more cosmopolitan Joni Mitchell, Young draws on the mythology and national aspirations of this country for inspiration. Nationalism may not be the highest human virtue. But if Herder was right, it is a way of grounding one's nobler flights in reality, allowing the abstract to be understood universally. The intensity and authenticity of Young's Americanness cast a new light on the rural nostalgia of the hippie movement, of which he is most certainly a spokesman. During the Vietnam War protests, hippies were attacked as traitors. The irony was that, all along, they were more romantically patriotic than their opponents.

Young's music does raise some questions, however. For instance: any art form widely appreciated by stoned white teenagers might seem to have unduly limited itself, even to those who uphold the expressive virtues of simplicity. Drugs helped open up people's imaginations in the sixties: Young himself once readily conceded that "when you're writing a song or mixing a record, to smoke a joint or take a drink or do a line of cocaine will produce some sort of avenue. Now, the avenue may be there anyway, and maybe someone else could go down that avenue without that, and maybe I could if I had to. But it affected my writing, no doubt about it." Yet while drugs can stimulate the imagination, they can also deaden the spirit. "If you want to get high," Young sang in 1982, "build a strong foundation." Whether or not fueled by drugs and alcohol, there is a lowest-common-denominator loutishness at too many rock concerts, and that element is certainly attracted to Young's concerts. He may sing in the most affecting manner about the death of his friends, but the crowd still cheers brutishly at the drug references. Young has determinedly refused to avoid this dilemma by aiming his music "higher." When teenagers graduate from hard rock, it is not necessarily to more refined kinds of music, as some sixties optimists assumed. They may descend instead to Neil Diamond and Barry Manilow; in other words, to schlock. But while there is an extraordinary, violent power to some of Young's best hard-rock music—the reiterated dissonant guitar chords at the end of side two of the *Rust Never Sleeps* album must be called artistic, since they have left "entertainment" so far behind—the only answer to this question of audience is that he appeals to other sensibilities, as well. Adults buy popular music in far greater numbers than is sometimes assumed, and not all of what they buy is schlock: there is a sophisticated adult audience for composers like Young, Randy Newman, Bruce Springsteen and Jackson Browne. That the majority of Young's concert audience is young (as opposed to young and stoned) is of less concern. True, a concentration on teen themes might seem to circumscribe an artist. But Young's themes are broader than that, and in any case the issues that concern teenagers have long been the essence of romantic poetry, which can appeal to young and old alike: it's the art that counts.

A more troublesome worry is the relationship between all successful rock performers and the commercial music industry in this country. There are those who question the ability of any mass art to maintain the subtlety and independence of more esoteric work. Virgil Thomson has gone so far as to argue that any music suffers that makes money. In addition, there is the widespread suspicion, at least among aficionados of less popular music, that anything could be popular with the proper promotion. This theory—held by lovers of classical music, jazz fans, new-wave rock critics, Adorno and Rzewski alike—is that whatever is advertised and played on the radio will sell. Its logical extension is that if only Anton Webern were played as often as, say, Christopher Cross, he, too, would sell albums in the millions.

There can be little doubt that the lowest, most prevalent level of American popular culture is crude or, worse, bland—much commercial television, many films, lots of popular music. This is formulaic stuff crafted in the most cynical manner. But that does not mean that only popular entertainment with artistic pretensions is any "good." Much wonderful entertainment, in films and in popular music, was made with no pretension other than to entertain. People actually *want* to hear what is popular. Were radio bolder in its programming, a tougher rock might be more popular than it is now. But critics who think the public will buy anything have a pessimistic estimation of the public. Much of what is popular seems in fact better than similar music that is less popular; the public is not that dumb.

A case can be made that better popular art has emerged in music than in other art forms since the mid-fifties. The creative decisions involving a pop record are usually made by a much smaller number of people than is involved in a film or a television program—typically, the artist and a producer. And those creative choices are less likely to be compromised by nervous executives than in film or television. Record executives aren't smarter, but a record costs less than a film or a television series. A record company with many artists can afford to take chances as long as a reasonable number of them actually sell records. A million-selling artist has considerable leverage with his record company. He represents large potential profits, and the executives are willing to humor him. This is the opposite of a star trapped by audience expectations. If he wants to change his style, he can, and Young and many others have. Sometimes their sales decline, but sometimes they increase, and even if they don't the record companies are likely to remain tolerant for several albums at least.

But commerce and rock artistry can clash, too. If a rock artist is *too* restlessly experimental, he will encounter record-company resistance: he may be challenged not only by pre-rock revanchists but by capitalism itself. The big record companies first ignored rock, then gingerly embraced it, then became obsessed with it to the exclusion of nearly everything else. The reason so much interesting new-wave, jazz and classical music is being released on marginal labels is that the big record companies seem fixated on only the broadest popular audience—just like the network television programmers. The proliferation of minor labels is the musical equivalent of what should happen with the proliferation of cable television, and what has already happened to AM and FM radio— a fragmentation of taste and styles that may accurately reflect individual musical tastes, but diminishes the chances of a quality mass art.

Young's struggle to maintain personal and artistic integrity and still speak to the country at large addresses that exact issue, but it has not been without reverses, and his failures are sometimes his own fault. Young's work has an erratic, self-indulgent side. It is all well and good for him to evoke a Cageian notion of audience creativity: "Songs must make the listener's mind work," he has said. "They don't have to finish the story, but leave whoever's hearing it out there with a sort of canvas to draw his own pictures." But too often his lyrics lapse from the evocative to the awkwardly prosaic. Like Dylan, he strives to avoid the sterility of recording-studio "perfection." Yet sometimes his songs themselves seem sloppily, incompletely conceived. This is the musical equivalent of the self-indulgence demonstrated in *Journey Through the Past* and, to a lesser but still troubling extent, in his *Live Rust* concert film. Self-indulgence and eccentricity, in the rock world or outside it, are often the price of any outsider's originality, however. In Young's case, he has found enough kindred souls to sustain a mass audience while remaining true to himself, which seems a fairly noble achievement for an artist in a democracy. "I'm lucky," he once said. "Somehow, by doing what I wanted to do, I manage to give people what they don't want to hear and they *still* come back. I haven't been able to figure that out yet."

20

ART-ROCK & THE FUSION OF RACES & STYLES

TALKING HEADS

For all its individuality and excellence, Neil Young's rock & roll speaks with a folkish voice; if his music can be equated with high art, it has attained that status through a popular idiom. Talking Heads approach the equation of art and rock from the other direction. Although they sell hundreds of thousands (but not millions) of records, and fill concert halls (but not arenas) with their live appearances, they remain unabashed artists who have chosen to work in a popular style. As such they epitomize the feverish crossover experiments in lower Manhattan since the sixties.

Rock may have been born as rebellious entertainment, but it soon developed artistic self-awareness. This fall from innocence is normally dated from the Beatles' *Sgt. Pepper's Lonely Hearts Club Band* of 1967, a "concept album" with the most imaginative usage of the recording studio for collage effects and overdubs that was possible at the time. "Art rock" as it developed in the late sixties and early seventies seemed a primarily British phenomenon, measured by bands that sold significant quantities of records. This movement, typified by such groups as Yes, Procol Harum and Emerson, Lake and Palmer, is best seen as a blend of middle-of-the-road sentimentality and empty virtuosity augmented by the recording studio. Concerned with translating traditional classical music into rock, these bands allied inflated late-romantic bathos with studio trickery and supplemented their own groups—which usually featured a flashy synthesizer player—with actual symphony orchestras. The best work to emerge from this genre either approached the febrile intensity of new jazz, as in Robert Fripp's King Crimson, or attempted a marriage of large-scale thematic form and rock, as in the Who's *Tommy*—a "rock opera" that, like *Einstein on the Beach,* was performed at the Metropolitan Opera House in concert form by the group itself.

New York art-rock was always different. Echoing the grimness of lower Manhattan, it was tougher, more aggressive, more concerned with reducing rock to its primitive basics and making an art out of that. New York bands accepted the advances of technology as a given, as today's equivalent to printed notation. But they did not become enamored of it, or let it determine their music. "Evolution" into primitivism might seem retrogressive, and so it struck the entrenched rock superstars of the time. But especially in New York this fascination with basics was merely a rock extension of the whole lower-Manhattan art world's devotion to minimalism and rigorous structuralism. Rock reflected and even epitomized the common interests of an artistic community.

The pioneers of New York art-rock were the Velvet Underground. When the band first got together in 1966, the artist Walter DeMaria played drums with it informally, testifying to the connection between art and rock. But the leaders were Lou Reed and John Cale. Reed was a poet and a rock guitarist. Cale was a Welsh violist who had been trained at the Royal Conservatory of Music in London, had studied composition with Copland and Xenakis at Tanglewood and had worked for several years with La Monte Young in New York. This mixture of sensibilities produced a spare, raw, defiant rock & roll, marked by brutal excitement and Reed's tough vulnerability. The Underground was ahead of its time commercially; young audiences were interested in earnestly idealistic folk-rock, bright British pop-rock and the even cheerier Los Angeles rock. Or perhaps the band wasn't really commercial at all, but a new kind of "art trip," anticipating Philip Glass's kinship with the late-seventies rock-club scene. The hip intelligentsia loved the Velvet Underground from the start, and Andy Warhol became its impresario.

When the Underground broke up in 1970, the scene didn't die. It was reborn at a curious assemblage of performance spaces and boutiques called the Mercer Arts Center, which became a true meeting place for the avant garde and rock & roll. The Arts Center was the original home of the Kitchen, which since its founding in 1971 has been New York's principal center for "downtown" experimental music and video art. The center was also the home of the New York Dolls, who emerged from the glitter-rock of the time to become the direct antecedents of New York's mid-seventies "punk."

Another pioneer was Patti Smith. Smith was a poet first, and began her transformation by chanting over a rock guitar played by Lenny Kaye, then better known as a rock critic. Gradually the band filled out, and by the mid-seventies, before she veered into megalomania and personal confusion, Smith managed an exhilarating blend of cosmic poetry in the Ginsberg-Burroughs tradition with a rock that grew ever heavier and more assertive. Eventually the rock took over, and since her musicians were never very good in the abstract, she obliterated her own individuality.

By that time, however, the "punk," later to be called "new wave," movement was in full flower. The word "punk" has by this time become inextricably linked with safety pins and spitting, first in London and then, three years late but full of fight, in Los Angeles and suburbia everywhere. This flamboyant, often speeded-up rock and exuberant, nihilistic life-style never really caught on in New York; the Dolls and, later, the Ramones helped inspire the movement, but didn't realize it fully themselves. Instead, New York "punks" remained truer to the original meaning of the word— dour and sullen romanticizations of lower-class rebels of the Brando-Dean variety. Much of their music was truly rudimentary, although as creators of a scene they did pose a valuable alternative to the ever slicker products of mid-seventies mainstream pop. But, as in all scenes, the dross served as context for a few wonderful bands. Those bands included the Ramones (clever conceptualists), Television (soaring guitar duets and a messianic lead singer), Blondie (witty eclectics with a stunning woman singer, and ultimately the most commercially successful of the lot) and Talking Heads, a term that derives from close shots of participants in television talk shows.

Talking Heads' original three members, who came from middle- and upper-middle-class backgrounds, attended the Rhode Island School of Design. Just as so much of the early experimental music in lower Manhattan was supported by the art world rather than conventional contemporary-music organizations, so, too, some of the best rock & roll in both Britain and America has come from visual-arts schools. In Britain, this was partly because such schools offered talented under-achievers a better education than the more conventional alternatives to Oxford and Cambridge. But in both countries, the pattern suggests that there was something about the esthetics of mid-century visual style that was congenial to both "classical" and rock vanguardists.

In Rhode Island, David Byrne, the Heads' eventual composer, singer and guitarist, and Chris Frantz, the drummer, had a band called the Artistics—subsequently nicknamed or retitled the Autistics. Eventually the two found themselves trying to put together a new band in New York. They needed a bass player, and turned to their design-school classmate Martina Weymouth, who didn't play the instrument but was eager to learn. The band made its debut as a trio in the summer of 1975; added a fourth member, Jerry Harrison, on keyboards and guitar in 1977; and recorded its first LP that year. Harrison, a Harvard graduate, had been a member of a pioneering neo-primitive group, the Boston-based Jonathan Richman and the Modern Lovers.

Despite their artistic selfconsciousness, the Heads were neither slumming artists nor artsified rock primates. They occupied a delicate no-man's-land between the two, and derived much of their excitement from the tension. "Serious" composers and artists were attracted by rock & roll for several reasons. First, as in the late sixties, there was a kinship between minimalism and structuralism on the one hand and a stripped-down, abstracted rock & roll on the other. By the mid-seventies, the SoHo gallery scene had become institutionalized, and the strictly visual arts were losing the creative impetus that had driven them in earlier decades. Performance art and rock performance offered a fresh challenge to many young artists. Rock entailed fewer technical demands than classical music, and seemed less of a closed craft guild. It provided at least the possibility of self-support. Above all, it was the actual musical language that people—not "the people" so much as fellow artists— preferred to speak. "The art scene had started to seem elitist," Byrne explained in 1979, "aimed at a small band of initiates who knew what all the right references were. I thought the idea was to reach people and get feedback." "Every once in a while," Harrison added, "we'll meet some artist who says, 'I think using rock & roll for your art form is *brilliant*.' I find that repellent." "I don't like to think of myself as an artist playing at having a band," Byrne said three years earlier. "I've gotten to the point where I think of myself as a performer—almost an entertainer. We take it very seriously, but it is entertainment."

The music of Talking Heads in the mid-seventies was far removed from "punk rock." Like all rock, it was rhythmically simple (or primally satisfying) in its underpinning of solid common time. But it was also precise and delicate, marked by incessant repetition in the bass line, a clipped tightness in the drumming and scratchy, coloristic chording from the guitar. At times there seemed to be an Eastern influence, intimations of Bali in bells and other fragile percussion effects. But evocations of the ethereal were quickly countermanded by the driving intensity of the band and the fractured peculiarities of the vocal part. At this point in his career, Byrne's singing was a squawk: there is no better word. His forced, cracked tenor could barely intone a note without breaking, and his stiff, bug-eyed performance style, born of terrified nervousness, was more fascinating than enthralling.

People gradually got used to Byrne's idiosyncrasies even as he smoothed out his singing with voice lessons and a newfound confidence. There were a few false steps along the way—the band's first commercial single was over-produced in a conventional rock manner that blunted its originality, and the addition of Harrison at first thickened the sound without enlarging it. But Byrne soon found a way to sort things out, and the band's growth thereafter was impressively steady. A song called "Memories Can't Wait" on the Heads's third album, *Fear of Music,* can serve as an example of the group's mature artistry. The instrumental context is an ominous, dark guitar riff, throbbing with anxiety. Byrne, singing in a more baritonal voice than usual, emits a series of almost conversational, schizophrenic fragments:

> *Do you remember anyone here?*
> *No you don't remember anything at all*
> *I'm sleeping, I'm flat on my back*
> *Never woke up, had no regrets*

The chorus evokes the alienation of the outsider, with imagery drawn from the rock world:

> *There's a party in my mind . . . and it never stops*
> *There's a party up there all the time . . . they'll party till they drop*

A later verse continues:

> *Take a walk through the land of shadows*
> *Take a walk through the peaceful meadows*
> *Try not to look so disappointed*
> *It isn't what you hoped for, is it?*

Through all of this, the dark, insistent music presses forward, full of busy echo and filter effects that never impede the music's directness. The impression is of technology gone crazy, and of a hyper-sensitivity in which every little sonic gesture has dizzying ramifications. Yet underneath it all, rock's dance impetus pushes on, threateningly. Suddenly the music shifts into the major, which lightens the mood without alleviating it, and Byrne drives into the final stanza, the last line repeated over and over in a howling upward whoop over a pounding reiterated figuration in the bass:

> *Everything is very quiet*
> *Everyone has gone to sleep*
> *I'm wide awake on memories*
> *These memories can't wait.*

You can dance to this music, if you want to; it has the beat. But most people find themselves compelled to listen.

Much of the song's impact derives from its atmospheric production. In the version of this same song on the group's live album *The Name of This Band Is Talking Heads,* the music is stripped of its studio effects, and sounds poorer as a result. Production has become part of creation: Brian Eno, the album's producer, once entitled a lecture "The Recording Studio as Compositional Tool." Recording technology today is capable of breaking down a musical texture into separate tracks that can be erased and replaced at will, and equally capable of creating musical effects that no live instrumentalist could equal without electronic aid. The very nature of composition has been changed as a result. The musically literate and the illiterate alike can use the studio to compose, and the recorded document is as much a permanent record as printed notation was in pre-electronic days. Joni Mitchell, another musical illiterate and superb composer, has likened the process to musical painting.

Fear of Music, released in 1979, was the second Talking Heads LP produced by Eno, who by this time had become almost a fifth band member in the studio. Eno had his own roots in the British art-rock movement, but in a leaner style than that of the more inflated groups. He attended art school and was an early member of a band called Roxy Music. He left that group in 1973 to become a solo artist, although, rather like Glenn Gould, he works almost exclusively in the studio. With Eno, however, reclusiveness is more a matter of nerves than philosophy. But it is also part of his own coming to terms with the pressures of mass success. Eno may not be a rock idol on the level of a Dylan. But he has an intense cult following, and he tries to avoid being trapped by that following. "Adulation is annoying because it creates a false momentum in you," he has said. "If you know that people have been absolutely overwhelmed by something you did, you are much more inclined to repeat it, even if you have doubts about it. That restricts your experimental freedom."

Eno's work has established him as one of the more fascinating figures in rock, and since the late seventies he has based his activities in New York. Essentially, he is a collaborator. Sometimes his collaborations appear under his own name, sometimes they are co-credited and sometimes he is listed as producer. Most of what is credited to him alone is overtly avant garde—his "ambient" environmental records (reminiscent in sound of Max Neuhaus's pieces) and his video studies of city skylines. Eno stands as a fine symbol of the art-rock interchange not only in New York but worldwide. His activities include all manner of avant-garde pursuits, from process music to sound and video documentation to aural collages to third-world excursions. In all these activities it is possible to accuse him of copying less well-known originators. Eno does not always deny the charge, adducing a distinction between their "research" and his translation of that research into listenable music. But it is not so simple as that. Eno brings his own distinctive character to anything he touches. And his personal manner, at once lucid and detached, suits the mood of contemporary avant-gardism very nicely.

His records with Talking Heads show an ever larger role from album to album. By the last, *Remain in Light,* he had co-written several of the songs as well as producing it. Eno's influence pushed the band into a more ornate texture that did not preclude intensity. This process was similar to the way minimalists like Reich and Glass enriched their vocabularies—to the point where they can hardly be called minimalists any more—yet retained a clear linkage with their origins.

Eventually Eno and Byrne took to collaborating independently of the band, which prompted separate projects by Frantz and Weymouth (who had by then married) and by Harrison. The first Byrne-Eno collaboration was called *My Life in the Bush of Ghosts,* a name taken from Amos Tutuola's novel about a young boy's mythic wanderings through Africa. It was recorded before *Remain in Light* but released after it, for both legal and artistic reasons. Here their shared interest in African music and culture became overt—the music, in direct borrowings of African rhythms and percussion; the culture, in the models Africa offered for communal music-making and for a society in which art had a clear functional role. The record also makes use of "found" vocal tracks taped from the radio and other sources that were superimposed over the instrumentals. The disc's African polyrhythms, that jumping skein of rhythmic counterpoint found in any African communal drum session, were carried over onto *Remain in Light,* and the concerts that followed the release of that album—in which live correspondences had to be devised for the multiple overdubs achieved in the studio—found the band transformed into a ten-member ensemble, half of which was black. The second disc of the band's two-record live album documents those performances, and they are a joy.

The extent to which white rock is a pale imitation of black models has long been a nagging issue. Early rock was a blend of black rhythm and blues and white up-tempo country music, but there are those who would discount the latter influence. Certainly black performers—Chuck Berry, for instance—have been rewarded poorly in comparison with lesser white performers—Pat Boone, for instance. Yet after one has recognized this discrimination, one must also remember the white contributions to the dialogue. Contemporary American black music owes a debt to white models—the Scottish-Irish folk heritage and even classical music. Today, when whites take a black song style, they sometimes simply bleach it, but they can also invest it with a different kind of structural clarity and rigor. It may not be "better"—some may even find it stiff—but it may well conform more readily to the dominant white culture in this country. It isn't just that white audiences are more comfortable identifying with and fantasizing about white performers, although that is of course part of it, and natural, too. But we all, blacks and whites, participate in American culture. All of us contribute something to what we borrow, making a hybrid that would be impossible without the interchange. With Talking Heads' soul and African inspirations, this exchange is particularly clear. The music would be unthinkable without the New York art-rock movement, its British equivalent and the modern recording studio. What makes *Remain in Light* fascinating is the very dialectic between Byrne's tense singing and the band's clear-cut formal clarity, in the foreground, and the roiling polyrhythms below.

Byrne's closeness to Eno led to resentments from the other band members. Byrne, they complained, was drifting away from the band and willfully autocratic in his dealings with them, and Eno's influence had become obtrusive. As if in answer, Byrne undertook a solo project without Eno, an overtly "artistic," full-length dance score for Twyla Tharp called *The Catherine Wheel*. Here the African influences were even more direct, with actual African instruments played by an ethnomusicologist. But otherwise for all the personal success Byrne enjoyed from its reception, this score did not differ much from what the Heads do as a group. Eventually, the original four members patched up their differences, and Eno was not involved in recording their fifth studio album, *Speaking in Tongues*. The dissidents were further mollified by the critical and, in the case of Frantz and Weymouth, commercial success of their own solo projects, which helped clarify their creative contribution to Talking Heads as a whole.

These solo projects and collaborations are hardly surprising in the context of the furious cross-pollination that had come to characterize the lower-Manhattan arts scene by the beginning of the eighties. It was *expected* that artists would innovate in as many media as were open to them. New York was attracting a diverse and cosmopolitan group of artists, of whom Eno was only one example. The very nature of the most exciting musical innovation seemed to involve fusions of heretofore distinct styles—rock and classical music, jazz and rock, music and video, performance and dance. Of all these mixtures, the kind of art-rock epitomized by Talking Heads seemed especially vital. Bands like the Heads tried to make art and win an audience, too. The newer bands were even more overtly part of a selfconscious artistic tradition; although some of them still talked about commercial success, they had precious little hope of it. Instead, they made a more hermetic music that borrowed textures, instruments, volume and even attitudes and dress from rock, but then exploited them experimentally in a manner akin to the post-Cageians. The movement was epitomized by Glenn Branca, who had emerged from a late-seventies art-rock band called Theoretical Girls and by the early eighties was making massive sonic onslaughts as indebted to Edgard Varèse as to any rock predecessor. He even called some of his pieces symphonies, and scored No. 1 for eleven electric guitars, winds and a barrage of percussion. His is the loudest music I have ever heard—so loud that no record has yet been able to capture its impact. (His first LP, *The Ascension,* comes reasonably close.)

This interchange among members of the downtown arts community was symbolized by the frequent benefits artists mounted for worthy causes. The annual St. Mark's Poetry Project benefits, where Patti Smith got her start in the early seventies, were the prototypes. As good an example as any was two nights of concerts at a huge Times Square disco called Bond's in June 1981 for the benefit of the Kitchen. Participating artists included "serious" composers—Glass, Reich, Maryanne Amacher; "jazz" musicians— Oliver Lake, George Lewis, Julius Hemphill; art-rockers—Branca, Rhys Chatham; rockers with artistic inclinations—Red Decade, the Love of Life Orchestra, Todd Rundgren, DNA, the Raybeats, the Feelies, Jim Carroll, the Bush Tetras; a rap group—Fab Five Freddy and Friends; dancer-composers—Meredith Monk and Laura Dean; dancers—Douglas Dunn's company; a performance artist—Laurie Anderson; a poet—John Giorno; and video pieces by such as Robert Ashley, Robert Wilson, Nam June Paik, Brian Eno and Talking Heads. Hardly anything looked or sounded alike. But it was demonstrably the product of a cohesive artistic community.

It might be objected that such movements are suspiciously fashionable—seducing artists into trendiness and deflecting them from their true work. If the outsider has an honored place in American musical culture, then a hothouse scene like lower Manhattan's might seem antithetical to isolated originality. In a sense, it is; that's the danger of capitals. Eno himself has said that while New York is a good place for work, he likes to retire to England when he has to *think.* But as I have also indicated, an outsider's sense of self has as much to do with an inner state of mind as with outer geographical location or material circum- stances. Neil Young is an outsider, and he may have made more money than everyone else in this book combined. Besides, for an art work to be seized upon by the fashionable may not be all bad. It is fashionable, in fact, to deride the fashionable, to assume that if something appeals to trendies it is automatically superficial. Yet many great musical works of the past have been enormous, fashionable hits in their time; to think otherwise is to romanticize historical reality. For a piece of new music to appeal to a fashionable audience may indicate that it has the strength to reach beyond a narrow peer group, in the same sense that a composer indicates vitality if he attracts the interest of other artists.

Both Byrne and Eno have expressed restiveness at the limits of rock as an idiom for sustained artistic evolution. Eno is investing much of his energy into avant-garde musical collaborations, "ambient" music and video. Byrne will surely write more theater pieces and has complained about the strictures of the song form: "There's very little rock that interests me, and I often think that I'm pretty much indicative of what other people are thinking. I don't take it personally because, as I said, I don't feel we play rock music any more."

Maybe, maybe not; the lines get blurred at this point, and the need to sort things out into categories becomes less imperative. Whether the band thrives as a quartet or in some mutation, Talking Heads have already proved themselves one of this country's most creative combinations of artistic integrity and popular appeal. "We're in a funny position," Byrne said in 1979. "It wouldn't please us to make music that's impossible to listen to, but we don't want to compromise for the sake of popularity. It's possible to make exciting, respectable stuff that can succeed in the marketplace." But the band's ambitions go further than that, as have its accomplishments to date. The Heads once found themselves as guests on that archetypical teenage rock television show, Dick Clark's *American Bandstand*. Each member was asked his ultimate ambition, and the three men hemmed and hawed. Tina Weymouth, with a sly smile, was more direct: "We want to change the face of music," she said.

BIBLIOGRAPHY AND DISCOGRAPHY

There are no comprehensive listings here of books and articles by and about my subjects, or their complete work lists or discographies. Instead, I mention writings that shaped my thinking about these composers and the issues they suggest. I also mention pieces from which I have drawn significant quotations, and recordings that are referred to in the text or seem otherwise important.

INTRODUCTION

The best single survey of twentieth-century art music by an American author is the second edition of Eric Salzman's *Twentieth-Century Music: An Introduction* (Prentice-Hall, Englewood Cliffs, N.J., 1974). In addition, the *Dictionary of Contemporary Music*, edited by John Vinton (who replaced Salzman in the middle of the project; E. P. Dutton, New York, 1974), is still a very useful, wide-ranging if now somewhat dated reference source, with many comprehensive general articles. And, of course, the relevant individual entries and general articles in *The New Grove Dictionary of Music and Musicians*, edited by Stanley Sadie (Macmillan, London, 1980), should not go unmentioned, along with the new and updated entries in the forthcoming *New Grove Dictionary of Music in the United States*.

A good history of recent musical avant-gardism is the British critic Paul Griffiths's *Modern Music: The Avant Garde Since 1945* (George Braziller, New York, 1981). Another British critic, Michael Nyman, has addressed a narrower subject in his *Experimental Music: Cage and Beyond*

(Schirmer, New York, 1974). This is full of information and insights, but unfortunately skewed by Nyman's distance from the American scene, afflicted with indefensible categorizations and, in a fast-moving field, decisively dated. *Breaking the Sound Barrier: A Critical Anthology of the New Music*, edited by the late Gregory Battcock (E. P. Dutton, New York, 1981), is something of a grab-bag, but does offer a few interesting essays by both composers and critics.

For American music, H. Wiley Hitchcock's *Music in the United States: A Historical Introduction* (second edition, Prentice-Hall, Englewood Cliffs, N.J., 1974), *Wilfrid Mellers's Music in a New Found Land: Themes and Developments in the History of American Music* (Alfred A. Knopf, New York, 1965; republished in paperback by Hillstone, New York, 1974) and Charles Hamm's *Music in the New World* (Norton, New York, 1983) are sound and readable and, crucially, they treat this country's music in both its cultivated and vernacular traditions. Walter Zimmermann, a German journalist, provides a rather eccentric collection of interviews in his hard-to-find *Desert Plants: Conversations with 23 American Musicians* (Walter Zimmermann and A.R.C. Publications, Vancouver, 1976). Robert Ashley gave me access to the manuscript of his forthcoming book version of *Music with Roots in the Aether*, which contains interviews with or articles by eight American experimentalists and essays about them by eight younger composers. Cole Gagne and Tracy Caras's *Soundpieces: Interviews with American Composers* (Scarecrow Press, Metuchen, N.J., and London, 1982) offers question-and-answer interviews with twenty-four living American composers, and includes up-to-date work lists. And, finally, *American Music Recordings: A Discography of Twentieth-Century U.S. Composers*, edited by Carol J. Oja (Institute for Studies in American Music, Brooklyn College, 1982), is a simply invaluable resource.

1 ERNST KRENEK

The principal collections of Krenek's writings in English are *Music Here and Now* (W. W. Norton, New York, 1939), *Exploring Music* (October House, New York, 1966) and *Horizons Circled: Reflections on My Music* (University of California Press, Berkeley, 1974). Krenek's essay "A Composer's Influences" was first printed in *Perspectives of New Music* and reprinted in *Perspectives on American Composers,* edited by Benjamin Boretz and Edward T. Cone (W. W. Norton, New York, 1971). Andrew Porter has written a detailed and highly favorable essay on Krenek's music for *The New Yorker,* reprinted in *Music of Three More Seasons: 1977–1980* (Alfred A. Knopf, New York, 1981). I also made use of Olive Jean Bailey's "The Influence of Ernst Krenek on the Musical Culture of the Twin Cities" (Ph.D. thesis, University of Minnesota, 1980), reprinted by University Microfilms International, Ann Arbor, 1982.

Nearly all of the domestically available recordings of Krenek's music are on the Los Angeles Orion label. Representative examples include a record of his orchestral music (with *Horizon Circled*) conducted by the composer on ORS 78290 and chamber and vocal music (with *The Santa Fe Timetable,* the accordion piece and the score for two pianos and electronic tape) on ORS 75204. Another orchestral disc, with Krenek conducting the Los Angeles Chamber Orchestra, is on Varèse International VR 81200. There is a modern recording of the opera *Jonny Spielt Auf* on the Austrian Amadeo label, AVRS 5038.

2   MILTON BABBITT

Benjamin Boretz's quotations come from the Babbitt entry in Vinton's *Dictionary of Contemporary Music;* the article as a whole, devoted almost exclusively to Babbitt's theory, offers a reasonable balance of fidelity and comprehensibility in the explication of that arcane subject. Gregory Sandow's article about Babbitt, "A Fine Madness," is in the March 16, 1982, *Village Voice.* I have also made use of the Babbitt interview in *Soundpieces.* "Who Cares If You Listen?" was reprinted in *Contemporary Composers on Contemporary Music,* edited by Elliott Schwartz and Barney Childs (Holt, Rinehart and Winston, New York, 1967). It also appears in a sometimes stimulating compendium called *Esthetics Contemporary,* edited by Richard Kostelanetz (Prometheus Books, Buffalo, N.Y., 1978), where its title is that of Babbitt's own choosing, "The Composer as Specialist." "One Hundred Metronomes" by Edward T. Cone appeared in the autumn 1977 issue of the *American Scholar.*

Babbitt's *Philomel* has been reissued on New World 307. *A Solo Requiem* is coupled with music by Mel Powell on Nonesuch N-78006. *All Set,* for jazz ensemble, is on Nonesuch H-71303.

3 ELLIOTT CARTER

The principal Carter collections are *The Writings of Elliott Carter: An American Composer Looks at Modern Music,* edited by Else and Kurt Stone (Indiana University Press, Bloomington and London, 1977), which contains "Music and the Time Screen," and *Flawed Words and Stubborn Sounds: A Conversation with Elliott Carter* by Allen Edwards (W. W. Norton, New York, 1971). In addition, there is a Carter interview in *Soundpieces.* David Schiff's *The Music of Elliott Carter* (Eulenberg Books, London, and Da Capo Press, New York, 1983) is the first extended analysis of the music. Andrew Porter's encomium is reprinted in *Music of Three More Seasons,* and Ned Rorem's polemic was on a mimeographed sheet slipped into the Alice Tully Hall program of the Jan. 29, 1982, New York premiere of his *Remembering Tommy* at the Juilliard Contemporary Music Festival.

Particularly interesting or well-realized recordings of Carter's music include, in chronological order of composition, the Elegy (1943) on Nonesuch D-79002; *The Minotaur,* a ballet suite (1947), on Mercury Golden Imports SRI 75111; the Sonata for cello and piano (1948) and the Sonata for flute, oboe, cello and harpsichord (1952) on Nonesuch H-71234; the Eight Pieces for Four Timpani (1949 and 1966) and the Brass Quintet (1974) on Odyssey Y-34137; the String Quartets Nos. 1 (1951) and 2 (1959) with the Composers Quartet on Nonesuch H-71249; the String Quartets Nos. 2 and 3 (1971) with the Juilliard Quartet on Columbia M-32738; *A Mirror on Which to Dwell* (1976) with Speculum Musicae, coupled with the *Symphony of Three Orchestras* (1977) with Pierre Boulez and the New York Philharmonic, on CBS M-35171; and *Syringa* (1978) with the Concerto for Orchestra (1970), CRI SD 469.

4 JOHN CAGE

Silence: Lectures and Writings was published by the Wesleyan University Press (Middletown, Conn., 1961) and reprinted as a paperback by the M.I.T. Press (Cambridge, Mass., 1966). Other Cage books include *A Year from Monday: New Lectures and Writings* (Wesleyan, 1967), *M: Writings '67–'72* (Wesleyan, 1973), *Empty Words: Writings '73–'78* (Wesleyan, 1981), *X: Writings '79-'82* (Wesleyan, 1983) and *For the Birds,* a conversation with Daniel Charles (Marion Boyars, Boston and London, 1981). There are also *John Cage,* edited by Richard Kostelanetz, a compendium of miscellaneous writings and information (Praeger, New York, 1970), and Cage interviews in *Soundpieces* and *Desert Plants*. Virgil Thomson's "Cage and the Collage of Noises" was most recently reprinted in *A Virgil Thomson Reader* (Houghton Mifflin, Boston, 1981), and I also made use of my own interview with Cage in the March 12, 1982, *New York Times*.

Henry Cowell's *New Musical Resources* was originally published by Alfred A. Knopf, New York, in 1930. It was reprinted with new material in 1969 by the Something Else Press, New York. There is a "descriptive bibliography" entitled *The Writings of Henry Cowell* by Bruce Saylor, a monograph published in 1977 by the Institute for Studies in American Music of Brooklyn College. Rita Mead has provided a detailed history of *Henry Cowell's New Music, 1925–1936: The Society, the Music Editions, and the Recordings* (UMI Research Press, Ann Arbor, 1981). And *American Composers on American Music*, edited by Cowell, first published in 1933 and republished in 1962 by Frederick Ungar, New York, offers a fine picture of American musical life between the wars.

There are many records of Cage's music. His keyboard works, mostly for prepared piano, can be heard in a two-disc collection with Jeanne Kirstein on Columbia M2S 819. Joshua Pierce has made other prepared-piano records on the hard-to-find Tomato label, TOM-2-1001 and TOM-7016. One of Cage's better-known electronic scores is *Fontana Mix*, on Turnabout TV 34046S. There are two different versions of *Variations IV* on Everest 3132 and 3230. A rather modest account of *HPSCHD*, which was worked out in collaboration with Lejaren Hiller, is available on Nonesuch H-71224. Tomato TOM-2-1101 offers the first two books of the more recent *Etudes Australes* for piano, as performed by Grete Sultan. A glimpse of Cage's charming personality as a reader of his own texts can be found on *Indeterminacy*, a Folkways set (FT 3704) with obbligato music by David Tudor.

5   RALPH SHAPEY

The Shapey quotations are taken from my interview with him in the May 10, 1981, Arts and Leisure section of the *New York Times*; from another interview by Shulamit Ran (a composer-colleague at the University of Chicago) in the same section of the *Times* dated May 8, 1977, and from *Soundpieces*.

Rituals and Shapey's notes for it are on CRI SD 275. Other important Shapey recordings include *Praise*, an oratorio from 1961, on CRI SD 355, and the thirty-one *Fromm Variations* for solo piano of 1973 on CRI SD 428.

6   DAVID DEL TREDICI

The Del Tredici quotations come from my interview with him in the Oct. 26, 1980, *New York Times* Arts and Leisure section and from his own notes to the recording of *Final Alice*. John Corigliano's remarks are taken from an article about him by Bernard Holland in the *New York Times* Sunday Magazine of Jan. 31, 1982. Erich Leinsdorf's comment about *Final Alice* is from my interview with him in the Jan. 13, 1980, Arts and Leisure section of the *New York Times*.

The Chicago Symphony *Final Alice* recording is on London LDR 71018. As of this writing, none of the other *Alice* pieces has been released, although *In Memory of a Summer Day* has been recorded by Leonard Slatkin and the St. Louis Symphony for release by Nonesuch Records in 1983. Some of Del Tredici's earlier music is on CRI SD 294. Recorded examples of Corigliano's music include the Clarinet Concerto (with Stanley Drucker and the New York Philharmonic conducted by Zubin Mehta) on New World 309 and the soundtrack album to Ken Russell's film *Altered States* on RCA ABL 1-3983; Corigliano has excerpted music from that soundtrack into a concert suite entitled *Three Hallucinations*.

7   FREDERIC RZEWSKI

The Rzewski quotations are from the interview in *Desert Plants*, and those by Wolff are from his program notes to the recording of *The People United Will Never Be Defeated*. Rochberg's speech was presented at the Conference on Contemporary Music of the 92nd Street Y on Jan. 25–26, 1981, in New York. I have also quoted him from Theodore W. Libbey, Jr.'s notes to the recordings of Rochberg's Fourth, Fifth and Sixth String Quartets.

Rzewski's *Coming Together*, *Les Moutons de Panurge* and *Attica* are on Opus One 20. *The People United* can be found on Vanguard VSD 71248, performed by Ursula Oppens. The *Four Pieces* along with one of the *Four North American Ballads*, played by the composer, are on Vanguard VA

25001, and Paul Jacobs plays the entire *Ballads* set, with music by William Bolcom and Aaron Copland, on Nonesuch D-79006. Speculum Musicae's account of *Song and Dance*, coupled with a John Harbison piece, is on Nonesuch H-71366. The work of Musica Elettronica Viva, the Rome-based live electronic music group of which Rzewski is a member, can be found on Mainstream MS/5002 (out of print) and BYG Actuel 529326 (a French import). Rochberg's Third Quartet is on Nonesuch 71283, and his Fourth, Fifth and Sixth Quartets make up a boxed set, RCA ARL2-4198.

8 ROBERT ASHLEY

There is a particularly interesting Ashley chapter in *Soundpieces*, and a less helpful one in *Desert Plants*. The book version of *Music with Roots in the Aether* will include an Ashley essay and an article on him by the composer Robert Sheff (who performs as Blue Gene Tyranny). Ashley's mimeographed statement on *Perfect Lives (Private Parts)* is entitled *And So It Goes, Depending,* and was copyrighted 1980, and there is also a mimeographed plot synopsis that was distributed at live performances of the opera. Charles Shere's essay on *Perfect Lives* appeared in Vol. 3, No. 1 (the final issue, spring 1982) of *New Performance* magazine.

I wrote a general overview of the experimental-music scene for the catalogue of the 1980 New Music America festival in Minneapolis, published by the Walker Art Center there. Roger Reynolds's *Mind Models* was published by Praeger, New York, 1975. La Monte Young's writings and scores are contained in La Monte Young and Marian Zazeela (his wife), *Selected Writings* (Heiner Friedrich, Munich, 1969) and *An Anthology*, edited by Young (Heiner Friedrich, no city, 1970).

A disc of music by members of the Sonic Arts Union (Lucier, Ashley, Behrman, Mumma) entitled *Electric Sound* and including Ashley's *Purposeful Lady Slow Afternoon* was once available on Mainstream MS/5010. "She Was a Visitor" from *That Morning Thing* is on *Extended Voices*, produced by Behrman, Odyssey 32 16 0156. An Italian import, Cramps CRSLP 6103, has *In Sara, Mencken, Christ and Beethoven There Were Men and Women*. Excerpts from *Perfect Lives (Private Parts)* are on Lovely Music LML 1001, VR 4904 and VR 4908, with the complete work (the title ultimately shortened to *Perfect Lives*) on Lovely Music LMC 4913 and 4947 (cassette only). Lovely Music VR 1002 offers *Automatic Writing*.

9 PHILIP GLASS

There are Glass interviews in *Soundpieces, Desert Plants* and *Music with Roots in the Aether*. A young Belgian critic named Wim Mertens has written a book called *Amerikaanse repetitieve muziek* (W. Vergaelen, Bierbeek, 1980), published in 1983 in England by Kahn and Averill and in New York by Alexander Broude as *American Minimal Music*. On the occasion of the Dutch premiere of *Satyagraha* in 1980, a booklet about the opera was published by Standard Editions, New York. Steve Reich's *Writings About Music* was published by the Press of the Nova Scotia College of Art and Design, Halifax, and New York University Press, 1974.

Glass's major recordings include *Solo Music* (Shandar 83515), *Music with Changing Parts* (Chatham Square LP 1001/2), *Music in Twelve Parts*, Parts One and Two (English Virgin CA2010), *Einstein on the Beach* (Tomato TOM-4-2901), *Dance* Numbers One and Three (Tomato TOM-8029) and *Koyaanisqatsi* (Antilles ASTA 1). *Satyagraha* has not been recorded; his first CBS album, *Glassworks* (FM 37265), provides a good sampler of his various idioms. The two recordings of the rock band Polyrock co-produced by Glass are on RCA AFL1-3714 and AFL1-4043. Riley's *In C* is on Columbia MS-7178. Major Reich recordings are on Deutsche Grammophon DG-2740106, ECM 1129 and ECM 1168.

10 LAURIE ANDERSON

The best collection of writings and information about Anderson is a catalogue called *Laurie Anderson: Works from 1969 to 1983*, edited by Janet Kardon and published by the Institute of Contemporary Art, University of Pennsylvania (Philadelphia, 1983). Early in her career, Anderson published little art books sold sporadically in art stores. Examples are *Notebook*, published by the Collation Center, Artist Book Series No. 1, distributed by Wittenborn Art Books, New York, 1977, and *Words in Reverse*, Top Stories No. 2, no city, 1979. Material for my chapter was taken from "Laurie Anderson: Performance Artist," by Mel Gordon, *Drama Review*, June 1980; from my own interview with her in the *New York Times*, Oct. 27, 1980; and from Eileen Phillips's "O Super

Artist, O Superstar" in the Oct. 17, 1981, *New Musical Express*. RoseLee Goldberg's *Performance: Live Art 1909 to the Present* (Harry N. Abrams, New York, 1979) provides an extensive history of performance art.

Anderson's first LP, *Big Science* (Warner Bros. BSK 3674), consists of "songs from *United States I–IV*" and includes "O Superman." The single of "O Superman," backed by "Walk the Dog," was released in this country first by One Ten Records (no catalogue number) and then, in the same packaging, by Warner Bros. on WBSP 49876. In 1984, she released a second LP, *Mister Heartbreak* (Warner Bros. 25077-1). Her work also appears on a number of compendiums, all interesting in themselves: *Airwaves*, One Ten Records OT 001/2; *New Music for Electronic and Recorded Media*, 1750 Arch Records S-1765; and three of the poet John Giorno's Poetry Systems releases, *Big Ego* (GPS 012-013), *The Nova Convention* (GPS 014-015) and *You're the Guy I Want to Share My Money With* (GPS 020). Hard-to-find records in experimental, jazz and rock idioms may often be obtained through the New Music Distribution Service, 500 Broadway, New York, N.Y. 10012.

11 DAVID BEHRMAN

There is a Behrman interview in *Music with Roots in the Aether*, along with an essay about him by Paul DeMarinis. His early *Runthrough* is on the same out-of-print Mainstream Sonic Arts Union album that also contains Ashley's *Purposeful Lady Slow Afternoon* (MS/5010). The best recorded example of Behrman's mature work is the combination of *On the Other Ocean* and *Figure in a Clearing* on Lovely Music LML 1041. Charles Dodge's *Earth's Magnetic Field* is on Nonesuch H-71250.

12 MAX NEUHAUS

Neuhaus's *Program Notes* was published in Canada by the York University Faculty of Fine Arts in 1974. His other written materials are all mimeographed. There are no recordings of his electronic music; Neuhaus takes his mission as a "site" composer seriously.

13 WALTER MURCH

Material for this chapter was derived from Murch's notes on the production of *THX 1138*, provided by him; unpublished conversations between us; a chapter on Murch in an unpublished book on film sound by Larry Blake; "Making Beaches Out of Grains of Sand" by Jordan Fox in *Cinefex* magazine, Dec. 1980; "The Art of the Sound Editor: An Interview with Walter Murch" by Larry Sturhahn in *Filmmakers Newsletter,* Dec. 1974; and "Murch: The Virtuoso of Movie Sound" by Betty Spence in the *Los Angeles Times* Calendar section, Aug. 30, 1981. Dale Pollock's *Skywriting: The Life and Films of George Lucas* (Harmony Books, New York, 1983) contains interesting information about the evolution of the San Francisco film scene. There is a book about Glenn Gould called *Glenn Gould: Music & Mind* by Geoffrey Payzant (Van Nostrand Reinhold Ltd., Toronto, 1978).

As mentioned in the text, no record of the soundtrack to *THX 1138* was released. The best recent example of Murch's film work can be heard on the soundtrack to *Apocalypse Now* (Elektra DP-90001).

14 THE ART ENSEMBLE OF CHICAGO

A good jazz history is Marshall Stearns's *The Story of Jazz* (Oxford University Press, London, 1956). Quotations from members of the Art Ensemble were taken from a press biography issued in April 1980 by ECM Records; from Rafi Zabor's "Profile: The Art Ensemble" in *Musician* No. 17, April 1979, and from John Litweiler's "The Art Ensemble of Chicago: Adventures in the Urban Bush," in the June 1982 *Down Beat.* Pleasants's *The Agony of Modern Music* was first published by Simon & Schuster, New York, in 1955. The Carter quotation comes from *Flawed Words and Stubborn Sounds,* and Robert Palmer's remarks are from his article in the March 28, 1982, *New York Times* Arts and Leisure section.

Art Ensemble records include *The Paris Session* (Arista Freedom AL 1903), *Live at Mandel Hall* (Delmark DS-432/433), *Fanfare for the Warriors* (Atlantic SD 1651), *Certain Blacks* (Inner City 1004), *Nice Guys* (ECM-1-1126), *Full Force* (ECM-1-1167) and *Urban Bushmen* (ECM-2-1211). There is also a variety of solo and duo albums by ensemble members available on the ECM, 1750 Arch, Muse, Nessa, Black Saint, Delmark, AECO, Sackville, Cecmo and India Navigation labels.

15 KEITH JARRETT

The Jarrett quotations come from "The Inner Octaves of Keith Jarrett" by Bob (now Robert) Palmer, *Down Beat,* Oct. 24, 1974, and "Keith Jarrett's Keys to the Cosmos" by Mikal Gilmore, *Rolling Stone,* Jan. 25, 1979. The Giddins comment was reprinted in his collection *Riding on a Blue Note: Jazz and American Pop* (Oxford University Press, New York and Oxford, 1981).

Jarrett's voluminous recorded output can be discussed in several categories. Ensemble records with his American collaborators include *Expectations* (Columbia PG 31580), *Fort Yawuh* (Impulse AS-9240), *The Survivors' Suite* (ECM-1-1085) and *Eyes of the Heart* (ECM-T-1150). An example of his work with his Scandinavian group is *Nude Ants* (ECM-2-1171). A collaboration with the drummer Jack DeJohnette called *Ruta + Daitya* is on ECM 1021. *Hymns/Spheres* (ECM-2-1086-87) is an organ disc, and *The Moth and the Flame* (ECM-D-1202) offers both piano and organ. Solo piano albums include *Facing You* (ECM 1017), *Solo-Concerts* (ECM 1035-37), *The Köln Concert* (ECM 1064-65), *Staircase* (ECM-2-1090), the ten-disc *Sun Bear Concerts* (ECM 1100) and *Concerts* (ECM-3-1227). The more overtly classical albums are *In the Light* (ECM 1033-34), *Luminessence* (with Jan Garbarek, saxophone, ECM 1049), *The Celestial Hawk* (ECM-1-1175) and *Ritual,* with Dennis Russell Davies at the piano (ECM-1-1112). His recording of piano music by Gurdjieff is on ECM 1174.

16 ORNETTE COLEMAN

The Coleman material was obtained from "Ornette Coleman Makes Waves" by Robert Palmer, *Rolling Stone,* Aug. 25, 1977; Coleman's own "Ornette Coleman: Harmolodics and the Oldest Language" in *Musician* No. 12, May 1–June 15, 1978; "Ornette Coleman: The Long Winding Road Back to L.A." by Leonard Feather, *Los Angeles Times* Calendar section, March 1, 1981; "Ornette, Ready for Prime Time" by Michael Shore, *Soho News,* July 1, 1981; "Focus on Sanity" by Brian Case, *Melody Maker,* June 27, 1981; "Ornette Coleman: Harmolodic Stompdown," by Robert Palmer, *New York Rocker,* Oct. 1981; and Quincy Troupe's "Ornette Coleman: Going Beyond Outside," in *Musician* No. 37, Nov. 1981. The Schuller quotation is from Martin Williams's notes to *The Shape of Jazz to Come.*

Coleman's recordings before the 1970's include *Live at the Hillcrest*

Club (Inner City IC-1007), *Something Else!* (Contemporary 7551), *The Shape of Jazz to Come* (Atlantic 1317), *Change of the Century* (Atlantic 1327), *Free Jazz* (Atlantic S-1364), *The Music of Ornette Coleman* (RCA LSC-2982) and *The Great London Concert* (Arista Freedom AL 1900). More recently, there have been *Skies of America* (Columbia KC 31562), *Dancing in Your Head* (A&M SP-722), *Body Meta* (Artists House AH 1), *Soapsuds Soapsuds* with Charlie Haden (Artists House AH 6) and *Of Human Feelings* (Island/Antilles AN 2001).

17   EDDIE PALMIERI

John Storm Roberts's *The Latin Tinge: The Impact of Latin American Music on the United States* (Oxford University Press, New York and Oxford, 1979) has been challenged by ethnomusicologists, but it remains the only general study of this broad subject. I also made use of Roberts's "Eddie Palmieri on Salsa" in *Stereo Review*, Feb. 1976, and "Eddie Palmieri, Salsaman" by Edmund Newton in the *New York Post*, Sept. 27, 1975.

Palmieri's records include *Eddie Palmieri and his Conjunto "La Perfecta"* (Alegre LPA 817), *Justicia* (Tico SLP-1188), *Harlem River Drive* (Roulette SR 3004), *The Sun of Latin Music* (Coco-109XX), *Lucumi Macumba Voodoo* (Epic 35523) and *Eddie Palmieri* (Barbaro B 205). Most are out of print or difficult to find outside Latin communities.

18   STEPHEN SONDHEIM

Background books include Alec Wilder's *American Popular Song: The Great Innovators, 1900–1950* (Oxford University Press, New York, 1972); Gerald Bordman's *American Musical Theater: A Chronicle* (Oxford, 1978); and Bordman's less ambitious *American Operetta from H.M.S. Pinafore to Sweeney Todd* (Oxford, 1981). I made use of Craig Zadan's *Sondheim & Co.* (Equinox/Avon, New York, 1976), updated in the Da Capo Press edition (New York, 1984), and a *Newsweek* Sondheim cover story by Charles Michener entitled "Broadway's Music Man" in the April 23, 1973, issue. Arlene Croce's *Follies* review was in the July 1971 *Stereo Review.*

Sondheim cast albums include *A Funny Thing Happened on the Way to the Forum* (Capitol SW-1717), *Company* (Columbia OS 3550), *Follies* (Capitol SO-761), *A Little Night Music* (Columbia JS 32265), *Pacific*

Overtures (RCA ARL1-1367), *Sweeney Todd* (RCA CBL2-3379) and *Merrily We Roll Along* (RCA CBL1-4197). In addition, there are several collections and revues that offer miscellaneous Sondheim songs, some from failed or stillborn projects or cut out of Broadway shows before the first night. These include *Side by Side by Sondheim* (RCA CBL2-1851), *Sondheim/A Musical Tribute* (Warner Bros. 2WS-2705) and *Marry Me a Little* (RCA ABL-4159).

There are two modern recordings of Gershwin's *Porgy and Bess*, the more theatrical (and hence superior) Houston Grand Opera version on RCA ARL3-2109, and the more symphonic Cleveland Orchestra account on London 13116. Weill's *Street Scene* is not available on records. Bernstein's *West Side Story* is on Columbia JS-32603, and his *Candide* is on Columbia OS-2350, with the 1973 revision on Columbia S2X-32923.

19 NEIL YOUNG

There are no coherent, critically distinguished histories of rock & roll. The best book on rock is Greil Marcus's *Mystery Train: Images of America in Rock 'n' Roll Music* (E. P. Dutton, New York, 1975). The revised edition of *The Rolling Stone Illustrated History of Rock & Roll*, edited by Jim Miller (Random House/Rolling Stone Press, New York, 1980), is also valuable. For Young specifically, I used "Neil Young: The Last American Hero" by Cameron Crowe in the Feb. 8, 1979, issue of *Rolling Stone;* "Neil, Feelin' Groovy!" by Ray Coleman in the April 10, 1976, *Melody Maker;* and my own article about him in the Nov. 27, 1977, Arts and Leisure section of the *New York Times*.

Decade (Warner Bros. 3RS 2257) is a particularly well-chosen, three-disc compendium of Young's work up until 1976, and comes complete with his laconically apt program notes. Important individual albums include *After the Gold Rush* (Reprise 2283), *Harvest* (Reprise 2282), *Time Fades Away* (Reprise 2151), *On the Beach* (Reprise 6317), *Tonight's the Night* (Reprise 2221), *Zuma* (Reprise 2242), *Rust Never Sleeps* (Warner Bros. HS 2295) and *Trans* (Geffen GHS 2018).

20 TALKING HEADS

Fan books are mostly disposable, but *Talking Heads* by Miles (Omnibus Press, London, 1981) is smarter than the norm, primarily because of its subjects. For background, my own chapters "Art Rock" and "The Sound of Manhattan" are in the revised edition of *The Rolling Stone Illustrated History of Rock & Roll*. I also used my "Talking Heads: Cool in the Glare of Hot Rock" in the March 24, 1976, *New York Times*; "Talking Heads: Psychodramas You Can Dance To" by Mikal Gilmore in the Nov. 29, 1979, *Rolling Stone*; and Adam Sweetling's "A Head of His Time" in the Aug. 1, 1981, *Melody Maker*. A good overview of the downtown New York art-rock scene appeared in the June 1982 *New York Rocker*.

The five Talking Heads studio albums are *Talking Heads: 77* (Sire SRK 6036), *More Songs About Buildings and Food* (Sire SRK 6058), *Fear of Music* (Sire SRK 6076), *Remain in Light* (Sire SRK 6095) and *Speaking in Tongues* (Sire 23883). The two-disc live album, released in 1982, is called *The Name of This Band Is Talking Heads* (Sire 2SR 3590). David Byrne's solo albums are *My Life in the Bush of Ghosts*, a collaboration with Brian Eno (Sire SRK 6093), and *The Catherine Wheel* (the "songs" are on Sire SRK 3645; the complete score is on Sire cassette only M5S 3645). Other Talking Heads solo projects are Tina Weymouth and Chris Frantz's Tom Tom Club (Sire SRK 3628 and 23916-1) and Jerry Harrison's *The Red and the Black* (Sire SRK 3631).

The best Velvet Underground record is *Live 1969* (Mercury 7504). Patti Smith's best is *Horses* (Arista 4066). Examples of Eno's work include *No Pussyfooting* (Island HELP 16), a synthesizer-guitar duet disc with Robert Fripp; *Taking Tiger Mountain by Strategy* (Island ISLP 9309) and *Another Green World* (Island ISLP 9351), both "rock" records; and *Discreet Music* (Obscure 3) and *Ambient Music No. 1 Music for Airports* (PVC 7908), both avant-garde background music. Some of Eno's discs flicker in and out of print. Glenn Branca's *The Ascension* is on 99 Records 99-01 LP, and his Symphony No. 1 (*Tonal Plexus*), on ROIR (pronounced "roar") A 125 (cassette only).

INDEX

A

ABC Leisure Magazines, 138

Abrams, Muhal Richard, 169–70

abstract composers, 54, 61, 62, 67, 73, 76, 96, 115

academic establishment: composers in, 32–4, 60–1, 68, 69, 98, 100, 120, 122; and serialism, 25, 26, 30, 33–4, 36

acoustics, 99, 119, 140, 144; *see also* sound

Adams, John, 80

Adorno, Theodor W., 22, 92–4, 231

African influence, 11, 51, 166, 167, 169–70, 171, 174, 196, 200, 202, 241–2, 243

"After the Ball," 210

Aida (Verdi), 57

Air, 170

Akalaitis, JoAnne, 116

Altered States (film), 158

Amacher, Maryanne, 148, 149, 244

ambient music, 149–50, 241, 245

American Composers Orchestra, 64, 130

American Graffiti (film), 156

American music, 50, 77–8, 134; accessibility of, 5, 93, 145; art music, 4, 6, 7, 10, 16–18, 22–4, 48, 117, 165; commercialization of, 93, 95, 120, 127, 231–2; dialogue between vernacular and cultivated, 3–5, 7–8, 204; diversity of, 6, 9, 17, 35–6, 138; fusions in, 3, 5, 12, 35–6, 243–5; influences on, 9–10, 15–17, 226; prejudices in, 5–6, 209; *see also individual musical forms*

American Scholar, 34

amplification: audience response to, 193; in experimental music, 105, 109–10, 119, 121; in jazz, 133, 194; in rock, 74, 105, 115, 121, 133, 143–4, 192–3, 194, 224, 227, 228; in theater, 193; *see also* electronic music

Amsterdam, Holland, 118

anarchism, 84, 110, 187–8; *see also* Cage, John

Anderson, Laurie, 11, 123–32, 218; music of, 130; as performance artist, 124–7, 129–32, 172, 244

Anderson (*continued*)
  Works: *As: If,* 124; *Big Science,*
  125, 127, 130; *It's Cold Outside,*
  130; *Mister Heartbreak,* 130;
  "O Superman (for Massenet)," 127;
  United States I–IV, 125; "Walk the
  Dog," 125
Ann Arbor, Mich., 33, 96, 98, 99
Ansermet, Ernest, 76, 192
Antheil, George, 17
Anyone Can Whistle (show), 214
Apocalypse Now (film), 156, 161
Art Ensemble of Chicago, 11, 164,
  170–6, 189; improvisation by,
  171–3; recordings, 170–1
  Work: *Urban Bushmen,* 170
Artforum, 116
Artistics, the, 237
artists, 43, 62, 128; appeal of
  innovative music to, 62–3; and
  minimalism, 104, 115–16; patrons
  of, 68; visual, 145, 148, 152–3
Artists House, 196
art music: American, 4, 6, 7, 10, 16–
  18, 22–4, 48, 117, 165; European,
  14, 45, 209–10; third-world, 77,
  129, 172, 188, 192; Western, 7–8,
  47, 51, 76, 112, 164–6, 171, 192,
  226
art-rock, 11, 12, 102–3, 127, 234–
  45; innovations and fusions in,
  243–5
arts, the: affinity to composers, 62–3,
  107, 115–16, 127–8, 237, 243–4;
  conceptual, 96, 104, 109, 119, 145;
  defined, 226; innovations and
  fusions in, 243–5; minimalism in,
  104, 115–16, 235, 237; and
  modernism, 21; and science, 31–2,
  143, 146; visual, 237; *see also*

individual arts; New York, N.Y.:
  downtown (SoHo) arts community
Ashbery, John, 40
Ashley, Robert, 10–11, 96–108, 116,
  119, 124, 135, 137, 244;
  experimental music, 96, 98–101;
  interest in spontaneity in jazz, 99–
  100; mixed media, 101–8, 128,
  129, 218; and sound, 99, 103, 104,
  144
  Works: *Automatic Writing,* 103;
  *In Sara, Mencken, Christ and
  Beethoven There Were Men and
  Women,* 101; *Music with Roots in
  the Aether* (book), 98, 139; *Perfect
  Lives (Private Parts),* 102–3, 104,
  105–7, 108, 125; *Purposeful Lady
  Slow Afternoon,* 101; "She Was a
  Visitor," 101, 104; *That Morning
  Thing,* 101; *Wolfman, The,* 105
Aspen Festival, 72, 110
Association for the Advancement of
  Creative Musicians (AACM), 169–
  70
atonality, 20, 76–7
Attica Prison uprising, 85
audiences: and amplification, 193;
  composers' attitude toward, 10,
  30–4, 45, 63, 81–3, 89, 104–5;
  creativity of, and experimental
  music, 52, 53–4, 57, 97, 101, 103,
  109–10, 119, 140, 147, 154, 160–
  1, 233; nostalgia in, 168–9, 195,
  202; response to complexity and
  innovation, 42, 63, 64, 109, 165,
  244–5; selfconsciousness of, 80,
  227; stylistic pressure from, 119–
  20, 122, 224, 232, 240; *see also
  individual musical forms*
avant-gardism, 14, 27, 39, 87, 124,

236; atonality, 20; classical, 71, 84, 85, 97, 131, 136, 165, 172, 180, 195–6; contemporary, 116, 241; fusion, 12, 243–5; jazz, 187, 195–6; musical theater, 113, 116, 117, 212; operas, 99; political spirit, 84, 85, 92; radical, 213; recordings, 137; *see also* New York, N.Y.: downtown (SoHo) arts community

B

Babbitt, Milton, 10, 11, 25–36, 47, 96, 97, 135, 144, 188; and abstraction, 53–4, 115; as academic, 25, 26, 30, 33–4, 72, 213, 220; attitude toward audience, 30–2, 42, 54; complexity of music, 25, 28–32, 36, 40, 53–4, 143; interest in mathematics, 26–7, 31, 54; program notes of, 27–8; and serialism, 18, 25–36 *passim*, 38, 60, 71, 213
    Works: *All Set*, 28, 35; *Aria da Capo*, 27; *Dual*, 27–8; *Philomel*, 29; *Solo Requiem*, 28; String Quartet No. 3, 28; "Who Cares If You Listen?" (essay), 30–1, 36, 82
Bacewicz, Grazyna, 78
Bach, Johann Sebastian, 86
ballet, 38, 52
Band, the, 230
Barbaro, 207
Barnard College, 124
baroque music, 166; neo-, 180
Bartók, Béla, 165, 180, 183
Barwood, Hal, 159
Bauhaus, 56, 61
Beatles, the, 174, 197, 223, 226; *Sgt.*

Pepper's Lonely Hearts Club Band, 234
Beats, the, 56
bebop, 165, 168, 171, 172, 194; *see also* jazz
Becker, John J., 98
Beckley, Connie, 132
Beeson, Jack, 212
Beethoven, Ludwig van, 42, 57, 66, 87, 88, 89–90, 130, 203; Eighth Symphony, 131; *Fidelio*, 90; Ninth Symphony, 90, 151–2
Behrman, David, 99, 133–44; electronic music, 11, 133, 135, 139–43; equipment and technology of, 139–40, 141, 146
    Works: *Figure in a Clearing*, 140–1; *On the Other Ocean*, 140–1; *Runthrough*, 139; *Sound Fountain* (with DeMarinis), 140
Behrman, S. N., 136
Bell Laboratories, 134, 146
Benson, George, 176, 184
Berg, Alban, 19
Bergman, Ingmar, 215
Bergsma, William, 110
Berio, Luciano, 78; *Sinfonia*, 78–9
Berklee School of Music, 177
Berlin, Irving, 210
Berlin, Ger., 92, 212
Berlioz, Hector, 32, 66
Bernstein, Leonard, 6, 76, 132, 192, 217–18; *Candide*, 211, 212; *West Side Story*, 205, 211, 214
Bernstein, Sid, 197
Berry, Chuck, 242
Billings, William, 16
Bishop, Elizabeth, 40
black music, 174–5, 202, 222; jazz, 11, 22, 100, 164–73, 177; popular,

black music (*continued*)
11, 22, 167, 196, 199; rock, 242;
spirituals, 209, 226
Black Stallion, The (film), 156
Blackwell, Ed, 187
Blakey, Art, 176, 177
Blank, Les, 202
Bley, Carla, 196
Blitzstein, Marc, 91
Blondie, 236
blues, 171, 179, 187, 189, 192, 222,
226, 242
Bond's, 244
Book of the Dead, 102
Boone, Pat, 242
Boosey & Hawkes (publisher), 65
Boretz, Benjamin, 25, 26–7
Boston, Mass., 69
Boston Globe, 80
Boston Symphony Orchestra, 79, 80,
180
Boulanger, Nadia, 17, 38, 110, 111,
117, 177
Boulez, Pierre, 26, 41, 121, 134, 146;
Domaine Musical Series, 111
Bowie, David, 224
Bowie, Lester, 170, 172, 173, 174
Brahms, Johannes, 87, 88
Branca, Glenn, 121–2, 127, 243–4;
The Ascension, 244
Brant, Henry, 158
Braxton, Anthony, 85, 136, 170, 183
Brecht, Bertolt, 91, 92
Britain, 4, 37, 93–4, 211; rock in,
194, 234, 235, 237, 240, 242; *see
also* United Kingdom
Broadway musicals, 4, 11, 22, 210–
20; audience at, 212–13, 215;
comedy, 210, 212; orchestration
for, 217–18; revivals, 212; and

rock, 219; *see also* musical theater
Brooklyn Academy of Music, 125
Brooklyn College, 138
Brown, Earle, 58, 146
Brown, James, 196
Browne, Jackson, 94, 231
Bruckner, Anton, 118
Buffalo Springfield, 223
Burden, Chris, 128
Burroughs, William, 75
Bush Tetras, the, 244
Busoni, Ferruccio, 22, 61
Byrds, the, 222, 223
Byrne, David, 12, 237–9, 241–3,
245; *Catherine Wheel, The*, 243;
My Life in the Bush of Ghosts (with
Eno), 241–2

C

cabarets: revival of, 219–20
Cage, John, 10, 16, 17, 47–8, 50–9,
79, 96, 137, 146; and audience, 52,
53–4, 57, 103, 160–1; circus
concerts of, 53; electronic music of,
52–3; experimental music, 47, 50–
9, 84, 97, 104, 105–6, 110, 118–
19, 187; interest in rhythm, 50,
51–2; Oriental influence on, 52,
55–7, 58–9; percussion scores, 50,
51; prepared piano scores, 51–2,
57
Works: *Atlas eclipticalis*, 53; *Etudes
australes*, 53; *4'33"*, 52, 103, 151;
Freeman Etudes, 53; *HPSCHD*, 53;
Imaginary Landscape No. 1, 52;
Indeterminacy (recorded writings),
53; *Roaratorio*, 54; *Seasons, The*, 52;
Silence (writings), 53, 54–6, 119;

String Quartet, 52; *Variations IV*, 53

Cale, John, 235

California, 15, 48, 186

Camerata, 162

Cardew, Cornelius, 93

Cariou, Len, 217

Carnegie Hall, 151, 180

Carroll, Jim, 244

Carroll, Lewis, 72, 73, 75

Carter, Elliott, 10, 12, 37–46, 47, 58, 79, 106, 166, 182, 197; and American culture, 43–5, 48, 91; complexity of music, 40–4, 74, 228

Works: First String Quartet, 38–9, 44; "Music and the Time Screen" (essay), 39, 46; *Symphony of Three Orchestras*, 41, 45; Third String Quartet, 40, 41, 45

Castro, Fidel, 200

Cavalleria Rusticana (Mascagni), 217

chamber music, 40, 41–2, 61

Chance, James, 197

Chaplin, Charles, 43

Charles Lloyd Quartet, 177

Chatham, Rhys, 122, 244

Chatham Square, 196

Chávez, Carlos, 50

Cherry, Don, 186, 187

Chicago, Ill., 60, 66, 68–9, 98; jazz in, 164, 169, 195

Chicago Symphony Orchestra, 64, 72

Chicago Tribune, 72

Childs, Lucinda, 116

Chilean leftist music, 86

China, 93

choral music, 38, 61, 101, 102

Chowning, John, 135

Christensen, Jon, 178

Christo, 145, 148, 152

chromaticism, 18–19, 73

Clark, Dick: *American Bandstand*, 244

Clark, Tom, 229

classical music, 3–4, 10, 71, 81, 98, 130, 145, 168; amplification in, 74; fusion with other musical forms, 5, 35, 77–9. 164–5, 167–8, 176–85, 242, 243; jazz influence on, 164–5; neo-classical, 37, 38, 39, 56, 76, 88, 131, 180, 183; new music, 71, 193; recordings, 137, 176, 194, 232; relation to society of, 7, 90, 94; traditionalists, 6, 7, 14–15, 40, 43–5, 47, 77, 146, 195; *see also* orchestras

Clinton, George, 6, 196

Coco, 205

Cocteau, Jean, 39

Coleman, Ornette, 11, 182, 185–98, 203; funk-jazz, 186, 189, 191, 192–4, 196, 201; harmolodic theory of, 186–9

Works: *Change of the Century*, 187; *Dancing in Your Head*, 190–1; *Free Jazz*, 187; *Of Human Feelings*, 191; *Oldest Language, The*, 191; *Shape of Jazz to Come, The*, 187; *Skies of America*, 189–90, 191

Cologne, Ger., 134

Coltrane, John, 187

Columbia-Princeton Electronic Music Center, 26, 134–5

Columbia Records, 189, 190, 191; Masterworks, 137

Columbia University, 26, 33–4, 39, 124, 136

Como Park Conservatory, 147

Company (show), 214, 215, 216, 218

complexity in music, 3, 5, 10, 61; and

complexity in music (*continued*)
audiences, 42, 165; electronic
music, 142–3; equation between
excellence and, 43, 166, 226; jazz,
166, 182–3, 187; and performers,
34, 41–2, 49, 74–5; *see also*
individual composers
composers: academic, 32–4, 60–1,
68, 69, 98, 100, 120, 122; affinity
to artists and poets, 62–3, 107,
115–16, 127–8, 237, 243–4;
attitude of society toward, 30–2,
152–3, 203; attitude toward
audiences, 10, 30–4, 45, 63, 81–3,
89, 104–5; Boulanger's training of,
17, 38, 110, 111, 117, 177; in
capitals, 48, 69, 132, 244;
collaboration among, 96, 106–7,
128, 173–4, 218; early rejection of
works (lag theory), 45, 63, 65, 105;
ensembles of, 121; goals of, 31,
81–2, 119; innovation through
imitation, 112; inspirations of, 38,
181–2; jealousy and hostility
among, 5–6, 34–5, 65, 81, 110,
114, 184; and music publishers, 65
need for record exposure, 138–9;
opposed to fixation on performers,
65; outsiders, 8–9, 44, 48–9, 58,
60, 64–7, 69–70, 82, 121, 128,
184, 185, 197, 244; patrons of, 31–
3, 34, 35, 42, 67–8, 81, 91, 122,
127–8; -performers, 130, 136;
pressures on, 82–3, 119–20, 224;
selfconsciousness of, 7–8, 16, 17,
227; and text, 39, 40, 73–5, 101–
6, 125; women, 11, 124, 131–2
composition: eclectic, 75, 76–7, 78,
86–7, 89, 120, 158, 179–80; and
recording studio technology, 240;

relation between theory and
practice in, 29–30; repetition in,
74, 81, 85, 104, 113, 115, 204,
228; text-sound, 101–6, 125
computer music, 52–3, 138–9, 140–
1, 143, 225; centers for, 134–5; *see
also* electronic music
Cone, Edward T., 33, 34–5; "One
Hundred Metronomes," 34–5
consonance, 74, 97, 112; of nature, 76
contemporary music, 26–7, 86, 98,
111, 114, 216; avant-gardists, 116,
241; opera, 107–8, 115, 117–18;
and orchestras, 34, 41–2, 51, 74–
5, 79–82; traditionalists, 15, 77,
106, 110; *see also* new music
Conversation, The (film), 156
Coolidge, Clark, 53
Cooperative Studio for Electronic
Music, 98
Copland, Aaron, 5, 17, 18, 38, 43, 50,
91, 235
Coppola, Francis Ford, 156, 158, 160,
161
Corea, Chick, 178, 194–5
Corigliano, John, 74–5, 82, 158
corporations: as patrons, 68
counterpoint, 39, 62, 74, 114
country music, 93, 168, 192, 209,
222, 227, 242; audiences, 204, 223;
concert circuits, 201–2; -rock, 223
Cowell, Henry, 4, 16, 17, 24, 48, 49–
50, 96, 97; *New Musical Resources*
(book), 49–50; *Quartet Romantic*,
49
Crane, Hart, 40, 45
Crazy Horse, 223, 225
Creative Construction Company, 170
critics, 7, 12, 42–3, 78, 80, 100–1,
105, 116, 128

Croce, Arlene, 218
Crosby, David, 223
Crosby, Stills and Nash, 223
Crosby, Stills, Nash and Young, 223
Cross, Christopher, 231
Crow Indians, 190, 191
Crumb, George, 6, 78, 81
Cubans, 199, 200, 204, 206
culture, *see* society and culture
Cunningham, Merce, 50, 58, 137, 140

D

Dada, 61, 127
Dallapiccola, Luigi, 61
dance, 63, 107, 115, 116, 128, 173, 243, 244; Latin music for, 198, 200, 201, 206; popular music for, 192, 196
Daniels, Charlie: "In America," 94
Danielsson, Palle, 178
Darmstadt, Ger., 26
Davidovsky, Marion, 135
Davies, Dennis Russell, 118, 130, 180, 212
Davies, Peter Maxwell, 121
Davis, Clive, 137
Davis, Miles, 6, 177, 178, 189, 191, 197; *Bitches Brew*, 194
Dean, Laura, 116, 244
Debussy, Claude, 165
DeJong, Constance, 117
Del Tredici, David, 10, 35, 71–83, 84, 96, 110, 172, 180; audience response to, 72, 79; fusion with popular music by, 78–9; use of tonality, 72–4, 76–7, 82–3

Works: *Alice* series, 72, 73–5, 78, 79, 80; *Final Alice*, 72, 73–4, 79, 81, 82; *Happy Voices*, 80
DeMaria, Walter, 235
DeMarinis, Paul, 139–40
democracy: and music, 22–3, 31, 35–6, 91; and racism, 167, 169–70
Deschanel, Caleb, 159
Desprez, Josquin, 14
Dessau, Paul, 92
Diamond, Neil, 231
disco, 196, 206–7, 220; funk-, 196–7
dissonance, 14, 62, 73, 74, 76, 77, 97, 112, 165, 231; jazz, 165, 168, 182–3, 187
DNA, 244
Dodge, Charles, 138–9; *Earth's Magnetic Field*, 139
Dramaturg, 80–1
Dresher, Paul, 122
drugs, 113; and rock, 224–5, 230
Dunn, Douglas, 109–10, 244
Dupree, Cornell, 205
Dvořák, Anton, 210
Dylan, Bob, 6, 94, 126–7, 194, 202, 222–3, 225, 226, 233, 240; "Blowin' in the Wind," 95

E

"ear music," 29, 42, 53, 63, 192
Eckhart, Meister, 56
ECM, 168, 178
Einstein, Albert, 62
Eisler, Hanns, 85, 92
electronic music, 7, 11, 49, 85, 87, 96, 133–44; and audience, 141–2, 154; centers for, 134–5; complexity of, 142–3; and

electronic music (*continued*)
  computers, 134–5; and
  environmental composers, 145,
  146, 149, 153; and
  experimentalists, 52, 101, 103, 136;
  humanized, 133; improvisation in,
  136, 139; and jazz, 136; and live
  performance, 136, 140–1; *musique
  concrète,* 11, 134, 154–5, 160; in
  performance art, 125, 127; and
  pop, 194; recordings, 138; and
  rock, 121–2, 130, 135, 143–4,
  194, 225, 240; and serialism, 25,
  26, 28, 34
Elektra-Asylum, 138
Emerson, Ralph Waldo: "The
  American Scholar," 16
Emerson, Lake and Palmer, 234
Eno, Brian, 143, 149–50, 244, 245;
  and Talking Heads, 240–3;
  Music for Airports, 150; *My Life in
  the Bush of Ghosts* (with Byrne),
  241–2
ensembles, *see* groups
environmental composers, 11, 145–
  53; ambient music, 149–50, 241,
  245; and audience, 150–1; and
  electronic music, 145, 146, 149,
  153; intrusion of, 152
Epic, 206
Erickson, Robert, 100
Europe, 15, 91; art music, 14, 45,
  209–10; film directors from, 159;
  music directors from, 79, 211; jazz
  in, 168, 177, 196; *Klangfarbenschule*
  compositions in, 63, 78, 179;
  musical culture, 3–4, 5, 8, 11, 13,
  16, 43–4, 91–2, 100, 211;
  serialism in, 21–2, 25–6, 35; tours
  of American contemporary music

in, 116–17, 118, 125
Europop, 206
Evans, Gil, 201
experimentalists, 7, 10, 18, 45, 78, 86,
  87, 93, 131, 226; and amplification,
  105, 109–10, 119, 121; and
  creativity of audience, 52, 53–4,
  57, 97, 101, 103, 109–10, 119,
  140, 147, 154, 160–1, 233;
  criticism of, 34–5, 101, 105, 110,
  146; defining, 97–8; leadership, 4,
  17, 24, 47, 49–50, 57–9, 84, 96,
  98–101, 118–19; multi-media, 10,
  99, 101–6; Oriental influence on,
  52, 55–7, 58–9, 97, 112–13, 131,
  174; patrons of, 67–8; and sound,
  99, 103, 104; traditionalists, 77,
  106, 110; *see also individual
  composers;* New York, N.Y.:
  downtown (SoHo) arts community
expressionism, 21, 28; abstract, 28,
  54, 62, 115
"eye music," 29, 53, 192

F

Fab Five Freddy and Friends, 244
Fahey, John, 204
Fania All Stars, 200
Fauré, Gabriel, 118
Favors Maghostut, Malachi, 170
Feelies, the, 244
Fela Anikulapo Kuti, 202
Feldman, Morton, 58, 146
film composers, 5, 81, 154, 157–63;
  musique concrète tradition, 11, 154–
  5, 160; sound editing, 11, 154–7,
  160–3; *see also* Hollywood
Five Spot, 187

folk music, 4, 8, 51, 93, 183, 202, 204, 210, 226–7; audiences, 203; fusion with other musical forms, 49, 167; influence of, 4–5, 57, 165, 183, 209; political, 85–6, 202; purists, 226; -rock, 130, 223, 225, 226, 228, 235; and rock, 12, 225, 226–7; Scottish Irish, 167, 226–7, 242

Follies (show), 214, 215, 216, 218

Ford Foundation, 110

42nd Street (show), 212

Foster, Stephen, 209

foundations: as patrons, 32, 35, 68, 81, 110–11, 122

Frankfurt school, 92

Frantz, Chris, 237, 241, 243

Freeman, Betty, 67–8, 81

French music, 4, 41, 78, 116–17, 131, 134; influence of, 10, 15–16, 17, 18, 22, 37–8, 41; *musique concrète* tradition, 11, 154–5

Freyer, Achim, 118

Friml, Rudolf, 213

Fripp, Robert, 235

Fromm, Paul, 67, 68, 81

funk, 93, 145; -disco, 196–7; -jazz, 186, 189, 191, 193, 196–7, 201; -pop, 167

Funny Thing Happened on the Way to the Forum, A (show), 214

fusion, 3, 5, 35–6; avant-garde, 12, 243–5; *see also individual musical forms*

G

galleries, 116, 196, 237–8; performance art in, 107, 125, 127–8

gamelans, 51, 57, 85

Garbarek, Jan, 178

Germany, 15, 78, 92, 116, 118, 134, 168, 202, 211; culture of, 21, 23–4; influence of music of, 10, 17, 38, 41

Gershwin, George, 5, 210; *Porgy and Bess*, 211, 212

Gesualdo, Don Carlo, 203

Gibran, Kahlil, 181

Giddins, Gary, 183, 184

Gilbert, W. S., 210, 214

Gillespie, Dizzy, 198

Ginsberg, Allen, 56

Giorno, John, 244

Glanville-Hicks, Peggy, 180

Glass, Philip, 38, 109–22, 128, 196, 244; in downtown New York arts community, 115–16; ensemble of, 109–10, 114, 118, 121–2, 135; European tours of, 116–17; minimalist music, 11, 104, 110, 113–16, 118, 241; operas of, 11, 115, 117–18; Oriental influence on, 112–13; rhythmic complexities, 77, 104, 109, 111, 113–15, 119, 121; and rock, 11, 112, 118–22, 235; theater compositions, 113, 116, 117; use of amplification, 121, 192

Works: *Dance*, 116; *Einstein on the Beach* (with Wilson), 107, 114, 117–18, 120, 235; *Music in Twelve Parts*, 115, 117; *Music with Changing Parts*, 109–10, 116; *Satyagraha*, 117–18, 120, 212

Gluck, Christoph Willibald, 203

Godfather I (film), 156

Godfather II (film), 156

Goldsmith, Jerry, 158

Gordon, Peter, 102–3
Górecki, Henryk, 78
gospel, 171, 179
Gottschalk, Louis Moreau, 16
Gould, Glenn, 162, 179, 240; *The Idea of North*, 162
government: as patron, 33, 35, 68, 91
Graham, Larry, 196
Grammy Awards, 206
Grand Union, 173
Griffes, Charles Tomlinson, 16
Group for Contemporary Music, 34, 61
groups, 34, 121, 158; and improvisation, 172–3, 178
Gruenberg, Louis: *The Emperor Jones*, 212
Guarneri String Quartet, 171
Guggenheim Museum, 116
Gurdjieff, G. I., 180, 181
Guthrie, Woody, 202
Gypsy (show), 214

H

Haden, Charlie, 177, 178, 187
Halprin, Ann, 100
Hamm, Charles: *Music in the New World*, 3
Hammerstein, Oscar II, 213
Hancock, Herbie, 178, 194–5
happenings, 52–3, 85, 99, 101, 107, 124, 127, 129
harmony, 39, 114–15, 139–40, 141, 192
Harris, Roy, 5, 17, 18, 91
Harrison, Jerry, 237–8, 241
Harrison, Lou, 17, 48, 50, 112
Hartmann, Thomas de, 181

Harvard College, 84, 136
hashish, 113
Haydn, Franz Joseph, 8, 131
"head music," 53
Heinrich, Anthony Philip, 16
Helps, Robert, 72
Hemphill, Julius, 244
Hendrix, Jimi, 197
Henri, Pierre, 155
Herder, Johann Gottfried von, 23, 230
Higgins, Billy, 186, 187
High Fidelity, 30
Hindemith, Paul, 24, 61, 180; *Gebrauchsmusik*, 92
hippie movement, 111, 204, 230
Hitchcock, H. Wiley: *Music in the United States: A Historical Introduction*, 3
Hofmannsthal, Hugo von, 214
Holland, 116–17, 118, 152
Hollander, John, 29
Hollies, the, 223
Hollywood: films, 231–2; musicals, 4, 210, 227; *see also* film composers
Hollywood Bowl, 151
Hovhaness, Alan, 180
Hudson River Museum, 140
humor, 130–1
hymns, 179

I

I Ching, 47, 52, 54
Idea of North, The (radio program), 162
immigrants, 4, 91, 158; influence on music by, 4, 10, 15, 18, 24, 67, 202–3
improvisation, 166, 181; criticism of,

165–6, 182; in electronic music, 136, 139; in jazz, 36, 136, 164, 165–6, 168, 171–3, 178, 187, 193, 195, 196, 201

Indian influence, 51, 56, 111–13

Institut de Recherche et de Coordination Acoustique/Musique (IRCAM), 134

intellectuals: American, 8, 9, 17, 23, 32, 66, 164–5, 167, 211; black, 174; and jazz, 164–5, 167; and political music, 92–3; and rock, 227, 236

International Society for Contemporary Music (ISCM), 18, 49, 50

Intrusive Burials (film), 156

Irakere, 200

Israel, Steven Ben, 85

Italy, 89

Ives, Charles, 4, 16, 39, 44, 48, 53, 64, 78–9, 97, 119, 180

the Light, 180; *Köln Concert,* 179, 184; *Moth and the Flame, The,* 179; *Ritual,* 180; *Solo Concerts,* 179; *Staircase,* 179; *Sun Bear Concerts,* 179

jazz, 4, 11, 28, 39, 63, 82, 85, 92–3, 95, 97, 130, 131, 244; amplification in, 133, 194; arrangers, 201; audiences, 168–9, 190, 195; avant-garde, 187, 195, 196; black, 11, 22, 100, 164–73, 177; complexity in, 166, 182–3, 187; cool, 168, 171; cooperatives, 169–73; defined, 164–5; dissonance in, 165, 168, 182–3, 187; and electronic music, 136; European, 168; "free," 168, 171, 172, 187–9; funk-, 186, 189, 191, 193, 196–7, 201; fusion with other musical forms, 5, 35, 77, 164–5, 167–8, 176–85; -gamelan, 85; history, 168–9, 171; improvisation in, 36, 136, 164, 165–6, 168, 171–3, 178, 187, 193, 195, 196, 201; Latin, 198; new, 116, 166, 169, 173, 195–7, 235; opera, 15; pop-, 168, 193–5; punk-191; recordings, 137, 164, 169, 176, 184, 194, 196, 232; rhythm in, 164, 166; rock-, 94, 193–5, 196–7, 205, 243; spontaneity in, 99–100, 171; traditionalists, 168, 176, 192, 194–5; white, 167–8

Jenkins, Leroy, 170, 183

Jimenez, Flaco, 202

Joachim, Joseph, 41

Johnson, J. J., 200

Johnson, Mimi, 103, 140

Jonathan Richman and the Modern Lovers, 237

Jones, Brian, 191

J

Jackson, Ronald Shannon, 191, 197

Jagger, Mick, 222

Jajouka, 191

Japanese culture, 43

Jarman, Joseph, 170, 172

Jarrett, Keith, 11, 176–85; diversity of, 11, 177–8; and jazz groups, 177–8, 183, 187; orchestral composing, 182–3; piano performances, 178–82; success of, 176, 178–9, 184

Works: *Celestial Hawk, The,* 180; *Concerts,* 179; *Facing You,* 178; *In*

Journey Through the Past (film), 225

Joyce, James, 54, 75

Judd, Donald, 109, 116

Juilliard School of Music, 26, 43–4, 78, 110

Julia (film), 156

K

Kagel, Mauricio, 78

Kandinsky, Wassily, 77–8

Kaye, Lenny, 236

Keene, Christopher, 180

Kerala, India, 112

Kern, Jerome, 35, 210, 213

Kim, Earl, 33, 72

King Crimson, 235

Kirk, Rahsaan Roland, 177

Kitchen, the, 97, 105, 125, 136, 236, 244

Klangfarbenschule, 63, 78, 179

Klee, Paul, 61

Klemperer, Otto, 92

Kline, Franz, 62

Kool/Newport/New York Jazz Festival, 197

Kooning, Willem de, 62

Korngold, Erich Wolfgang, 158

Koussevitzky, Serge, 50

KPFA, 100

Krenek, Ernst, 10, 14–24, 47, 61, 165; and serialism, 19–24, 28 Works: *Ballad of the Railroads*, 14; "Composer's Influences, A" (essay), 20–1; *Horizon Circled*, 19; *Jonny Spielt Auf*, 15, 22; *Santa Fe Timetable, The*, 14

Kroesen, Jill, 102–3

Kroll Opera, 92

Krupa, Gene, 146

L

labor unions, 34, 41, 65, 160

Lacy, Steve, 85

LaFaro, Scott, 187

La Guardia Marine Air Terminal, 150

Lake, Oliver, 244

Lansbury, Angela, 217

La Perfecta *conjunto*, 203, 204

Latin music, 11, 198–208; fusion with other musical forms, 205–6

League of Composers, 18, 49, 50

Leinsdorf, Erich, 81

Lewis, George, 136, 143, 166, 169, 183, 244

Lewis, Jerry, 117

LeWitt, Sol, 116, 124

Liddell, Alice, 73

Lieberson, Goddard, 137

Ligeti, György, 78

Liszt, Franz, 130

literature: and music, 39, 40, 73–5

Little Night Music, A (show), 214–15, 216

Living Theater, 85

Lomax family, 202

London Symphony Orchestra, 189, 223–4

Los Angeles, Calif., 15, 69, 158, 159–60, 186, 195, 223, 236

Lovely Music Ltd., 140

Love of Life Orchestra, 244

Lucas, George, 156–7, 158, 159, 160; *THX 1138*, 156–7, 158, 160, 161

Lucier, Alvin, 99, 135, 137, 143

Lutoslawski, Witold, 78

M

Ma, Yo-Yo, 168
Mabou Mines, 113, 116, 117
Mac Low, Jackson, 53
Madama Butterfly (Puccini), 57
Mahavishnu Orchestra, 194
Mahler, Gustav, 87
Mailer, Norman, 167
Mangione, Chuck, 176, 194
Manhattan School of Music, 98, 146
Manilow, Barry, 220, 231
Mantler, Michael, 196
Maoist composition, 173
Marcus, Greil, 173
Marcuse, Herbert, 92
marijuana, 113
Martinon, Jean, 64
Marxists, 22, 89–91, 92, 93–4
Massachusetts Institute of Technology, 134
Material, 197
mathematics: and composition, 26–7, 31, 42, 54
McCartney, Paul, 222
McLaughlin, John, 194
McPhee, Colin, 112, 180
meditational music, 112–13
Mee, William: "Alice Gray," 73
Melanie, 219
Mellers, Wilfrid, 226; *Music in a New Found Land*, 3
Mencken, H. L., 23
Menil family, de, 68
Menotti, Gian Carlo, 212
Merce Cunningham Dance Company, 137, 140
Mercer Arts Center, 236
Merrily We Roll Along (show), 216
Messiaen, Olivier, 63

Metropolitan Opera, 120, 212, 235
Mexicans, 199
Midler, Bette, 220
Midwest, the, 69, 98–9
Milan, Italy, 134
Milhaud, Darius, 72, 110
Milius, John, 159
Miller, Glenn, 167
Mills College Center for Contemporary Music, 33, 96, 98, 100, 101, 137
Mingus, Charles, 187
minimalism, 11, 44, 56, 76, 85, 88, 96, 103–4, 110, 113–16, 118, 127, 129, 137, 228, 235, 237
Minneapolis–St. Paul airport, 150
Mitchell, Joni, 230, 240
Mitchell, Roscoe, 170, 172, 173–4
Mitropoulos, Dimitri, 50
mixed media: 10, 99, 101–8, 128, 129
modernism, 10, 14–15, 18, 20, 21, 44, 72, 74, 87, 158, 213; post-, 21
Molière: *Le Bourgeois Gentilhomme*, 23
Mona Lisa (da Vinci), 104
Mondrian, Piet, 43
Monk, Meredith, 107, 128, 129, 244
Monroe, Bill, 203
Moondog, 119
Moore, Douglas, 212
Morocco, 190–1
Morrow, Charlie, 148
Motian, Paul, 177, 178
Moye, Dougoufama Famoudou Don, 170, 174
Mozart, Wolfgang Amadeus, 32, 42, 81, 130, 203, 208, 216; *Abduction from the Seraglio, The*, 56–7, 210; *Magic Flute, The*, 210; *Musical Joke, A*, 131

Mumma, Gordon, 96, 98–9, 137, 139

Munkacsi, Kurt, 118

Murch, Walter, 11, 154–63, 172
Work: *THX 1138* (Lucas), 156–7, 160, 161

Murch, Walter (painter), 155, 159

museums, 116, 196

Musica Elettronica Viva (MEV), 85, 136

Musical Quarterly, 49, 116

musical theater, 22, 38, 162, 171, 172; audiences, 212–13, 215; avant-garde, 113, 116, 117, 212; collaboration in, 96, 106; and experimentalists, 10–11, 107, 128; minstrel shows, 210; revues, 210; *see also* Broadway musicals; Hollywood

musique concrète, 11, 134, 154–5, 160

Mussorgsky, Modest Petrovich, 48

Muzak, 145, 152

Myers, Paul, 190

mysticism, 11, 26, 56, 77–8, 89, 97, 113, 227

N

Nancarrow, Conlon, 39, 44, 50, 69

Nash, Graham, 223

Nashville, Tenn., 202, 227

National Endowment for the Arts, 68, 69, 73

nationalism, 10, 17–18, 230

National Public Radio, 147

Neuberger Museum, 149

Neuhaus, Max, 52, 145–53; environmental composer, 11, 145–9, 150–3, 241; use of electronic music by, 145, 146
Works: *Radio Net*, 147; *Times Square*, 147–8, 151, 152; *Water Whistle*, 146–7

New England, 48

Newman, Randy, 219, 231

new music, 77, 87, 110, 116–17; and amplification, 133; classical, 71, 193; recordings, 137–8; uptown and downtown, 116, 123–4; *see also* contemporary music; jazz: new; New York, N.Y.: downtown (SoHo) arts community

New Music America festivals, 97, 105, 149, 150

New Music Distribution Service, 138, 196

New Music Edition, 49

Newport Jazz Festival, 189

New World Records, 49

New York, N.Y., 18, 34, 48, 87, 98, 199; avant-gardism in, 85, 109, 116, 127; Broadway theater in, 215; cabaret revival in, 219–20; downtown (SoHo) arts community, 63, 85, 97, 109–10, 115–16, 119, 122, 123–4, 127, 128–9, 131–2, 136, 191, 195–7, 234, 235–44; environmental music in, 147–8, 151, 152; establishment of composers in, 60–1, 67, 69–70, 72; experimentalists in, 58, 63, 66, 68–9, 96–7, 102, 111, 113–14; homosexual subculture in, 215, 220; jazz in, 177, 186–7, 195; painting and sculpture in, 61, 115, 123; performance art in, 128; rock in, 118, 234, 235–44

New York City Opera, 217

New York Dolls, 236

New York Philharmonic Orchestra, 41
New York State Council on the Arts,
68
New York Times, 31
New York University, 26
92nd Street Young Men's–Young
Women's Hebrew Association, 87
Nonesuch Records, 137, 138
Norteño music, 203
North, Alex, 158
Northeastern establishment, 10, 16,
18, 23, 25, 26, 35, 98
Nova Scotia, 115–16
Nyman, Michael: *Experimental Music*,
97

O

Obrecht, Bill, 130
Odyssey Records, 101
Old and New Dreams, 187
Oliveros, Pauline, 48, 100
ONCE (group and festivals), 98–9,
105
opera, 57, 216, 217; American, 11,
22, 115, 117–18, 210–12;
American companies, 40, 69, 80;
audiences, 40, 107, 211–12; avant-
garde, 99; collaboration in, 106–7,
128; comic, 131; European
tradition in, 11, 211; and
experimentalists, 10–11, 101–8,
114–15, 117–18, 128; folk, 212;
jazz, 15; rock, 235
operetta, 210
Opus One, 85
orchestras, 121; and art-rock, 234–5;
conductors of, 65, 74, 79–81; and
contemporary music, 34, 41–2, 51,

74–5, 79–82; *Dramaturg* for,
80–1; rehearsal time, 41, 65, 74–5,
121; scores for, 34, 38, 40, 61; and
unions, 34, 41, 65; vocal solos with,
73–4
Orff, Carl, 115
Oriental philosophical influence, 52,
55–7, 58–9, 97, 112–13, 132,
174
Orquesta Aragón, 200
Ortega, Sergio: *"¡El Pueblo Unido
Jamás Será Vencido!,"* 86
Outward Visions, Inc., 196

P

Pacific Overtures (show), 216–17
Paganini, Niccolò, 42
Paik, Nam June, 244
Palmer, Robert, 171, 191
Palmieri, Charlie, 199
Palmieri, Eddie, 11, 198–208; La
Perfecta *conjunto* of, 203, 204
Works: *Eddie Palmieri*, 207; *Harlem
River Drive*, 205; *Justicia*, 205, 206;
Lucumi Macumba Voodoo, 206;
"Seeds of Life, The," 205; *Sun of
Latin Music, The*, 205–6
Paris, France, 17, 23, 38, 57, 63, 76,
111, 134, 189
Parliament-Funkadelic, 196
Partch, Harry, 48, 119, 188
Parton, Dolly, 227
Pasatieri, Thomas, 212
patrons, 31–3, 34, 35, 42, 58, 67–8,
81, 91, 107, 122, 127–8
Peabody Conservatory, 110
Penderecki, Krzysztof, 78
performance artists, 11, 102, 107,

performance artists (*continued*)
127–9, 237–8, 243, 244; *see also*
Anderson, Laurie
Perle, George, 30
Persichetti, Vincent, 110
Perspectives of New Music, 27, 67
Peters (publisher), 65
Phillips, Liz, 149
Pink Floyd, 224
Pirates of Penzance, The (operetta),
159, 212
Piston, Walter, 136
Pleasants, Henry: *The Agony of
Modern Music*, 165
poetry, 11, 29, 40, 53, 62–3, 73, 102,
104, 106, 125–7, 128, 244
Polish composers, 78
political music, 89–95; folk songs,
85–6, 202; patronization of, 93–4,
95; *see also* Rzewski, Frederic
Pollock, Jackson, 54
Polyrock, 118
popular music, 3, 35, 88, 92–3, 97,
109, 130, 165, 168, 179, 221, 226,
229; audience, 190; black, 11, 22,
167, 196, 199; celebrities, 184;
commercialization of, 92–3, 95,
120, 127, 231–2; criticism of, 51;
dance, 192; division in styles of,
209–11; electronic music, 194; and
films, 158; funk, 167; fusion with
other musical forms, 4–5, 35, 77,
78–9; influences on, 209; jazz, 168,
193–5; New York, 132; popularity
of, 44, 81, 82, 93, 231–2; and
radio, 93, 127; recordings, 93, 127,
137, 195, 232; urban, 11, 209;
white, 167; *see also individual forms*
populism, 5, 6, 7, 10, 17–18, 38, 49,
90–1, 222

Porter, Andrew, 37
Pousseur, Henri, 136
Powell, Bud, 180
Powell, Mel, 22, 35, 36
prepared piano, 17, 57
Presser (publisher), 65
Prime Time, 191, 192
Prince, Harold, 214–15, 218, 220
Princeton University, 26, 33–4, 39,
71, 72, 84, 213
Procol Harum, 234
Public Theater, 197
Puccini, Giacomo, 15; *Madama
Butterfly*, 57
"Pueblo Unido Jamás Será Vencido!,
¡El," 86
Puerto Ricans, 199, 200
Pulitzer Prize (for composition), 64,
65, 67, 72
punk, 124; -jazz, 191; -rock, 225, 236
Purdie, Bernard, 205

Q

Quilapayún: "¡El Pueblo Unido Jamás
Será Vencido!," 86

R

racism, 164–7, 169–70, 185, 190
radio, 4, 5, 93, 100, 127, 137, 145,
151, 162, 190, 199, 202, 231–3
raga, 111
ragtime, 209
Rain People, The (film), 156, 161
Rakha, Allah, 113
Ramones, the, 236
Randall, James K., 72

rapping, 197, 244

rationalism, 10, 26, 39, 71, 86, 87

Ravel, Maurice, 43; *Bolero,* 115; *Valse, La,* 215

Raybeats, the, 244

RCA records, 118

record companies, 137–8, 190; private and minor labels, 138, 169, 184, 196, 232; and rock, 93, 194, 223, 231–3

recordings, 4–5, 74, 149–50, 151–2, 158; studios and technology for, 234–5, 240, 242; *see also individual musical forms*

Red Decade, 244

Redman, Dewey, 177, 178, 187

Reed, Lou, 235

reggae, 94

Reich, Steve, 6, 77, 100, 104, 110, 114, 115, 116–17, 121, 128, 241, 244; *Come Out,* 85

Reinhardt, Max, 224

Renoir, Jean, 226

Return to Oz (film), 156

Reynolds, Roger: Center for Music Experiment and Related Research, 100; *Mind Models,* 99

Rhode Island School of Design, 237

rhythm, 19, 39, 50, 51–2, 75, 192; complexities in, 77, 104, 109, 111, 113–15, 119, 121, 166; and jazz, 164, 166

Riegger, Wallingford, 136

Riley, Terry, 48, 100, 110, 116; *In C,* 114, 122, 137

Rimsky-Korsakov, Nikolai, 48

ritualists, 78–9, 87

Robbins, Matthew, 159

Robertson, Robbie, 230

Rochberg, George, 35, 76–7, 78, 84, 87–9, 180, 216; String Quartet No. 3, 87

Roche sisters, 132

rock, 11, 81, 92–3, 112, 131–2, 168, 221; amplification in, 74, 105, 115 121, 133, 143–4, 192–3, 194, 224, 227, 228; art-, 11, 12, 102–3, 127, 234–45; audiences, 119–20, 209, 224, 225, 230–2, 240; black, 242; British, 194, 234, 235, 237, 240, 242; and Broadway, 219; clubs, 118, 196, 224, 225; concerts and festivals, 105, 121, 204, 224–5; country-, 223; critics of, 222, 227, 228–9; and drugs, 224–5, 230; and electronic music, 121–2, 130, 135, 143–4, 194, 225, 240; folk-, 130, 223, 225, 226, 228, 235; and folk music, 12, 225, 226–7; hard, 127, 196, 227, 231; influences in, 222, 242, 243; innovation and fusion in, 223, 232, 243; -jazz, 94, 193–5, 196–7, 205, 243; Latin, 198; Los Angeles, 235; merging of composer and performer in, 130; new-wave, 93, 124, 127, 207, 225, 236; opera, 235; performers, 12, 173–4, 222–3, 227–8; and political music, 94; progressive, 136; punk-, 225, 236; and record companies, 93, 194, 223, 231–2; and roll, 28, 194, 221, 223, 225, 237; soft, 93, 196; and theatrical art, 224; and video, 162, 243; and youth rebelliousness, 222–3

Rockefeller, Nelson A., 85

Rodgers, Richard, 210, 213; *Do I Hear a Waltz?,* 214; *Slaughter on Tenth Avenue,* 205

Rodriguez, Tito, 199

Rollins, Sonny, 187, 189

romanticism, 11, 21, 30, 32–3, 77, 93, 166, 184, 203, 229–30, 231; neo-, 22; return to, 10, 61–3, 66–7, 71, 84, 85, 86–9, 158, 180

Romberg, Sigmund, 213

Rome, Italy, 84, 92, 136

Ronstadt, Linda, 130, 159, 219

Rooks, Conrad: *Chappaqua* (film), 111

Rorem, Ned, 35, 43

Rosenman, Leonard, 158

Rossini, Gioacchino, 132

Rotterdam, Holland, 117

Roulette, 97

Roxy Music, 240

Royal Netherlands Opera, 117

Rudhyar, Dane, 48

Rudner, Sara, 109–10

Ruggles, Carl, 16, 39, 44, 48, 64, 66, 69, 119

Rundgren, Todd, 244

Rush, Loren, 135

Russell, Ken, 158

Rzewski, Frederic, 10, 84–95, 96, 120, 136, 139, 231; political music of, 10, 84, 85–6, 89–90, 92, 93, 94–5; return to romanticism, 71, 84, 85, 86–7, 88–9, 180 Works: *Attica*, 85; *Coming Together*, 85; *Four North American Ballads*, 86, 94; *Four Pieces*, 86; *Moutons de Panurge, Les*, 85; *Pueblo Unido* variations, 86, 89; *Song and Dance*, 86

S

sacred music, 31

St. Louis, Mo., 195

St. Louis Symphony Orchestra, 79

St. Mark's Poetry Project, 244

salsa, 200, 204-8

Salzburg, Archbishop of, 81

Salzman, Eric, 61

San Diego, Calif., 69

Sanborn, John, 103

Sandow, Gregory, 28

San Francisco, Calif., 69, 100-1; filmmakers in, 158, 159–60, 162

San Francisco Chronicle, 49

San Francisco Conservatory, 80

San Francisco Symphony Orchestra, 80, 81

Sang d'un poète, Le (film), 39

Santana, Carlos, 198, 204

Satie, Erik, 43, 57

Scandinavian composers, 77

Scherchen, Hermann, 61

Schoenberg, Arnold, 24, 50, 60, 62, 129, 158, 172, 188; twelve-tone composition, 18–19, 21, 25–6, 27, 30, 43, 75–6

Schonberg, Harold C., 84

Schorske, Carl E.: *Fin-de-Siècle Vienna*, 20

Schreker, Franz, 22

Schuller, Gunther, 22, 35, 36, 67, 94, 165, 183, 186, 187

Schuman, William, 17, 18, 35

Schwann catalogue, 138

science: and art, 31–2, 143, 146

Scriabin, Alexander, 77

sculpture, 104, 115

serialism, 15, 18–36, 38, 39, 41, 49, 56, 60, 61–2, 71–3, 74, 76, 77, 78, 82, 84, 85, 86, 87, 88, 98, 105, 111, 114, 133, 142, 213; and academic establishment, 25, 26, 30, 33–4, 36; criticism of, 21, 34–5, 42, 47, 67; and electronic music,

25, 26, 28, 34

Serra, Richard, 115

Sessions, Roger, 26, 30, 33, 50, 72

Shankar, Ravi, 111, 112

Shapey, Ralph, 10, 60–70, 82, 121; as
academic, 60, 98; affinity to artists
and poets, 62–3, 115; as loner, 60,
64–7, 69–70; program notes of,
63–4; romanticism of, 61–3, 66–7
Work: *Rituals*, 64

sheet music, 4, 137, 210

Sheff, Robert (Blue Gene Tyranny),
102–3

Shere, Charles, 106–7

Shorter, Wayne, 194

Sills, Beverly, 217

Simon, Paul, 219

Singspiel, 210

ska bands, 94

Slonimsky, Nicolas: *Lexicon of Musical
Invective*, 42, 105

Smiles of a Summer Night (film), 215

Smith, Leo, 170

Smith, Patti, 127, 132, 236, 244

Smith, Rex, 219

Smithson, Robert, 145

society and culture, 23–4; American,
6, 8, 12–13, 16–17, 22–3, 43–5,
48, 57, 89–95, 109, 130, 211, 242;
attitude toward composer of, 30–2,
152–3, 203; crudity of popular
culture, 231–3; ethnic subcultures,
15, 198–9, 202–5; European, 3–4,
8, 13, 16, 43–4, 92, 211; racism in,
164–7, 169–70, 190; relation of
music to, 7, 21, 30–2, 89–95, 99,
152–3, 174–5, 221, 228; sixties
rebelliousness, 222–3

SoHo, *see* New York, N.Y.: downtown
arts community

Sollberger, Harvey, 61

soloists, 41, 61, 73–4, 173–4

Solti, Sir Georg, 72

Sondheim, Stephen, 11, 213–20;
collaboration with Prince, 214–15,
218, 220; criticism of, 217–19; and
opera, 217, 219
Works: *Anyone Can Whistle*, 214;
"Broadway Baby," 214; *Company*,
214, 215, 216, 218; *Do I Hear a
Waltz?* (lyricist), 214; *Follies*, 214,
215, 216, 218; *Funny Thing
Happened on the Way to the Forum,
A*, 214; *Gypsy* (lyricist), 214; *Little
Night Music, A*, 214–15, 216;
Merrily We Roll Along, 216; *Pacific
Overtures*, 216–17; "Poor Baby,"
216; "Send in the Clowns," 215,
220; *Sweeney Todd*, 216, 217; *West
Side Story* (lyricist), 214

Sonic Arts Union, 101, 136–7, 139

soul music, 93, 171, 196, 205

sound: -color, 63, 77–8; in electronic
music, 140, 144; emotion of, 161,
163; in environmental music,
145–51; and film, 5, 11, 81, 99,
154–7, 160–3; physics of, 76;
synthesized, 29, 133, 154–5; text-,
101–6, 125

Sound Fountain (museum installation),
140

Soundworks (aural art show), 149

South, the, 164, 186, 190

South American political folk songs,
86; *see also* Latin music

Soviet Union, 21, 77, 91

Specials, the: "Ghost Town," 94

Speculum Musicae, 34, 41, 86

Spielberg, Steven, 158

spirituals, 4, 209–10, 226

Springsteen, Bruce, 95, 231
Stanford University, 33, 134–5
Stein, Gertrude, 17, 212
Steinberg, Michael, 80–1
Sterne, Teresa, 138
Stills, Stephen, 223
Stockhausen, Karlheinz, 26, 78, 87, 136, 146
Stone, Sly, 196
Strauss, Richard, 74, 214
Stravinsky, Igor, 24, 76, 158, 165, 217; *Pulcinella*, 88; *Rite of Spring, The*, 104
structuralism, 85, 104, 110, 118, 137, 235, 237
Sturr, Jimmy, 202
Stuttgart, Ger., 118
Subotnick, Morton, 100
Sullivan, Sir Arthur, 210
Suzuki, Daisetz, 56
Sweeney Todd (show), 216, 217
swing, 171, 172
symphonists, 4, 17, 22, 33, 34, 35
synthesizers, 52, 134–5, 140–1, 225, 235
Syracuse Symphony Orchestra, 180

T

Talking Heads, 122, 234–45; art-rock, 11–12, 237–45; and Eno, 240–3 Works: *Fear of Music*, 239–40; "Memories Can't Wait," 238–40; *Name of This Band Is Talking Heads, The*, 240; *Remain in Light*, 241–2; *Speaking in Tongues*, 243
Tanglewood, 35, 67, 151
tape recorder, 134, 145, 155, 228–9

Taylor, Cecil, 6, 178, 183, 184
Taylor, Deems: *The King's Henchman*, 212
Taylor, James, 219
Tchaikovsky, Peter Ilyich, 144; Violin Concerto, 41
Teitelbaum, Richard, 136
television, 108, 162, 231–2
Television, 236
Texas, 185–6, 190, 202
Tharp, Twyla, 243
theater, 11, 162, 193; *see also* musical theater
Theoretical Girls, the, 243
Thomson, Virgil, 5, 9, 17, 38, 90–1, 144, 231; "Cage and the Collage of Noises" (essay), 58; *Four Saints in Three Acts*, 212; *Mother of Us All, The*, 212
THX 1138 (film), 156–7, 158, 160, 161
Tieghem, David Van, 102–3
Tin Pan Alley, 4, 219, 222
Tocqueville, Alexis de, 23
tonality, 51, 54, 97, 111, 112, 114–15, 186–8, 189; return to, 71–4, 76–7, 82–3, 85, 87
totalitarianism, 20–1
Townshend, Pete, 193, 222
traditionalists: classical, 6, 7, 14–15, 40, 43–5, 47, 77, 146, 195; contemporary, 15, 77, 106, 110; jazz, 168, 176, 192, 194–5
trance composers, 110
Tudor, David, 58, 137
Tunick, Jonathan, 218
Turetzky, Bertram, 52
Tutuola, Amos, 241
Tyner, McCoy, 205

U

Ulmer, James Blood, 191, 197
United Kingdom, 77, 90; *see also*
  Britain
United States: Latin community in,
  198–9; nationalism in, 10, 17–18,
  230; political art in, 91–2, 94, 95;
  see also American music;
  intellectuals: American; society and
  culture: American
University of California: at Berkeley,
  72, 150; at San Diego, 33, 100,
  134–5
University of Chicago, 60, 66, 98,
  110
University of Michigan, 98, 99
University of Southern California,
  155–6, 158, 159
urban popular song, 11, 209
Ussachevsky, Vladimir, 135

V

Varèse, Edgard, 50, 63, 243
Velikovsky, Immanuel: *Oedipus and
  Akhnaton,* 118
Velvet Underground, 235–6
Verdi, Giuseppe, 89–90, 132; *Aida,*
  57; *Falstaff,* 90
vernacular music, 3–4, 7–8, 204
video, 102–3, 107, 162, 243, 244,
  245
Viennese music, 20, 21, 28, 47, 56
Vietnam War protests, 230
Village Vanguard, 177
virtuosity, 5, 16, 37, 41–2, 43, 65, 86,
  97, 128–9

W

Waart, Edo de, 80
Wagner, Richard, 17, 29–30, 32, 59,
  63, 84, 89–90, 103, 162, 163, 188;
  Opera and Drama (book), 29;
  Rheingold, Das, 115; *Tristan und
  Isolde,* 75
Warhol, Andy, 236
Waring, Fred, 177
Warner Bros., 127
Warner Communications, 138
Weather Report, 194
Webern, Anton, 25, 61, 62, 231
Weill, Kurt, 5, 22, 61, 85, 91, 92,
  217; *Street Scene,* 22, 211, 212;
  Threepenny Opera, 22, 92, 212
Wesleyan University, 33
West, Hedy, 204
Weymouth, Martina, 237, 241, 243,
  245
Whiteman, Paul, 167
Whitman, Walt, 40, 44
Whitney Museum, 116
Who, the, 173, 222; *Tommy,* 235
Wilde, Oscar, 43
Williams, John, 158, 162
Williams College, 213
Willis, Thomas, 72
Wilson, Olly, 207
Wilson, Robert, 107, 128, 244;
  Einstein on the Beach (with
  Glass), 107, 114, 117–18, 120,
  235
Winding, Kai, 200
Wolf, Hugo, 75
Wolff, Christian, 58, 86, 93
Wolpe, Stefan, 60, 61, 62, 67, 92
World War I, 20, 38

Wuorinen, Charles, 30, 33, 34, 35, 61, 97, 121

X

Xenakis, Iannis, 78, 235

Y

Yes, 234–5
Youmans, Vincent, 213
Young, La Monte, 76, 103–4, 113–14, 186, 235
Young, Neil, 221–33; and folk music, 226–8, 234; performances, 224–5, 227–8, 230–1; romanticism of, 229–30, 231; simplicity of, 11–12, 225–6, 228

Works: "Cortez the Killer," 229; *Decade*, 225; *Everybody's Rockin'*, 225; *Harvest*, 221, 223–4; "Heart of Gold," 221; *Journey Through the Past* (film), 225, 233; "Like a Hurricane," 228; *Live Rust*, 233; "Love Is a Rose," 228; *Rust Never Sleeps*, 225, 227, 231; "Star of Bethlehem," 230; *Tonight's the Night*, 225; *Trans*, 225–6; *Zuma*, 225, 229

Z

Zawinul, Josef, 178, 194
Zen Buddhism, 55–6
Zukofsky, Paul, 66

ACKNOWLEDGMENTS

Grateful acknowledgment is made to the following for permission to reprint previously published material:

Laurie Anderson: Text from "Walk The Dog" by Laurie Anderson. © Ⓟ

Down Beat: An excerpt from "The Inner Octaves of Keith Jarrett" by Bob Palmer. Reprinted with permission of DOWN BEAT.

*The Herald Square Music Company: An excerpt from "*FOLLIES (BEAUTIFUL GIRLS)*" (Stephen Sondheim)* © *1971—*THE HERALD SQUARE MUSIC COMPANY *and* RILTING MUSIC, INC. *and* BURTHEN MUSIC COMPANY, INC. *Used by permission. All rights reserved.*

Index Music, Inc.: Excerpts from "Memories Can't Wait" by David Byrne. © *(PA 41-851) 8/3/79, Bleu Disque Music Co. Inc./Index Music, Inc.* ALL RIGHTS RESERVED.

Newsweek: Excerpt from "Broadway's Music Man" by Charles Michener. Copyright 1973 by Newsweek Inc. All rights reserved. Reprinted by permission.

The New York Times: Excerpts from "Interview with David Del Tredici" and "Interview with Erich Leinsdorf" by John Rockwell. Excerpts from John Corigliano interview with Bernard Holland and "The Art Ensemble of Chicago" by Robert Palmer. Copyright © *1980, 1982 by The New York Times Company. Reprinted by permission.*

Silver Fiddle: Excerpts from "Cortez the Killer" and "Love Is A Rose" by Neil Young. © *1975 Silver Fiddle. Used by permission. All rights reserved.*

Tree International: Excerpts from "My Tennessee Mountain Home" by Dolly Parton. Copyright © *1972* VELVET APPLE MUSIC.

Tommy Valando Publishing Corp.: Excerpt from "Pacific Overtures" by Stephen Sondheim © *1975 Revelation Music Publishing Corp. and Rilting Music, Inc. Lyrics reprinted by special permission.*

Wesleyan University Press: Excerpts from SILENCE *by John Cage. Copyright* © *1961 by John Cage. Reprinted from* SILENCE *by permission of Wesleyan University Press.*

ABOUT THE AUTHOR

John Rockwell was born in Washington, D.C., and raised in San Francisco. He graduated from Harvard College and received a Ph.D. in cultural history from the University of California at Berkeley. After working as a classical music and dance critic for the Oakland Tribune *and the Los Angeles* Times, *he began writing about music of all kinds for* The New York Times *in 1972.*